CARING IN AN UNJUST WORLD

CARING IN AN
UNJUST WORLD

Negotiating Borders
and Barriers in Schools

Edited by
Deborah Eaker-Rich
and
Jane A. Van Galen

STATE UNIVERSITY OF NEW YORK PRESS

Published by
State University of New York Press, Albany

For information, address State University of New York Press,
State University Plaza, Albany, N.Y., 12246

Production by Cathleen Collins
Marketing by Fran Keneston

Library of Congress Cataloging in Publication Data

Caring in an unjust world : negotiating borders and barriers in
  schools / edited by Deborah Eaker-Rich and Jane A. Van Galen.
    p.   cm.
  Includes bibliographical references and index.
  ISBN 0-7914-2799-4 (hc : alk. paper). — ISBN 0-7914-2800-1 (pb :
alk. paper)
  1. Teacher-student relationships—United States. 2. Interaction
analysis in education. 3. Social interaction—United States.
I. Eaker-Rich, Deborah, 1952–   . II. Van Galen, Jane. A.
LB1033.C297 1996
371.1'023—dc20   95-15811
                                                        CIP

10 9 8 7 6 5 4 3 2 1

Contents

Introduction

DEBORAH EAKER-RICH AND JANE A. VAN GALEN

A growing body of literature has drawn attention to the relational work performed in schools. In these analyses, the moral, "caring" work that frames the delivery of lessons, rather than the techno-rational facets of schooling, take center stage. This book offers another voice in the dialogue contained within the literature (Beck, 1994; Brabeck, 1989; Brown and Gilligan, 1992; Gilligan, 1982, 1990, 1993; Larrabee, 1993; Martin, 1992; Noddings, 1984, 1986, 1989, 1992) that is exploring "caring" in schools.

This fairly recent literature has explored the developmental and philosophical perspectives of what it means to *care*, at least in theoretical terms. A developmental notion of caring as an academic discourse, began with Carol Gilligan's 1982 work, *In a Different Voice*, in which she challenged previously accepted views of moral development by including a "different" perspective, demonstrated in her empirical work as being voiced most often by women. Gilligan's work brought into question the assumption, grounded in the developmental stage models of Lawrence Kohlberg and others, that the highest moral choices should be based exclusively upon universal principles of justice and detached, objective rationality. Gilligan posited instead the legitimacy of moral and ethical choices that are also based on norms of care, connectedness, and relationship. The *care* examined by Gilligan is far from being sentimental and servile. In Gilligan's (1993) words: "My critics equate care with feelings, which they oppose to thought, and imagine caring as passive or confined to some separate sphere. I describe care and justice as two moral perspectives that organize both thinking and feelings and empower the self to take different kinds of action in pubic as well as private life. Thus, in contrast to the paralyzing image of the

1

'angel in the house', I describe a critical ethical perspective that calls into question the traditional equations of care with self-sacrifice" (p. 209).

Although Gilligan intimated that her work had implications for education and set subsequent studies in schools, she did not choose to pursue those implications in her own work.

The work of Nel Noddings (1984) echoed Gillligan's call for renewed attention to the relational in moral reasoning and in social life. Moving beyond Gilligan's demonstration that relational considerations *do* underlay much moral reasoning (even while concern for connectedness and relationship have long been denigrated relative to moral reasoning grounded in logic principles of justice), Noddings called for education that places caring explicitly at the center of the work of schools. In her words, "I . . . argue that the first job of the schools is to care for our children. We should educate all our children not only for competence but also for caring. Our aim should be to encourage the growth of competent, caring, loving, and lovable people" (1992, p. xiv). Noddings's visionary work calls upon us to envision schools as they *might* be were they organized as "centers of care" (1992, p. 65).

The sentiment of caring is not something new to schools; as Miller (1990) and others have noted, teachers often speak of their work in relational terms that invoke the importance of teachers and students being and becoming caring persons. Educational researchers (Brabeck, 1989; Prilliman, Eaker, and Kendrick, 1994; Beck 1994; and the contributors to a recent special issue of the *Urban Review*, 25 no. 1, 1993) have begun to look at the relational work already to be found in schools, particularly at how *caring* is defined by teachers as well as how it is practiced. Although the caring relationships between many of the adults and children in schools may not yet resemble the theoretical models envisioned by Noddings, Gilligan, and others who have sought to bring caring to the center of theory and policy making, the most recent research does reveal an intentional caring as pedagogy. The recent work has drawn attention to the importance and complexity of caring and connectedness in current educational thought and practice. These authors have helped us to better understand schools and classrooms that are defined not only in terms of their technical and organizational components, but also in terms of the quality of relationships and the emphasis placed on the development of students as caring, ethical people.

As this emerging work has begun to shed light on the dynamics of care in classrooms and schools, the authors of these works have also begun to raise questions about what it means to give and to receive care in the heterogeneous settings actually encountered in educational practice. Foundational articulations of the theory of care in education have not yet grappled with the complexities of the *context* of care; namely, the multiple perspectives—the variety and differences—of culture and social positionality. These complications must inform theory. As the notion of caring continues to develop and gain prominence both in educational theory and in practice, it is imperative that theory and practice inform and enrich the other.

We have organized this volume to address the issue of caring across social barriers that emerge in heterogeneous settings as persons from different backgrounds attempt to establish caring relationships in schools. We have asked authors to consider several questions. We have asked them to address the issues of how the terms of relational work in schools are negotiated and defined when relationships within schools and communities are defined by ethnicity, class, and gender. We also asked the authors to consider the limits and possibilities of "caring" in schools that serve and reflect an unjust world.

These are important questions at this stage of the development of the literature in the field, because, as Noddings's argues, for a caring act to occur, it must be *interpreted* as caring by the one toward whom it is extended (1984, 1989, 1992). As she writes in *Caring: A Feminine Approach to Ethics and Moral Education* (1984): "When my caring is directed to living things, I must consider their natures, ways of life, needs, and desires. And, although I can never accomplish it entirely, I try to apprehend the reality of the other" (p. 14).

In her later works (1989, 1992), Noddings acknowledges the difficulties of knowing another's nature, needs, and desires when one party holds power over the other or is a member of a group that has historically dominated another. Given that many relationships in schools are constrained by such power discrepancies, we felt that these issues of caring across social borders merited further attention.

The authors in this volume address the difficulties and complexities of apprehending the reality of "others" when the caregivers or those receiving care or both are from historically marginalized groups. In casting a sociological lens on the philosophical discourse on caring, the studies and essays collected here consider how caring is defined, enabled, and constrained by social structures.

As such, this book has evolved into two major parts: Dilemmas of Caregivers and Dilemmas of Creating Schools as Centers of Care.

The first part, Dilemmas of Caregivers, confronts issues of caring from the perspective of, as Noddings uses the term, *the one caring*, or the caregiver. In her theoretical work, Noddings emphasizes reciprocity of the caring relationship. As she explains, "A *caring relation* is, in its most basic form, a connection or encounter between two human beings—a carer and a recipient of care, or cared-for. In order for the relation to be properly called caring, both parties must contribute to it in characteristic ways. A failure on the part of either carer or cared-for blocks completion of caring and, although there may still be a relation—that is, an encounter in which each party feels something toward the other—it is not a *caring* relation" (1992, p. 15).

As with Gilligan, Noddings does not endorse a sentimental or self-sacrificing "care." Instead, she speaks of one acting in the best interests of the other. For Noddings (1984), caring is central to the act of teaching:

> As a teacher, I am first, one caring.
> The one-caring is engrossed in the cared-for and undergoes a motivational displacement toward the projects of the cared-for. This does not . . . imply romantic love or the sort of pervasive and compulsive "thinking of the other" that characterizes infatuation. It means, rather, that one-caring receives the other, for the interval of caring, completely and non-selectively. She is present to the other and places motive power in his service. Now, of course, she does not abandon her own ethical ideal in doing this, but she starts from a position of respect or regard for the projects of the other. In the language of Martin Buber, the cared-for is encountered as "Thou," a subject, and not as "It," an object of analysis. During the encounter, which may be singular and brief or recurrent and prolonged, the cared-for "is Thou and fills the firmament." (p. 176)

To care in such ways may often be difficult. Caring becomes more difficult, as Noddings acknowledges, when it is attempted "at a distance"— either because of physical separation or because those who would care are "physically near but are still strangers" (1992, p. 115).

The stories conveyed in this part are stories of those who, because of circumstances of history, politics, intolerance, or social and economic domination, are strangers to those for whom they would demonstrate care. In these cases, the caregivers are women confronting the sexism that distances males and females, gay and lesbian teachers who are attempting to care within a homophobic culture that distances them from the students and peers for whom they care, and educational researchers and their participants within an urban school setting who are attempting to bridge the distances of status, purpose, and perspective that too often impede genuinely collaborative inquiry. Noddings cautions that "caring at a distance is fraught with difficulties" (1992, p. 116), and the chapters in this part both illuminate the nature of these difficulties and suggest avenues for ways that those on the margins may minimize the social and psychic differences between themselves and others.

In the first chapter of the part, "Caring and the Open Moment in Educational Leadership: A Historical Perspective," Jackie M. Blount profiles historical instances of caring school leaders. She examines the cases of such leaders, all of whom are women, during the evolution of educational administration and before, as Blount terms it, "the reification of school administrative structures and practices" that impose bureaucratic distance between teachers (many of whom are women) and administrators (many of whom are men). In presenting the historical perspective upon caring within school leadership, she effectively argues that current administrative structures and normative practice hinder and may even prevent the possibility of caring school leadership in the present. She leaves us to consider whether schools might not now be closer to models of centers of caring had this alternative, relational, style of leadership prevailed.

Jan Streitmatter, in her chapter dealing with "Justice or Caring," examines the practices and dilemmas of two female teachers who are attempting to promote gender equity, albeit in differing ways. Drawing from Gilligan's work, Streitmatter juxtaposes an equality versus equity framework and how these are potentially tied to two primarily distinct moral orientations for these teachers, those of justice and care. In so doing, she raises many conflictual issues regarding the appropriate questions that we as educators need to consider as we attempt, under the rubric of caring for children, to "equalize" past injustices and inequalities. The teachers described in this chapter both care about their students. Both attempt to minimize distance between female students and the more privileged positions of males in the society, and the analyses of the consequences of the approaches taken by each sheds new light on the ways in which *caring* and *justice* approaches may address the moral dilemma of sexism.

Chapters 3 and 4 deal with the often hidden dilemmas faced by gay and lesbian teachers who attempt to care for their students within a homophobic culture. In "Uncommon Caring: Male Primary Teachers as

Constructed and Constrained," James R. King points to the multiple layers of complexity inherent in the decision of any man to become a primary school teacher. These complexities are further exacerbated, as King illuminates, when these men happen to also be gay. Similarly, in "Lesbian and Gay Teachers: Forbidden to Care," Rita M. Kissen tells the turbulent and uncertain stories of homosexual teachers as they struggle to "really be there" and care for students while at the same time experiencing the very real apprehension, fear, and consequences that can, and do, result both from being "in" and "coming out" of the closet. These two chapters leave us with painful questions about the distances maintained between homosexual students and the teachers who would care for them and between the homosexual teacher and the students for whom they would care. As these chapters illustrate, the social inhibition attached to caring between homosexuals and others makes the engrossment of the caregiver in the "cared-for" difficult at best.

In the final chapter of this part by Jaci Webb-Dempsey, Bruce Wilson, Dickson Corbett, and Rhonda Mordecai-Phillips, we see the various actors within one urban school, including the researchers themselves, struggle with what is meant by "in the best interests of children." The authors, along with Noddings, contend that doing what is in the best interests of children is the basis of caring. We see within this chapter how notions of care are "bound" by race, class, gender, historical circumstance, and age. We also witness the lack of understanding resulting when well-intentioned actors view one another only from the distance of these boundaries. Webb and her colleagues explore the complications of trying to ascertain what borders can appropriately and productively be crossed in attempting to develop a consensus around what it means to care in this one school as the actors join together to create a school in which children do know that they are in a place that is centered on their care.

Part Two, Dilemmas of Creating Schools as Centers of Care, explores the complexities of moving beyond the one-on-one relational work on the part of particular teachers to the more complex task of creating and sustaining institutional norms of caring and connection.

The chapters in this section look at five "caring" projects, whether originally or explicitly articulated as such or not. The "projects," as described in these chapters, demonstrate successful, failed, and ongoing attempts to live out an ethic of care and relational work within schools.

Chapter 6, by Van Dempsey and Noblit, "Caring and Continuity: The Demise of Caring in an African-American Community, One Consequence of School Desegregation," lays out the historical and present consequences of desegregation efforts within one African-American community. In their analysis, we see those outside the community dispute the sustenance of a caring community that was created through continuity of purpose, place, and people (Noddings, 1992). In this case, the law, not the people within the caring community, determined who had the power to redefine the meaning and structure of what constituted a "good school." As a result, the community lost the "good school" as they had defined it, and with the loss of the school came the loss of the sense of a caring community that emanated from the school. In this case of "failed" caring, we see how the voices of power prevailed over those of connectedness.

In "Interpersonal Caring in the 'Good' Segregated Schooling of African-American Children," Emily V. Siddle Walker looks at the "good" segregated school from a slightly different perspective than that of Dempsey and Noblit. She asks us to explore issues of interpersonal caring within this school that seemingly provided a more successful schooling experience for some students than for others. As a result of this focus on interpersonal caring, she highlights the power dynamics that enable or restrict success as well as the importance of connectedness for these students. At the same time, she challenges the unitary, traditional focus of school reform that merely explains the lack of success among African-American students as attributable to institutional and cultural practices.

Jane A. Van Galen, in "Caring in Community: The Limits of Compassion in Facilitating Diversity," examines student life within a traditionally Catholic school undergoing diversification, whose participants explicitly voice an ethic of care as being one of the essential elements that makes their school successful. Upon in-depth analysis, "caring" appears to serve a social reproductionist role within the school as it is received differently along racial and gender lines. The manifestations of caring in this school serve to reinforce class, race, and gender roles among students. Van Galen's chapter suggests that well-intended teachers who may invest much in their relational work with students may, nonetheless manifest caring in culturally bound ways that limit, rather than support, students' personal and academic growth. Van Galen contends that disempowering relationships couched in a rhetoric of care may ultimately render the differential treatment of students invisible and unspeakable.

"Caring in One Urban High School: Thoughts on the Interplay Among Race, Class, and Gender" by Lynn G. Beck and Rebecca L. Newman portrays a case of the success of caring within a school in which many factors work against the success of the students. Beck and Newman look at the various characteristics of caring as it is enacted among women, diverse racial groups, and classes in this urban high school. They provide us with a positive scenario of the possibilities of a school organized around a negotiated and agreed-upon ethic of caring for all participants.

In Chapter 10, "Caring as Empowerment: School Collaboration and Community Agency," the authors, Carmen Mercado and members of the Bronx Middle School Collaborative, describe a school-based, collaborative, integrated research and pedagogical project. The project was undertaken to empower adolescent students from working class and ethnically diverse environments. This project demonstrates how students' opportunities and ability to research matters of essential importance to their own lives can result in academic excellence and learning to care about themselves and others as well. This collaborative project reinforces what Noddings argues should be the foremost goal of education: "living with those whom we teach in a caring community through modeling, dialogue, practice and confirmation" (Noddings, 1986, p. 502).

We believe this book to be an important addition to the literature regarding the complexities of caring within the traditional structures and practices of schools. The chapters here confirm that talk of caring and relational work permeates the life of schools and was part of school life long before the emergent and overdue academic interest in the subject. We believe that the chapters demonstrate the rich opportunities for exploring the complexities of relational work in schools. While we join many within the academy who are calling for caring schools, we believe that it is important to learn much more about the caring that is now taking place in settings and situations in which relational work might be expected to be problematic. Yet as we solicited manuscripts for this book and spoke to others about our work, we found that in spite of widespread consensus around the importance of caring in schools on the part of teachers, parents, administrators, and students, the practice of caring, as so much of school life, is not subject to critical reflection. We found few teachers, administrators, or even teacher educators who have studied the caring literature and who ground their relational work in this literature or who even had talked among themselves about what it might mean to care in meaningful ways. The work of caring teachers seems to us to exist in a world that is, as yet, distinct from the work of academics who call upon teachers to reconsider their practice.

Thus, we offer this volume as part of the dialogue between educational theory and practice. We have been reminded in the process of working on this book with others that we will be most effective as we apply theoretical constructs to the analysis of caring when we encourage those engaged in this vital relational work to speak back to us. As Noddings notes, knowledge across cultural groups (such as those in the academy and those in schools) is best acquired in relation (1992, p. 114). Our hope for this book is that a theory of caring will help to shape practice, that closer looks at practice will help to move the theory forward, and that the dialogue between academics and practitioners will continue in the interest of both "cultures" contributing their parts to the creation of schools that are working in the best interests of *all* children.

REFERENCES

Beck, L. G. (1994). *Reclaiming Educational Administration as a Caring Community*. New York: Teachers College Press.

Brabeck, M. (1989). *Who Cares? Theory, Research, and Educational Implications of Care*. New York: Praeger.

Brown, L. M. and Gilligan, C. (1992). *Meeting at the Crossroads*. New York: Ballantine Books.

Gilligan, C. (1982). *In a Different Voice*. Cambridge, MA: Harvard University Press.

———. (1990). *Making Connections: The Relational Worlds of Adolescents at Emma Willard School*. Cambridge, MA: Harvard University Press.

———. (1993). "Reply to Critics." In M. J. Larrabee, ed., *An Ethic of Care: Feminist and Interdisciplinary Perspectives*. New York: Routledge.

Larrabee, M. J., ed. (1993). *An Ethic of Care: Feminist and Interdisciplinary Perspectives*. New York: Routledge.

Martin, J. R. (1992). *The School Home: Rethinking Schools for Changing Families*. Cambridge, MA: Harvard University Press.

Miller, J. (1990). *Creating Spaces and Finding Voices: Teachers Collaborating for Empowerment*. Albany: SUNY Press.

Noddings, N. (1984). *Caring: A Feminine Approach to Ethics and Moral Education*. Berkeley: University of California Press.

————. (1986). "Fidelity in Teaching, Teacher Education and Research for Teaching." *Harvard Educational Review* 56: 496–510.

————. (1989). *Women and Evil.* Berkeley: University of California Press.

————. (1992). *The Challenge to Care in Schools: An Alternative Approach to Education.* New York: Teachers' College Press.

Prilliman, R., Eaker, D., and Kendrick, D. M., eds. (1994). *The Tapestry of Caring: Education as Nurturance.* Norwood, NJ: Ablex Publishing.

Part One

Dilemmas of Caregivers

CHAPTER 1

CARING AND THE OPEN MOMENT
IN EDUCATIONAL LEADERSHIP

A Historical Perspective

JACKIE M. BLOUNT

INTRODUCTION

School administrators first emerged from American classrooms in the mid-1800s in a broad movement that paralleled the rise of differentiated managerial classes in industry. Principal teachers, as these administrators were called, assumed logistical, fiscal, and curriculum management responsibilities while maintaining their instructional duties at reduced levels. Meanwhile full-time teachers forfeited their independence by degrees. The teaching principalship was one of the first school administrative positions, but soon the trend to consolidate and form ever-larger school systems created the need for additional administrators such as full-time principals, supervisors, and superintendents.

Variety characterized school administration during these early years. First, teachers, young and old, rural and urban, college and normal school educated, male and female, all could become principals and eventually district administrators—though usually a woman could not assume such work if doing so made any man subservient to her. Second, early school and district administrators came to their work by various routes, such as through local elections or school board appointments. Third, early administrators performed a broad range of duties, depending on publicly perceived needs and individual priorities. Finally, local school administrators operated relatively free of the constraints of a prescribed set of managerial practices. Essentially, even though an administrative class had evolved, standards of selection and practice had not, a situation that constituted an open moment in the direction of school administration.

During this open moment that lasted into the early decades of the twentieth century, two important strands of leadership practice emerged. The first, what I will call *traditional school administration*, was shaped by a powerful group of nationally prominent educational leaders who sought to define and standardize administrative practice; to control access to school administrative positions; to build alliances with powerful corporate, academic, and governmental organizations; and to solidify a rigidly hierarchical bureaucratic structure. In general, adherents to this view conflated *administration* with *leadership* in that they regarded administrators as leaders by virtue of position. Military and business organizational models informed this view as did evolving notions of scientific-social efficiency.

The second strand of school leadership practice, what I will call *caring leadership*, was shaped by Deweyan progressives and supporters of the women's movement. Caring school leaders viewed their work as the development and nurturance of relationships with teachers, students, parents, community members, and other administrators. They tended to pursue social reform agendas, including applying Dewey's notions of democracy to school governance. Although some of these leaders were women, clearly not all women administrators were caring leaders.

Education scholars have tended to chronicle and analyze traditional school administration through the years, primarily by describing the evolution of contemporary administrative structures and practices. Caring leadership, however, has received far less attention. In the following pages I will describe caring school leadership using Noddings's notion of *caring* as a theoretical base. I will then portray the work of several caring leaders from the early twentieth century, exploring some of the events that transpired as traditional and caring leaders worked with and against each other until the open moment in school leadership selection and practice decisively ended.

CARING SCHOOL LEADERSHIP

Nel Noddings, in her groundbreaking work, *Caring: A Feminine Approach to Ethics and Moral Education* (1984), offers an incisive analysis of caring. She describes caring as "rooted in receptivity, relatedness, and responsiveness" in that it is grounded in individual relationships between persons where each strives to meet the other morally (p. 2). Affect is an acknowledged and valued part of such a relationship and is not rejected or minimized through logical analysis or hierarchical arrangements of eternal principles. Reliance on these principles, Noddings contends, divorces persons from considering the unique relational and situational contexts in which they must make ethical decisions. This separation ultimately dulls sensitivity to the needs and concerns of others and weakens the bonds of a caring relationship.

The caring relationship is asymmetrical where at any time one person, the *one-caring*, is engrossed in the needs and well-being of the other, the *cared-for*. To the cared-for the attitude and actions of the one-caring are of great importance and as a result, "the cared-for glows, grows stronger, and feels not so much that he has been given something as that something has been added to him (pp. 20–21)." As the one-caring accepts this response from the cared-for, the caring act is completed.

The caring leader and follower relationship is analogous in several ways to Noddings's description of the one-caring–cared-for relationship. First, in a caring relationship each person willfully engages in a mutual bond. The one-caring does not enjoy a caring relationship unless such attention is received and in some way reciprocated by the cared-for. The cared-for does not participate in a caring relationship unless the one-caring chooses to be engrossed in his welfare. The active commitment of each is essential. Similarly, caring leaders inspire the action and dedication of others who are free to choose whether or not to follow. Leaders exist, then, in relationship with followers. Because *follow* and *lead* are intentional act verbs, those who follow or lead do so willingly. When persons choose to follow or lead, they consider the contexts of their situations and their relationships with others.

Second, just as the one-caring is concerned for the growth and well-being of the cared-for and finds her intentions and actions completed in his receiving that care, the caring leader also is engrossed in the welfare of followers and finds her efforts completed in their happy reception of her care.

The caring leader is not disconnected from the responses of followers, but instead derives strength and direction from their acceptance of her concern.

Finally, just as the caring relationship changes as contexts shift, caring leader-follower relationships are situationally based and constantly negotiated rather than standardized and structure bound. Caring leaders minimize their reliance on relatively static policies and organizational forms in making ethical decisions, but instead consider the contingencies of each new situation as they strive to improve the welfare of followers. In this sense, caring leaders do not necessarily have much in common with administrators, who primarily uphold and perpetuate organizational structures and attendant rules.

Traditional views of school leadership, on the other hand, hold that *leadership* and *administration* are synonymous, that is, leaders are persons who display a defined set of leadership traits, exhibit leadership behaviors, or assume institutionally defined roles of leaders (Maxcy, 1991). The administrators who perform this work tend to serve as functionaries whose roles are carefully defined and hierarchical positions fixed. As such, administrators find themselves expendable. They can be replaced by others who also meet the same structure-bound requirements. Traditional views of leadership, then, disconnect individuals from their unique webs of relationships in work settings and instead impose standard sets of structures, roles, and relationships. In sum, traditional leaders can operate regardless of the presence of caring. The caring leader cannot.

CONTEXTS

The events and culture of turn-of-the-century America significantly shaped the lives, work, and relationships of both traditional and caring school leaders. With the rapid urbanization of the time, for example, large numbers of rural agricultural workers and immigrants gravitated to the industrial Northeast and Midwest, a trend that created densely populated urban centers. Cities strained to accommodate the basic needs of vast numbers of new inhabitants. Urban school superintendents faced a multitude of complex projects, such as rapid school construction, teacher hiring-training-retention, acquisition of suitable curricular materials, and management of social functions of schools in response to increased societal needs. At this time, the search for effective means of handling these problems dominated discussion among superintendents throughout the nation (Tyack, 1974; and Callahan, 1962).

Urbanization and industrialization affected not only public institutions such as schools, they also transformed institutions as private as the traditional family. Where once family members had worked in home-based enterprises, industrialism increasingly required workers to report to factory sites for long hours of monotonous labor in exchange for regular wages. As a result, families segregated internally into those who worked outside the home, usually men, and those who remained at home to perform domestic duties, usually women (Matthaei, 1982).

This segregation to the home effectively limited women's educational, economic, and political opportunities in comparison with the priviledges enjoyed by men. Women typically received little instruction beyond that required for simple literacy because they were not expected to work in the public sphere, where greater educational achievement might have been necessary (Solomon, 1985). Also, women could not express their opinions at the ballot because representative democracy remained a male privilege.

Eventually some women could not contain their frustration with an absence of educational opportunities, limited economic possibilities outside the home, and lack of voice in political decision making. Following the Seneca Falls Women's Rights Convention in 1848, thousands and eventually millions of women rallied together in a broad social movement that reached beyond the boundaries of the home and allowed a variety of women to connect in friendship.

Many of these women looked for ways to educate themselves and each other. They fought for admission to post-secondary educational institutions and then enrolled in record numbers. This thirst for formal education was paralleled by an explosion of women's community study groups and women's clubs (Solomon, 1985, p. 63). Women's clubs grew in popularity to the extent that by 1909 one of the larger organizations, the General Federation of Women's Clubs, could boast a membership of 800,000 women. At the time this represented one-tenth of the female population of the United States. Many women belonged to other such clubs as well (Gribskov, 1980, p. 79).

Some women's clubs eventually turned their missions beyond study and toward social reform in such areas as public education, economic and political opportunities for women, public sanitation, child labor, and other social concerns resulting from rapid changes in the population and economy. Members learned they could accomplish many of their goals by pressuring legislators and pushing for the inclusion of women in policy making and public administrative positions such as school superintendencies. The power of these groups increased dramatically as women won the right to vote state by state.

Many women teachers, administrators, and other educators joined various groups within the womenís movement, not a surprising fact since by 1910 nearly a half million women around the country worked in education in some capacity (U.S. Office of Education, 1921, p. 10). Groups emerged that pushed for the betterment of schools, student experiences, and teachersí working conditions. One such group, the National Congress of Parents and Teachers Associations, quickly grew to a million and a half members in the 1920s (Cott, 1987, p. 87). Teachers' organizations also expanded rapidly during these years, as they rallied for improved classroom conditions and equal pay for women teachers. Publications sprouted bearing such names as *The Women's Voice and Public School Advocate*.

THE CARING SCHOOL LEADERSHIP OF THREE WOMEN

Within the context of industrialization, urbanization, and the growth of a strong nationwide women's movement, some women rose to prominence in school systems around the country. I will discuss the lives and works of three of these women whom I consider caring leaders: Ella Flagg Young, Julia Richman, and Susan Dorsey. Young worked throughout her long education career in the Chicago city schools, eventually superintending the system from 1909–1915 with a brief break in 1913. Richman began her teaching career in the New York City schools and was later promoted through the ranks to district superintendent in 1889, a position she held until her death in 1912. Susan Dorsey, like Young and Richman, taught in the school system she would eventually superintend. In 1920, Dorsey assumed the top administrative position of the Los Angeles city schools, a role she held through 1929. In the following sections I will highlight aspects of these womenís careers that demonstrate their distinctively caring leadership.

Relationships with Teachers

In the early years of this century, frustrated urban teachers often believed that school administrators cared little about conditions in the classroom. Class sizes increased; supplies of educational materials dwindled; student and teacher turnover soared; salaries—especially for women who received a fraction of men's—hardly kept pace with living costs; teacher evaluations sometimes reflected administrative whims that teachers endured with little recourse; and children attended school while suffering from overwork, abuse, hunger, and other problems associated with massive social dislocations of the time. To compound teachers' frustrations, some school boards started filling administrative positions with college educated men who had little, if any, teaching experience. Because administrators had previously risen through the teaching ranks, teachers became angry, and teacher-superintendent relationships often deteriorated as a result (Murphy, 1990; Tyack, 1974; and Callahan, 1962).

Young, Richman, and Dorsey, however, enjoyed great support from teachers and teacher organizations. They maintained strong bonds with teachers throughout their careers. During her nine years as superintendent, Susan Dorsey did not forget the teachers with whom she had once worked. She maintained strong ties with them in part by laboring tirelessly for higher teacher salaries, sabbatical leaves, and job tenure. Throughout her career, teachers admired and respected Dorsey and even elected her president of the Southern Section of the California Teachers' Association (Sicherman et al., 1980, pp. 506–508; and McGregor, 1953).

Julia Richman felt so strongly about maintaining connections with teachers that she converted the building in which she lived to a social center for teachers in her district. Some teachers even lived at Teachers' House, a place where Richman also met with school leaders to plan for the social needs of the district's students (Sicherman et al., 1980, p. 151).

Ella Flagg Young built extraordinarily deep and long-lasting relationships with teachers. While still a teacher in the Chicago schools, Young's exemplary instructional style attracted notice and soon led to her appointment as director of the Chicago Normal School. In this role she regularly held social and professional meetings at her own house, meetings that were enthusiastically attended by all of the teachers in her school. Once appointed superintendent, Young remained connected with teachers by campaigning for higher salaries and greater teacher participation in school administration. She developed strong friendships with many individual teachers in the Chicago city school system including Margaret Haley, the president of the Chicago Teacher's Federation. At times teachers called on Young to mediate disputes within the federation, so respected was her ability (Smith, 1979, pp. 122–127). An active contingent of teachers around the country eventually elected Young president of the National Education

Association, the first woman to hold such a position. Although powerful male school administrators primarily controlled the organization at the time, Young won the election largely with the votes of newly enfranchised female teachers.

Clearly for Young, Richman, and Dorsey, the support of teachers was critical to their success. These superintendents worked diligently to maintain these bonds and improve the conditions of teachers.

Relationships with Community

These women leaders also worked actively in their communities, often by participating in women's service organizations. Susan Dorsey became a charter member of the Woman's Christian Temperance Union, later served on the Southern California Committee on the Cause and Cure of War, and worked as vice president of the Women's Law Observance Association. Julia Richman actively worked with the National Council of Jewish Women. Ella Flagg Young chaired a division of the General Federation of Women's Clubs during her terms as superintendent and campaigned relentlessly to sell war bonds in her retirement (Sicherman et al., 1980; Smith, 1979).

Numerous other women school leaders amassed lengthy records of public service as well. Laura Joanna Ghering, for example, served not only as the superintendent of the Kingfisher City Schools in Oklahoma, she also worked with the local Red Cross chapter, served as president of the County Health Commission, and actively participated in the Woman's Christian Temperance Union for twenty-five years. Bertha Palmer, state superintendent of public instruction in Minnesota, served as secretary of the Sunday School Association and worked in a state position of the Federation of Women's Clubs (Cook, 1928). Betsey Mix Cowles, superintendent of Painesville city schools in Ohio, worked as an organizer of women's groups and as the principal leader of the local Female Anti-Slavery Society. She actively crusaded for woman's rights as well, serving as president of the first Ohio Women's Convention (Sicherman et al., 1980).

Women school leaders generally worked in organizations that aimed to elevate the morality of society, at least in part because these organizations were open to their membership, but also because they wanted to labor for social improvement in their communities. These organizations in turn provided moral and political support for these women. In contrast, most traditional superintendents amassed records of participation in exclusive professional organizations and civic groups, many of which focused their efforts on economic development (Cook, 1928).

Concern for Students

In crowded urban centers many children suffered seemingly unending difficulties. Some worked long hours in dangerous factories and attended school intermittently. Other children had little to eat and only rags to wear. Many immigrant children spoke languages other than English. To some at the time, juvenile delinquency appeared ready to escalate out of control. Traditional school leaders responded to these problems through tighter control—by regimenting the school environment and standardizing curricula. In contrast, some caring school leaders of this time spoke not of the need for control, but rather for the desperate need to improve the conditions of children.

Ella Flagg Young, in particular, articulated the need for schools to understand and help children. She identified among her close friends the social activist Jane Addams and philosopher John Dewey, her mentor and doctoral advisor at the University of Chicago. Young argued forcefully for student empowerment by integrating Dewey-inspired democratic principles into the process of schooling.

While serving as the Chicago schools superintendent, Young faced chaotic and tumultuous social conditions as the city grew rapidly. Many of her urban superintendent peers around the country responded to similar challenges by standardizing curricula, school design, teacher behavior, administrative structure, schedules, . . . and generally imposing rigid structures in the practice of schooling to increase efficiency. Young, however, strongly believed that such measures contributed to powerlessness and isolation among school children and employees. She viewed her administrative and academic work as a social project geared toward dismantling and reconfiguring what she considered demeaning structures. Young described her views eloquently in her doctoral dissertation and book, Isolation in the Schools (1901): "So rapid . . . has been the unexpected development of problem after problem that the school has begun to lose ground in . . . its greatest work. Unification was confounded with uniformity by the leaders, reformers, and organizers in their efforts to make that systematic which was to a considerable degree chaotic. The human mind, the most delicate, the most sensitive, the most complex of all organizations, loses power, is arrested in its development, if its efforts are directed toward establishing unvarying conditions in its own environment and in that of others also" (pp. 45–48).

Young believed that efforts by school administrators to standardize and regiment the school environment would inevitably isolate students and teachers alike from their independence, intelligence, and each other. She thought that many school leaders tended to choose the easiest, most expeditious route through chaotic times by over-structuring schools rather than by striving to give students and teachers room to grow and develop. Young maintained that growth and development were possible only in an environment where individuals remained connected with one another. Isolation, according to Young, would weaken the school community and eventually the community at large.

A woman who acted on her beliefs, Young met with as many persons associated with the Chicago schools as she could, striving to build individual connections with teachers, administrators, community members, and with students. She also labored to distribute control to the school community rather than to concentrate it tightly in her own hands.

Much of the Chicago school community appreciated Young's efforts to improve the quality of schools at a difficult time. Community leaders spoke glowingly of her leadership and stouthearted concern. Teachers sponsored appreciation events in her honor. Students thanked her at public events. When school board members whom she had accused of corruption attempted to vote her out of office, Jane Addams led thousands of her supporters in a rally that effectively forced four board members to tender their resignations. The Chicago school community essentially reciprocated Young's caring leadership and from that support she derived some of the strength needed to continue her work (Smith, 1979; Sicherman et al., 1980).

Situational Decision Making

Ella Flagg Young, Susan Dorsey, and Julia Richman each served in rapidly growing districts with large, diverse populations and significant economic changes. While traditional school leaders implemented standardized procedures to control seemingly unstable school environments, these three women handled crisis situations with a keen sensitivity to the uniqueness of the situations. In the end, local media and national education journals alike lauded the sometimes novel solutions these women implemented.

During Dorsey's nine year term as Los Angeles superintendent, the student population expanded from 90,609 to 222,670, roughly a 250 percent increase. She managed this growth by launching a massive bond campaign that generated millions of dollars and great public support. Through her close, attentive guidance, the Los Angeles school system became "one of the finest in the country with an alert, professionally trained teaching staff and well-equipped, beautiful buildings." Her flexible decision making and creative solutions soon earned her the reputation as "the greatest administrative genius in the history of American education" (*NEA Journal*, 1946, p. 136).

Of all the school districts in New York City, Julia Richman chose to superintend the crowded Lower East Side. In response to the immense needs of the district's students, Richman set up a series of special schools to help older students, those who got into trouble, skipped school, or were disabled (Sicherman et al., 1980, p. 151). On noticing that some students seemed hungry, she began a school lunch program. For students with poor, uncorrected vision she instituted school optical exams. She was particularly concerned with the difficulties faced by immigrant children in adjusting to their new country. To help these children she encouraged teachers to be mindful of student needs and adjustments. She also wrote textbooks for students to use. Whenever she perceived problems, especially those connected directly with students, Richman searched diligently for unique and workable solutions.

Young, Richman, and Dorsey did not lead through standard procedures, but rather they continuously evaluated the complex, shifting needs of their school systems and found ways to make things work. They considered the welfare of their school communities in their analyses and avoided basing their decisions exclusively on rules. Rule-based decision making would have diminished the possibility of caring leadership by focusing attention on polarized abstractions rather than on the contingencies of school leader-follower relationships.

Some of the similarities among these women are striking. They each maintained very close associations with teachers in their systems; they were exceptionally effective at working with teachers organizations and resolving disputes; they were deeply committed to social service and action in their communities; they worked actively to maintain high-quality, caring relationships with diverse members of their school systems; they were well appreciated in their communities on an ongoing basis; they expressed deep concern for the welfare of students in their districts and acted strongly on this concern; and finally, these women provided leadership that considered the complexities and continuously changing aspects of their relationships and contexts. In short, Dorsey, Richman, and Young exemplify what I call *caring leaders*.

SHADES OF DEMOCRACY AND
THE DEMISE OF CARING LEADERSHIP

As effective and popular as these women were in their communities, their leadership styles did not spread among other urban superintendents of the time. Their bases of support were mostly local, decentralized, and unique. Most superintendents chose instead to follow the lead established by the centralized and almost exclusively male Department of Superintendence of the NEA, an organization that by the turn of the century had become arguably one of the most powerful education organizations in the country.

The Department of Superintendence utilized several tactics for building and consolidating its power. One of its major initiatives during the women's suffrage era was to transform school board memberships and superintendencies from elected to appointed positions. Because many of the women superintendents of the time had won their positions through the ballot, they stood to lose much in an appointive system. The department also championed scientific and efficient school standards to be implemented by well-trained, university educated professionals. At the time few women could enroll in university-level administrative preparation programs. This essentially meant that appointments contingent on such training effectively excluded women from administrative positions. Finally, the department's insistence on standardization led many school systems to adopt common administrative practices (Callahan, 1962) that left little room for the flexibility needed to build and maintain caring relationships.

One of the driving concerns of the Department of Superintendence, for example, was the reduction of school board size. As school boards contracted, superintendents found their work of implementing of board decisions easier. More important, however, as boards shrank each member represented a larger segment of the local population. To win board seats candidates increasingly needed large sums of money for their campaigns. As a result, wealthier members of communities soon replaced candidates of more humble means. Eventually homogeneity characterized school boards around the country as men from the business and professional communities and their wives dominated membership (Counts, 1927). Superintendents benefited from a boost in their prestige through association with these wealthier and more influential members of the community (Callahan, 1962, p. 150).

Soon the Department of Superintendence also lobbied for the complete elimination of the elected school board, replacing it instead with appointed members. In 1893, a committee of the department recommended that "city school boards should be small, appointed by the mayor, and divorced from partisan politics" (Callahan, 1962, p. 96–98). The committee further suggested that boards give appointed superintendents greater administrative power and longer contracts. Each of these proposed changes effectively increased superintendents' power, and the change from elected to appointed superintendencies also removed school administrators from direct public accountability, thus minimizing their relationship and connection with community constituencies.

The Department of Superintendence employed two arguments in defending these proposed changes. First, they contended that "The public schools should be absolutely free from the domination of those who would prostitute them to political or personal ends." Second, they explained that "The management of the schools should be in the hands of educational experts clothed with adequate power, protected in their tenure of office, and held responsible for results" (AASA, 1966, p. 88). Because the department believed superintendents were becoming increasingly expert in their work, they should be trusted to carry out their duties without interference from political figures. Both arguments served to elevate the professional stature of the superintendency. These views, however, amounted to adding a bureaucratic layer between school administrators and the school communities they served.

Ellwood Cubberley, Stanford's educational administration scholar from the early years of this century, believed that, although democracy was important for the governance of the country, it did not necessarily extend to school employees. He "praised democracy abstractly but scorned the notion that teachers should participate democratically in determining school policies." He argued instead that schools should "give up the exceedingly democratic idea that all are equal, and that our society is devoid of classes . . . and to begin a specialization of effort along many new lines in an attempt to adapt the school to the needs of these many classes in the city life" (Tyack and Hansot, 1982, p. 128). Essentially he believed that in a class-based society only some should benefit from full democratic privileges. The school leader, though, should enjoy autocratic power, which would effectively minimize reciprocity between a leader and those whom he would administer.

Ella Flagg Young maintained that such added layers not only produced isolation between educators, but also between educators and students. In addition to the problem of isolation, some women leaders found Cubberley's notion of democracy problematic. Margaret Haley, president of the Chicago Federation of Teachers and close friend of Ella Flagg Young, believed that democratic principles should be practiced consistently throughout public schooling. Said Haley:

> Practical experience in meeting the responsibilities of citizenship directly, not in evading or shifting them, is the prime need of the American people. However clever or cleverly disguised the schemes for relieving the public of these responsibilities by vicarious performance of them, or however appropriate those schemes in a monarchy, they have no place in a government of the people, by the people, and for the people, and such schemes must result in defeating their object; for to the extent that they obtain they destroy in a people the capacity for self-government. . . .
>
> Misdirected political activity in lowering the democratic ideal, reacts to lower the educational ideal. On the other hand, a false or incomplete educational ideal fails to free the intelligence necessary for the work of constructing a democracy out of our monarchical inheritance. . . .
>
> Two ideals are struggling for supremacy in American life today: one the industrial ideal, dominating thru the supremacy of commercialism, which subordinates the worker to the product and the machine; the other, the ideal of democracy, the ideal of the educators, which places humanity above all machines, and demands that all activity shall be the expression of life. If this ideal of the educators cannot be carried over into the industrial field, then the ideal of industrialism will be carried over into the school. Those two ideals can no more continue to exist in American life than our nation could have continued half slave and half free. If the school cannot bring joy to the work of the world, the joy must go out of its own life, and work in the school as in the factory will become drudgery. (Haley, 1904, pp. 145–152)

Haley essentially argued that power should be distributed throughout the educational community; that for students, teachers, and administrators to understand democracy they should be trusted to practice it on a daily basis; and that members of the school community must be able to work closely with each other, understand each other, and live with a base of connectedness. She argued that democracy is an ongoing community process that depends on strong relationships among diverse members of society. Aaron Gove, superintendent of Denver Schools and Haley's opponent in this debate that appeared in the 1904 *NEA Proceedings*, argued instead that power should be concentrated in the hands of administrators whom school communities should trust. He contended that the democratic work of citizens ended with the election of those who could then appoint "professionals."

Although this debate focused overtly on issues of power, control, and definitions of democracy, it also revealed remarkable differences in relationship values in school districts. In effect, Haley's conception of the role of school administration, which was inspired largely by Dewey, would have allowed greater room in school administration for caring leadership. After this debate, however, the Department of Superintendence eventually consolidated policy-making power around the nation and consequently succeeded in influencing standards for administrative practice that concentrated authority in the hands of superintendents and minimized possibilities for mutual, reciprocal, caring relationships with diverse members of school communities.

IS THERE STILL ROOM FOR CARING SCHOOL LEADERSHIP?

Although caring school leadership cannot be legislated or standardized at least in part because of its infinite variety and contextual dependence, mandated standardized practices can have the effect of limiting the possibility of caring school leadership. As I have argued, moves toward the standardization of administrative practice and increased isolation in administrative structures have effectively reduced opportunities for individuals to exercise caring school leadership from the superintendency. Those who succeed in serving as caring leaders must first overcome significant structural hurdles, must break the rules, must somehow defy the system.

The women superintendents I have profiled served as caring school leaders at a historical moment before the reification of school administrative structures and practices. Even though these women enjoyed some flexibility in the manner with which they carried out their duties, they still labored against significant difficulties. Because each of these women served in large school districts, they could not possibly know and develop caring relationships with each person in their school communities. Instead, although they undoubtedly cared for many persons in their districts, they ultimately *cared about* most of the others. Noddings regards *caring about* as different from caring for in that the one-caring sees the object of care as an abstraction. A reciprocal relationship does not necessarily exist when one *cares about* someone or something. Without reciprocity the one-caring does not necessarily receive joy in her work; she grows tired; her caring reserves become depleted. Young, Dorsey, and Richman were notable leaders not only for their caring commitment to their work, then, but also for the remarkable amount of energy they expended with relatively little replenishment. Caring school leadership was not sustained perhaps in part because it required so much of its adherents.

The historical examples of Young, Dorsey, and Richman raise questions about the possibility of caring leadership in contemporary school districts. As I have argued, problems of rigid administrative structures and normalized practice hinder, if not prevent caring school leadership. Also, however, whether genuine caring school leadership can exist where superintendents know large portions of their school communities only as abstractions is a question that needs further exploration. When critical dialogue begins around this and related questions, the moment for caring school leadership may reemerge or perhaps open fully for the first time.

REFERENCES

AASA. (1966). "The Centennial Story." In M. C. Nolte, ed., *An Introduction to School Administration: Selected Readings*. New York: Macmillan Publishing Company.

Callahan, R. E. (1962). *Education and the Cult of Efficiency: A Study of the Social Forces That Have Shaped the Administration of the Public Schools*. Chicago: University of Chicago Press.

Cook, R. C., ed. (1928). *Who's Who in American Education: A Biographical Dictionary of Eminent Living Educators of the United States*, Vol. 1. Hattiesburg, MS: Who's Who in American Education.

Cott, N. (1987). *The Grounding of Modern Feminism*. New Haven, CT: Yale University Press.

Counts, G. S. (1927). *The Social Composition of Boards of Education: A Study in the Social Control of Public Education.* Chicago: University of Chicago.

Gribskov, M. (1980). "Feminism and the Women School Administrator." In S. Knopp Biklen and M. Brannigan, eds., *Women and Educational Leadership.* Lexington, MA: Lexington Books.

Haley, M. A. (1904). "Why Teachers Should Organize." *Journal of Proceedings and Addresses of the Forty-Third Annual Meeting of the National Educational Association Held at St. Louis, Missouri.* Winona, MN: National Educational Association.

McGregor, G. (1953). "The Educational Career of Susan Miller Dorsey." *History of Education Journal* 5, no. 1: 15–17.

Matthaei, J. A. (1982). *An Economic History of Women in America: Women's Work, the Sexual Division of Labor, and the Development of Capitalism.* New York: Schocken Books.

Maxcy, S. (1991). *Educational Leadership: A Critical Pragmatic Perspective.* New York: Bergin and Garvey.

Murphy, M. (1990). *Blackboard Unions: The AFT and the NEA, 1900–1980.* Ithaca, NY: Cornell University Press.

Noddings, N. (1984). *Caring: A Feminine Approach to Ethics and Moral Education.* Berkeley, CA: University of California Press.

Sellers, M. S., ed. (1994). *Women Educators in the United States, 1820–1993.* Westwood, CT: Greenwood Press.

Sicherman, B., Green, C. H., Kantrov, I., and Walker, H. (1980). *Notable American Women: 1607–1950.* Cambridge, MA: Belknap Press of Harvard University Press.

Smith, J. K. (1979). *Ella Flagg Young: Portrait of a Leader.* Ames: Educational Studies Press and the Iowa State University Research Foundation.

Solomon, B. M. (1985). *In the Company of Educated Women: A History of Women and Higher Education in America.* New Haven, CT: Yale University Press.

Tyack, D. (1974). *The One Best System: A History of American Urban Education.* Cambridge, MA: Harvard University Press.

———— and Hansot, E. (1982). *Managers of Virtue: Public School Leadership in America, 1820–1980.* New York: Basic Books.

U.S. Government, Office of Education (1921). *Biennial Survey of Education, 1916–1918.* Washington, D.C.: Office of Education.

Young, E. F. (1900). *Isolation in the Schools.* Chicago: University of Chicago Press.

CHAPTER 2

JUSTICE OR CARING

Pedagogical Implications for Gender Equity

JAN STREITMATTER

The past ten years have seen an increasing interest in issues of gender, specifically focusing on women's rights, their perspectives, and their construction of the world as it may differ from that of men. This interest can be found in both recent media coverage as well as the longer history of scholarly attention.

Attention from the media has drawn the broader public into the discussion of gender issues. For example, *Time Magazine*, February 14, 1994, displayed a man with a pig's head on the cover, reading "Are men really that bad?" The gist of the article was that such extensive coverage of victimized women was creating a strong sense that male bashing and creation of negative stereotypes of men has become a formidable problem in North American society today. Reflecting the reverse perception of issues of bias against females, the February 13, 1994 edition of the *New York Times* ran an article that discussed the introduction of a bill into the House of Representatives that would prohibit sexual harassment and other forms of gender bias in schools. Opponents of the proposed bill discount it as unnecessary, citing gains made by girls in schools.

In the realm of scholarship, Gilligan's (1977) early work helped lay the foundation for our thinking about the possibility of fundamental fallacies in how academicians and clinicians view normal human development, specifically moral development. The framework through which we have worked, she contends, is male oriented without consideration of the possibility of a distinct female orientation. *In a Different Voice* (1982) brought into sharper focus the concepts of two moral orientations, caring and justice. Taking as the foundation for our understanding of the justice orientation, Gilligan (1982) discusses Kohlberg's (1969) stages of moral development. Kohlberg describes the highest level of moral decision making as being that which depends on an understanding of the higher laws of equality and justice, on a "principled conception of individual natural rights" (Gilligan, 1977, p. 510). Gilligan quotes a twenty-five-year-old man interviewed by Kohlberg whose response embodies the view of responsibility according to a justice orientation. "[What does the word *morality* mean to you?] Nobody in the world knows the answer. I think it is recognizing the right of the individual, the rights of other individuals, not interfering with those rights. Act as fairly as you would have them treat you. I think it is basically to preserve the human being's right to existence. I think that is the most important. Secondly, the human being's right to do as he pleases, again without interfering with somebody else's rights" (1977, p. 510).

This removed and fairly dispassionate view of individuals is consistent with the justice orientation. The essence or specific needs of the individual are not part of the rationale, rather a generalized notion of individual rights and needs define this orientation. This voice advocates equality, reciprocity, autonomy, obeying rules, and upholding principles.

Gilligan (1977, 1982) suggests that the very different orientation of caring describes the approach to resolving moral dilemmas that females are more likely to use. The basis of this approach was first described by Kohlberg (1969) in his sequence of developmental stages of moral development. Level 2, Stage 3 is known as *Interpersonal Concordance Orientation*, or the "good boy–good girl" approval-seeking orientation. He describes behavior at this stage as motivated by the need to please or help others, such as when children do things not because they believe them to be right, but because they believe that the actions will be praised. Kohlberg's research findings indicated that as both adolescents and adults, females tended to remain at this point in moral development.

Gilligan (1977, 1982) has enhanced and elaborated upon Kohlberg's narrowly constructed look at the thinking embodied in this orientation.

The caring perspective emphasizes responsibility to humans rather than to more abstract ideas and holds as most important the concern for connectedness to others and maintenance of relationships. Kohlberg (1969) described this orientation and the associated decision making as underdeveloped, whereas Gilligan argues that it is merely a different voice rather than a deficient one.

Since Gilligan's earlier work, others such as Lyons (1983, 1987) and Noddings (1984, 1992) have sought to further define *caring*. Lyons's 1983 study examined the moral orientations of males and females. She concluded that, although distinctive lines could not be drawn between the genders with regard to moral orientation, males were far more likely to use only a justice orientation, whereas females used either caring only or both orientations. Noddings's recent work, *The Challenge to Care in Schools* (1992) has taken caring as a concept that could be used to reshape schools in the interests of both females and males. She contends that schools that use caring as the essential component upon which all else is built will provide students with the opportunity to become caring adults who will construct a more sensible future.

The more recent work of Gilligan, Lyons, and Hamner, *Making Connections* (1990), tells the stories of girls at the Emma Willard School, many of whom speak of moral issues in ways that underscore their concern with caring, their attention to people, and the importance of their relationships with those people. These compelling stories tell of girls' emerging sense of self through voices that speak of the importance of relationships and people in those relationships, along with the tension of understanding what is fair and right. The teachers who took part in the four year study also speak. They talk about the changes in the ways they think about the girls, how and what they teach, as well as the changes in how they have thought about themselves over the period of their participation in the study. This work provides valuable insight for teachers, whether they teach in girls only or mixed gender classrooms. Another important work, one that speaks expressly to teachers about caring and justice orientations and the implications in classrooms, is Kay Johnston's (1992) examination of the connection between teachers' moral orientations and decision making in classrooms.

Johnston (1992) agrees with Tom (1984) that the relationship between teacher and student has an essential moral framework within which it functions; that teachers are moral craftspersons. Further, within the daily routine in the classroom, teachers are called upon to make multiple decisions that have an impact on their students and have a moral connotation to them. The students' academic and personal lives are affected by these decisions. Johnston contends that the majority of teachers make these decisions according to a justice orientation, with the goal of following the rules themselves, applying the same rules to all, and therefore assuring an equal approach to students' learning activities and behavior management. Within a context that integrates a caring orientation, Johnston suggests that teachers are in a position to construct relationships with their students that allow a more relative approach to decision making based on the needs of the individual student, the situation at hand, and what may represent fairness for that student at that moment.

Johnston's (1992) work provides a helpful blueprint for teachers in their rethinking the premise for general decision making in the classroom. What many are coming to see as the female voice or female moral orientation is important to consider as we teach and interact with students. It is an important means of empowering students, particularly females, whose voices otherwise might not be heard by the teacher or other students. However, according to the results of Lyons's (1983) work, there are important implications for male students as well, for whom a caring orientation may be a means of seeing the world.

Conceptually connected with the scholarship that addresses moral orientation is the work done by researchers examining the slightly broader concept of gender equity in schools. Considerable research about questions of females' place and power in schools has been conducted since the introduction of Title IX of the Education Amendment Act, 1972. The conclusions have been that, despite the prohibition of gender discrimination in schools, boys continue to be more empowered than girls in every respect. This uneven life by gender in schools is present in nearly every piece of schooling. For example, teacher and student interactions, curriculum, classroom organization, and teaching methods all reflect the dominance of males in the schooling enterprise (*The AAUW Report: How Schools Shortchange Girls* [1992] provides a good source for a review of much of the pertinent literature).

Some teachers, although it is a strikingly small group, are beginning actively to work toward gender equity in their teaching practice. They construct their understanding of what gender equity means to them and how it makes the best sense to rethink their teaching to address gender bias. Implied in their thinking and actions as teachers is the consideration of voice and moral orientation. As Johnston (1992) has suggested, the teacher's moral orientation is reflected as she or he makes the many decisions required during the teaching day. The teacher's caring or justice orientation or both is imbedded in the various aspects of teaching. Interactions with students are an important example of a component of teaching where the teacher's decision making reflects his or her moral orientation. The daily practice of teachers who integrate gender equity into their teaching reflects their interpretation and implementation not only of gender equity but also their own moral orientation(s).

The following is the discussion of two teachers as they use different interpretations and approaches to gender equity in their teaching. Within that context, their moral orientations are considered through an examination of their decision making in the area of interaction with students and specifically in their use of discipline. To create a clearer picture of the ways these two teachers think about gender equity, a brief discussion of their separate ways of constructing gender equity precede the teachers' stories.

GENDER EQUALITY OR GENDER EQUITY?

The label *gender equity* is used fairly universally to represent ways of thinking and acting that address gender issues. The term *equity* is used to describe the general concept. However, when one begins to consider how gender equity is operationalized, it becomes clear that there are essentially two ways to conceptualize it: within a framework of *equal* (or *equality* when the term is used as a noun) or within a framework of *equitable*. *Gender equity* is the general term for referring to gender-related practices, but it may be interpreted as equal treatment or equitable treatment. In using the conceptual framework of equality, one is particularly concerned about issues at the beginning, or schooling "inputs," which Secada (1989) defines as "what a school starts with when educating its students. Those resources-financial (monies), physical (books in a library, science lab equipment), and personnel (its teachers and how qualified they are)-are distributed (i) directly among schools and (ii) indirectly among the students who enroll in those schools" (1989, p. 70).

The actions of implementing "equal" treatment would involve assuring that students receive the same opportunities for access and participation. A teacher could put this into practice by providing the same or equivalent materials to all learners; being certain all learners participate actively and with the same frequency; assuring that all learners receive equal access to all aspects of the curriculum; and assuring that all curriculum materials have comparable "male" and "female" characteristics or models. Teaching that is sensitive to gender equity practices and that is structured through this conceptual framework of equality is concerned primarily with giving all students, female and male, an equal footing at the start (Secada, 1989).

Several points are implied through this framework. An approach of equality will enhance the learning opportunities of female and male students. How equal the achievement or attitudes and dispositions of the students will be at the end of the period is fairly open ended. The implication is that with an equal beginning, students will proceed according to their individual capabilities. Some will do better than others or will have different preferences, but there will not be an explicit difference between identifiable groups (Secada, 1989).

Gender equity through an "equitable" framework is approached differently. Its premise is that a particular group historically and habitually has been less advantaged within the system than another group. In the case of those committed to teaching equitably within the context of gender concerns, the group at risk is generally considered to be female learners, although there are certain circumstances within classroom life where it becomes quite clear that some males individually are the victims of gender bias. But when considering students as members of particular groups, females are arguably less advantaged when the final outcomes of academic achievement are measured (*AAUW Report*, 1992). Indeed, final outcomes tend to be the principal issues of concern when one adopts the framework of "equitable" as opposed to "equal." For instance, a teacher may stress participation of female learners in science over that for male learners if, for example, fewer females enter a science fair or score as highly on science tests as males.

The next step of implementing gender equity through an equitable framework is to enhance opportunities for the at-risk group, sometimes to the point of extending an unequal and greater amount of resources toward that group rather than equalizing resources between girls and boys. The rationale is that it is fair to work in a somewhat unequal fashion to remove the factors that have previously placed this group at risk for unequal achievement in the end. Gender-equitable teaching suggests that, without extra or different consideration, a particular group will not have the capability and opportunity to finish at the same level as the other group. Equal distribution of inputs, or resources such as quality of instruction, frequency of teacher interactions, and level of teacher expectation, is not sufficient to assure that there will be no significant difference between groups, female and male, when final outcomes are measured. Equitable teaching practices cannot assure the same outcomes for all individuals within a category, due to issues such as individuals' interests and levels of motivation. However, the goal is to attempt to provide for the possibility of equal outcomes given systematic societal biases.

The stories of Judy and Beth follow. Both are strongly committed to addressing gender equity in their teaching. The similarity ends there. Their underlying assumptions about gender equity differ as do their methods of approaching the issues with their students. Further, their decision making within the context of gender equity reflects different moral orientations.

JUDY

Judy directs and teaches in a preschool in a medium-sized school district. The preschool consists of four classes of a maximum of fourteen students each. Special-needs students are integrated with non-special needs children. Judy has a strong commitment toward gender equity in her teaching that adheres to the framework of equality. This is apparent in all aspects of her daily work with her preschool students and her staff, but particularly through her interactions with students. The following illustrates a typical series of interactions that Judy has with her students.

The school day begins at 9:00. The five boys and eight girls in Judy's class have arrived by 9:20, each accompanied by his or her mother. Judy greets each of the children in nearly an identical fashion. Boys and girls are spoken to in an adult tone of voice, reminded to stow their belongings in their cubbies. Even though two of the girls appear in designer outfits and another girl wears a frilly dress complete with party shoes, Judy does not comment on their appearance. Instead she remarks about their facial expressions and readiness for the day.

"It's good to see you this morning. I like the way you look ready to get started."

Judy intentionally keeps her praise gender neutral and steers away from commenting about physical appearance. She remarks: "Girls are too often complimented about their appearance rather than their ability. I don't comment about the girls' pretty clothes or hair."

In monitoring the students, she is careful about interacting with all the children equally. As they work, each child receives exactly the same amount of teacher interaction as the next. The quantity of academic interaction time (or in the case of preschool, center activity work) is intentionally doled out in equal amounts. Judy also is conscious of equalizing the content, or quality, of her interactions. As she engages each student in discussions and descriptions of her or his activities, she displays no preconceived notions about gender-based interests or abilities. The content of the discussion she holds with several girls in the home center is quite similar to the content of a later discussion with a boy playing in the same center.

Judy attempts to and succeeds in working with each child, whether girl or boy, in nearly an identical fashion. Her tone of voice and her words are as similar from one child to the next as she can possibly make them. This is true whether she is disciplining or complimenting a child. For example, when one girl takes a pencil from another girl, Judy reacts to the problem by saying "Susan, I would like you to remember our rule about respecting the rights of others. Taking another person's things is breaking that rule." Later in the day, when a boy knocks another boy down during an outside play period, she repeats the same words and in the same tone of voice. As she walks over to the two boys who have had the scuffle, she says to the aggressor, "Brian, I would like you to remember our rule about respecting the rights of others. Pushing another person is breaking that rule." At one point another day when a group of children were in the painting center, Judy remarks "Katherine, I like the way you are filling the entire paper with your work." Later, another group enters that center. As Steven paints, Judy repeats her words exactly to the male artist.

Judy's purpose in using this approach is several-fold. She believes firmly that each of the children in the class should be treated exactly as every other child, regardless of gender or special needs. She views herself as responsible for creating a classroom where equal inputs are provided. Because she is very familiar with the literature regarding teachers' tendency to give boys more and different kinds of attention than girls, she constantly monitors herself to be certain that her words and actions are the same for girls and boys.

As in all other aspects of her gender-equitable teaching practice, Judy constructs discipline within the framework of equality. Judy is concerned with discipline as a process issue; students who break classroom rules are spoken to in the same fashion and receive the same consequences regardless of gender. In Judy's classroom several of the boys are aggressive and loud. A situation occurred in the home center. This center is furnished with a cabinet with dishes, a table and chairs, dress-up clothes, and a variety of baby dolls. Judy has paid careful attention to making the center one that she believes will be attractive to girls as well as boys. The dress-up clothes include a variety of male and female clothes. Sequined gowns, aprons, construction hard-hats, men's work shirts, and a variety of men's and women's shoes are available for the children to try on. The babies are black, white, brown, and Asian. All are anatomically correct; three are female and one is male. A situation occurred in the home center that illustrates Judy's equality-framed discipline approach.

Two girls finish playing "house," setting the table for a meal and cradling their babies. They take off their aprons and leave the center for another activity. Before departing however, they begin to have a very loud conversation. Judy comes over to them from another side of the room and asks them to please play in a way that will not disturb others. They quiet down and move on to a different center.

The two oldest and largest boys then enter the center. After rummaging through the dress-up clothes and choosing large men's shirts to wear, they turn to the baby dolls. Each boy picks up one and begins to shake and shout at the dolls. The noise level begins to escalate as the boys become increasingly more violent in their "play" with the dolls, culminating with their stabbing, punching, and throwing the dolls against the wall. Judy calmly turns to the boys saying, "How can you play in the center more quietly?"

Despite the dramatic difference in the type of play of the girls and the boys, Judy speaks to both groups not only using the same words, but more important imposing the same rule; others' play should not be disturbed, and by being loud in a discussion, or by loudly beating up dolls, the same rule was violated.

These examples illustrate many of the subtleties present in Judy's interpretation of gender equity as well as her decision making, which is founded on a moral orientation. Judy moves through her day with her students in ways that are structured by a rigid adherence to the principles of equality and according to a justice orientation. She strictly monitors verbal and non-verbal interactions according to a set of rules and standards that she has set for herself and her students. The overriding rule is that no one's rights may be violated, whether that is played out in taking another person's property or in pushing someone down. Her gender-equity related reason for teaching and interacting the way she does is perfectly consistent with her belief in providing the identical resources to all of her students regardless of gender. She guards against what she believes is the constant tendency of nearly all teachers: giving boys more and different attention.

In strictly monitoring her verbal and nonverbal interactions according to a set of rules and standards and being certain to apply them to her students in a very equal way, she also is reflecting her moral orientation. In Judy's classroom, all students have the same rights, her expectations of the students are the same, and she redirects or praises students in accordance with the principle of justice. Judy believes that this is the most appropriate means for assuring that she treats all of her students equally.

The caring orientation described by Gilligan (1982) speaks to the importance of relationships, their development and maintenance. It is no surprise that in Judy's classroom, where the elements of a caring orientation are avoided, relationships across genders do not occur.* In fact, Judy's classroom reflects stark barriers between gender groups that have been constructed by the children and not addressed by Judy as she resists treating children differently, hearing different voices, or more directly suggesting that the children interact with those of the other gender. By the end of the school year, the boys remain within their group and the girls within theirs, with virtually no interaction. Judy has achieved the surface goal of providing equal inputs for the children, but any outward signs of changes in the children's sexist behaviors and attitudes are not present.

BETH

Beth teaches seventh and eighth grade science in a middle school with early adolescents from Native American and Hispanic cultures and of lower socioeconomic backgrounds. Beth's interpretation of gender equity in her teaching, as well as in other aspects of her life, is that of equity. She is concerned primarily with outcomes and secondarily with inputs. She believes that female students in the school and especially those in her classes are more at risk than the boys because of pervasive societal gender bias. Based on this belief, Beth consciously distributes her resources unevenly; her instructional time and attention and her energy outside of the classroom are directed more to the girls than the boys. To enhance girls' opportunities for

---

* Although there is evidence that children in this early childhood development period often choose to be with other children of the same gender (e.g., Hamachek, 1985), my recent research revealed that more aggressive gender-equity related interventions on the part of the teacher allow for the creation of a classroom climate where children work and play together in mixed-gender groups quite spontaneously (Streitmatter, 1994).

success in her science classroom and in the schooling process from middle school onward, Beth overcompensates in her approach to them in an attempt to equalize the eventual outcomes. That is not to say that the boys are systematically ignored; they are a strong presence in the classes. But Beth is very conscious of the tendency in any classroom for male domination, particularly in a domain such as science. When asked, given that her resources as a teacher are limited, should one group in the classroom receive more than the other, she replies: "Girls ought to get it. Of course. Although during the Women's Month Activities, I wish there was something for boys. But I always find my interest and concern are for the girls."

During one session in a seventh grade class, Beth engages her students in a typical question and answer period. Her pattern and style of interaction with her students illustrates her implementation of her equity approach to gender equity.

Beth goes through an introduction to acid rain without a pause. Following the introduction, she begins to ask review questions. "Where does acid rain come from?" A boy seated in the back shouts out an answer. Beth ignores him and calls on a girl seated in front who does not have her hand raised. "Sonya, where does acid rain come from?" The girl promptly answers correctly. Another question is put forth. Boys' and girls' hands go up. Beth calls on a girl with her hand raised, whose response to the question is only partially correct. "That's only part of the answer. What else can you add?" Beth asks Maria. Hands wave, but Beth waits a full fifteen seconds until Maria adds additional information to her answer. More questions follow. During that time Beth calls on boys, but the frequency by gender is not equal. In fact, she calls on about twice the number of girls than boys, many of whom have not volunteered to answer.

Beth consistently calls on girls more often than boys, ignores any student who shouts out answers (although in over 20 hours of observation in her classes, only boys shouted out answers), and frequently calls on girls whose hands are not raised. She is confident that the girls can do the work and get the right answers, and this expectation is relayed to the girls. Each one called on does know the answer and proves her success in science to herself and the rest of the group.

While the interaction pattern is a distinctive indicator of an equity framework in action, her moral orientation might appear initially as no different from that of Judy. However, speaking with Beth and gaining further insight to other aspects of her work in the area of gender equity point to a clear caring orientation.

At the beginning of each class period, the students rush in to beat the bell. Students cluster around Beth, asking her how she is, what she did the night before, or what she will do that weekend. Beth has a personal question for each student as well. "Jorge, how was basketball practice last night?" and "Shandra, how is your sister's baby doing now?" are examples. She knows each of the students as individuals, knows the parts of their lives that are not apparent to the casual observer, and believes that it is essential for the students to know that she cares about them as whole people. But again, she gives a bit more to the girls. An example is the series of programs that she runs during Women's Month each year.

> Some of the activities are just for fun, where there are all women. The university volleyball team comes out. We take the girls to see the women's university basketball team play. We also have lunch forums. One is about the different pressure points on girls and boys. Another is on domestic violence. Another thing we do is show a film in the seventh-grade language arts and social studies classes. It's about a son who wants to be a dancer and a daughter who wants to be a lawyer. It makes a point about parental expectation about gender. We do a mother-daughter luncheon. It's great. We had sixty girls and their mothers this year. They were in heaven. They got waited on for a change. I told a story about women achieving against great odds. A girl from school read a poem. I talked about how Women's Month got started and that we were here to celebrate what we do have, and the struggle women have had in the past.
>
> The girls need to have a voice and to see who they are. When they're with the boys, they don't get a chance to make decisions. The boys usually dominate. That's why it's so important to give them this.

Beth knows each girl and becomes acquainted with the many issues that are intertwined in their lives. As in nearly all underclass neighborhoods, poverty, early pregnancy, dropping out, and domestic violence are prevalent within these families. Beth sees her development of personal caring about the girls, as well as the development of programs such as the Women's Month activities as essential parts of her work toward empowerment of the girls in her school.

The structure of Beth's decision making in the classroom suggests that she makes use of both justice and caring orientations. Her choice of disciplinary procedures within the classroom reflects this combination. At the beginning of the school year, Beth explains the discipline policy and the rules. If a rule is broken the first time, the student's name is placed on the board. A check goes after the student's name if she or he does something wrong a second time, and so forth. Each check indicates 15 minutes after school in Beth's class.

Close observation of a number of Beth's classes indicated that each student, whether female or male, who broke a rule received a check mark. There was no gender differentiation here. Further, the numbers of check marks for girls was only one less than that for boys over time. Regardless of circumstance, at least during the class time, any student breaking the rules received the same punishment. However, after the school day, Beth used the detention time to interact with the students, especially the girls, in a way that gave both Beth and the students the opportunity to further establish their relationships. She did talk with the boys, but the bulk of her time went to the girls. For example, on one occasion, Suzette needed to make up time for two check marks that she had received for talking with her neighbor. Beth sat with Suzette and worked to get at the root of a problem that she suspected existed. During the 45 minutes (Suzette stayed past her detention time), Beth discovered that Suzette had left home to stay with a friend because her father's continued alcohol problem was creating an abusive situation. Beth promised to get help for Suzette and a day later had followed through.

GENDER EQUITY AND MORAL ORIENTATION

Judy and Beth present very different approaches both to their understanding of gender equity in their teaching and to decision making as seen through a lens of moral orientation. To begin with, each has a different goal for her gender equity work. Judy's principle concern is to create a place for children where each will receive identical treatment from her. Her underlying assumption is that this equal treatment will provide a foundation for each child to move on to Kindergarten and beyond, unimpeded by gender bias they will encounter in the future. Embedded in her equal treatment is a justice orientation to decision making. Establishing relationships with some children and perhaps not others is the antithesis to her goal. It is only through not establishing relationships with any child that she is able to ensure that she does not favor, or treat unequally, a child.

Beth proceeds quite differently. The relationships she establishes with her students enable her to create a special and empowering setting for all students, but especially the girls. Without knowing them and showing them that she cares about all aspects of their lives, she would not be as successful in creating science classes where girls succeed (sometimes in spite of themselves) and in creating opportunities where girls can envision many opportunities for themselves in the future.

Often during the course of a school year, but most often during Women's Month, people who are uneasy with Beth's approach ask "But what about the boys?" Beth explains that the boys in her classes receive plenty of attention. It is just that people are not used to girls being on an equal footing or even dominating because the norm is for boys to dominate. She thinks through the issue this way: "At the beginning of the year, the boys love me. I'm funny, charismatic, a jock, and have sports stories. So they can share some of that stuff. But by the second or third quarter, the girls have picked up that I listen, and that I care. And the boys like that, too—that I really care about them. The girls succeed in my class, and they're not used to succeeding in science. I have so many girls who say, 'Oh my God, I've always hated science.' I definitely share with the girls what they like to talk about. We like to talk about our families, boyfriends, friends."

Beth's interpretation of gender equity according to an equity framework, and her deep commitment to establishing close relationships with her students are intertwined. Her actions that provide unequal and greater resources to the girls are interrelated with her use of a caring moral orientation.

There is no easy measure that indicates which of the approaches toward gender equity is the better one. Does an equality approach, by virtue of giving the girls the same as the boys, provide the best context and enough subtle support to girls so that they, regardless of gender, have the full range of options open in life? Or does an equity approach, with emphatic attention to empowerment of girls by virtue of their gender, give them the additional support they may require to recognize their options?

Although an unqualified prescription for determining the better means of integrating gender equity and moral orientation in our classrooms probably cannot be identified without longitudinal studies of girls and boys in various classroom settings, in the interim it is important to go back to the essence of the issue surrounding our work with gender equity and caring in schools. How do we as educators create classrooms where each voice is heard to the extent that each student is empowered to reach her or his greatest potential? What does appear obvious is that a caring orientation to decision making provides an opportunity for girls' voices to be heard and for them to establish greater faith in their abilities. In Beth's classroom, this appears to be the case in both the girls' acquisition of science and in their recognition of their options in other aspects of their lives. These two components of her teaching create a more powerful setting than if implemented singly. Beth places high priority on gender equity issues and frames her decision making through a moral orientation that focuses on caring. Beth's teaching that connects an equity approach with a predominant caring orientation offers an illustration of a place that provides an empowering environment for the girls whose lives she touches.

ACKNOWLEDGMENT

This chapter is excerpted in part from J. Streitmatter, *Toward Gender Equity in the Classroom: Everyday Teachers' Beliefs and Practices*. Albany: SUNY Press, 1994.

REFERENCES

The AAUW Report: How Schools Shortchange Girls. (1992). Wellesley, MA: AAUW Educational Foundation, Wellesley College Center for Research on Women.

Gilligan, C. (1977). "In a Different Voice: Women's Conceptions of the Self and Morality." *Harvard Educational Review* 47: 481–517.

———. (1982). *In a Different Voice*. Cambridge, MA: Harvard University Press.

———, Lyons, N., and Hanmer, T. J. (1990). *Making Connections: The Relational Worlds of Adolescent Girls at Emma Willard School*. Cambridge, MA: Harvard University Press.

Hamachek, D. E. (1985). *Psychology in Teaching, Learning, and Growth*. Newton, MA: Allyn and Bacon, Inc.

Johnston, K. (1992). "Two Moral Orientations: How Teachers Think and Act in the Classroom." In A. Garrod, ed., *Learning for Life: Moral Education Theory and Practice*. Westport, CT: Praeger.

Kohlberg, L. (1969). "Stage and Sequence: The Cognitive-Developmental Approach to Socialization. In D. A. Goslin, ed., *Handbook of Socialization Theory and Research*. Chicago: Rand McNally.

Lyons, N. (1983). "Two Perspectives: On Self, Relationships and Morality." *Harvard Educational Review* 53:125–145.

———. (1987). "Ways of Knowing, Learning and Making Moral Choices." *Journal of Moral Education* 16:3.

Noddings, N. (1984). *Caring: A Feminine Approach to Ethics and Moral Education.* Berkeley: University of California Press.

———. (1992). *The Challenge to Care in Schools: An Alternative Approach to Schools.* New York: Teachers College Press.

Secada, W. G., ed. (1989). *Equity in Education.* New York: Falmer Press.

Streitmatter, J. L. (1994). *Toward Gender Equity in the Classroom: Everyday Teachers' Beliefs and Practices.* Albany: SUNY Press.

Tom, A. (1984). *Teaching as a Moral Craft.* New York: Longman.

CHAPTER 3

UNCOMMON CARING

Male Primary Teachers as Constructed and Constrained

JAMES R. KING

Teaching, particulary teaching in the primary grades has been construed as an act of caring. Primary teachers I know often say "We teach the child, not the subject." And in these times when traditional families may no longer be representative of school children's home lives, there is a call for men to participate in teaching at the primary grades. Yet, even with the invitation, men are not choosing to become teachers in primary grades. This chapter is an exploration of culturally constructed factors such as caring, gendered behavior, and sexual orientations that may have an impact on men's participation in primary teaching. After all, how each of us views each other becomes part of how the other sees oneself.

A public perception is that men who teach primary grades are often either homosexuals, pedophiles, or principals (in training). These commonly held, but seldom voiced, presuppositions have had a strong impact on men's decisions to teach young children. Furthermore, such perceptions ensure that the men who do choose to be primary teachers are frequently seen as "suspect." Although the rhetoric from the education culture overtly entices young men to consider elementary teaching, we covertly monitor those male teachers who are not married, and who "act funny." In this chapter, I do not intend to speak against the careful monitoring of who is,

47

and who is not, encouraged or not allowed to teach children. In fact, I believe it is crucial to evaluate prospective teachers' suitability for work with young children. Yet, as a former primary teacher, as a teacher trainer, and as a gay man, I wish to examine some of the frameworks that have been used in the covert monitoring of male primary teachers and suggest that some evaluation frameworks for prospective teachers are misguided. When primary education is viewed as a context of caring, men's work as caregivers can be seen as a problem.

UNCOMMON MEN IN A CONTEXT OF CARE

Teaching in the primary grades is a complex endeavor. Nais (1989) describes the experience as one that requires teachers who are comfortable teaching from their personal values, most especially "caring for" and "loving" children. Although caring is an important part of teaching at all levels, love and care as well as other nurturing behaviors are privileged attributes in primary teaching contexts. One could even say care is requisite or synonymous with primary teaching. Further, primary teachers are described by Nais as teaching in integrated ways. Nais intends to include both curriculum and relationships. That is, primary teachers integrate subject areas such as math, science, and literacy into cohesive, inclusive learning activities. Similarly, primary teachers interact with students, as well as other teachers, in ways that build and maintain close relationships and a sense of connectedness.

I agree with Nais's characterization of primary teaching and suggest that this dichotomy of academic subjects and relationships is likewise one that is imploded, causing even more thorough integration. So, subject area boundaries are breached and interpersonal relationships are part of the class curriculum. Integration of subjects and relationships leads to teaching in ways that hinge on social and affective reference groups. Social groups are found among colleagues, with student groups, and across levels of school hierarchy.

The caring and nurturing that characterize primary education culture are themes that are parallel to feminist views of females' moral development (Gilligan, 1982), feminist accounts of caring (Noddings, 1984), and women's ways of learning and knowing (Belenky, et al., 1986). In fact, Noddings's (1984) *Caring: A Feminist Approach to Ethics and Moral Education* and Nais's (1989) *Primary Teachers Talking* have much in common in their conceptualization of teaching as acts of caring. Noddings suggests that entering the profession of teaching is to enter a "very special—and specialized—caring relationship" (p. 174). She characterizes teachers' (the one-caring) professional moves as centered on students (the cared-for). "When a teacher asks a question in class and a student responds, the teacher receives not just the 'response' but the student [as well]" (p. 176). The answer is less important than the engagement between the student and the teacher. According to Noddings, teachers accomplish their focus on students by "be[ing] totally and *nonselectively* present to the student—each student—as he [sic] addresses me" (p. 180, emphasis mine). Although Noddings addresses these arguments to the ethics of teaching, I suggest that they are particularly well suited to primary teaching culture. Further, although it is my hunch that "nonselectivity" was intended by Noddings to indicate all students, I suggest that *all* of the teacher is also a crucial issue. Being there for children means freedom for the teacher to be there as a whole person. When Noddings (1984) writes about the need to "be there" it sounds like: "Th(e) picture is incomplete so long as I see myself only as the one-caring. But as I reflect also on the way I am as cared-for, I can see clearly my own longing to be received, understood, and accepted" (p. 49).

How we construct ourselves as caring persons, as teachers for our students, is a purposeful act. Teachers who are comfortable with who they are more likely "be there." On the other hand, those teachers who are preoccupied with life issues outside the classroom are less able to center on children and their needs.

For many, these attributions by Nais (1989), Noddings (1984) and others have tended to shape (or been reproductive of) a public perception of primary teaching as "women's work." When teaching is construed as an act of caring, then care as a gender identified behavior has extra significance. In fact, Noddings (1992) writes that "Women have learned to regard every human encounter as a potential caring occasion" (p. 24). I interpret this to mean that caring is essentialized as a feminine way of relating to or constructing social reality. Of course, Noddings argues for the appropriateness of males as the ones-caring as well as females. As Noddings (1984) writes, "It should be clear that my description of an ethic of caring as a feminine ethic does not imply a claim to speak for all women nor to exclude men . . . [Yet] there is reason to believe that women are somewhat better equipped for caring than men are" (p. 97).

I am suggesting that, although caring is associated with "the feminine," it is also true that men can and do provide appropriate caring. Further, that based on sexist cultural attitudes, caring is devalued when it is acted out by men. The conflating of caring and primary teaching has had predictable effects on men's participation. And in fact the numbers from a survey by the National Association for the Education of Young Children (1985) suggested that only about 5 percent of direct child-care providers were men. Yet, there is no systematic evidence suggesting that men are inappropriate persons to provide the nurturing and caring thought to be essential for learning contexts involving primary and preschool children. Therefore, it is important to examine how it might be that men are so dramatically underrepresented in the profession of primary education.

HEARING (AND IGNORING) THE CALL

Seifert (1988a) has suggested that men's experiences as fathers means that they can successfully engage in caring and nurturing behaviors. Yet, he is careful to point out that the caring provided by men as fathers is at least differentiated from that provided by teachers in the length of fixed units of time spent caring for their children. Teachers are required to care for longer intervals than the intervals for which fathers customarily provide care. It is also quite possible that fathers fill the role of number 2 caregiver, often a helper or a supplement to mom. In caring, men classroom teachers are on their own.

Seifert further suggests that the reasoning behind the rhetoric, "We need more men teaching primary grades," may also be problematic and negatively influences men's selection of primary teaching. His first argument to support the need for greater numbers of men in primary teaching is a "compensation hypothesis," which simultaneously suggests that men can provide "sex appropriate" role models for boys and offer children of both sexes models of caring, nurturing males. But Seifert sees these two issues as contradictory. It is quite possible that a sensitive, nurturing male could be perceived by others as providing a role model that is inappropriate for young boys. Some parents may not want their children exposed to nuturing, caring, and or what the parents may construe as "soft" males. It is not a perspective that I share, but one that I know to exist.

Sometimes when I teach primary grade students or when I talk with my young neighbors, I intuitively know the very real differences in myself when I center on the "cared-for" (Noddings, 1984). I can drop my adult privilege and enter a space that respects and values humans of all ages;

where participants agree to honor the "other" like self, tell "the truth," and suspend personal agendas. It is an experience redolent with senses of "being there." The payoff *is* being there. It is my personal connection with women's ways, the feminine, and a self-identified gay spirit (Roscoe, 1988) that enable these small connections. But crossing over what the larger culture considers gendered behaviors is risky business. I examine this paradox of gender related social behavior as it relates to sexual orientation in a following section of this chapter. For now, suffice to say that perhaps the role ambiguity and resultant confusion inherent in disrupting the expected gender related social behaviors is related to some men's decisions not to be primary teachers. Because they characteristically have greater numbers of employment options, men more readily choose other work alternatives in preference to early childhood teaching.

Seifert's (1988a) second argument, a "social equity hypothesis," proposes that men entering primary teaching may enhance the stature of what is perceived to be "women's work." This, too, is a problematic assumption that I examine in the following section.

PRIMARY TEACHING AND THE PROBLEM OF "WOMEN'S WORK"

Most germane to the arguments that follow is Seifert's discussion of gender bias regarding the society's construction of "early childhood teacher" or "primary teacher." In colleges of education, we systematically direct male students away from primary grades (Seifert, 1983). In the profession, teachers also gender type teacher's roles along traditional perceptions of gender. Seeing primary education as "women's work" is problematic for many reasons. First of all, from recent feminist perspectives, nurturing and caring (Noddings, 1992) or connected knowing (Belenky et al., 1986) are strengths that are particular, though not exclusive, to women's (and girls') experiences in our culture. So in that sense, being female can be seen as a predisposition for primary education, when teaching, especially primary teaching, is seen as caring (Noddings, 1984). My interpretation of the intent of this feminist essentialist argument is to create an understanding of women's perceptions and theories of the world and how those constructs might differ from patriarchal knowing. Yet, when that same feminine model of knowing and being is mapped into patriarchally controlled workplaces, such as schools, contradictory messages emerge. In fact, the special characteristics accorded women in these recent feminist epistemologies have also been used to devalue women's job skills and expertise in hierarchially organized and competitive workplaces. According to Reskin (1991): "women's assignment to child care, viewed as unskilled work in our society, illustrates these patterns. Women are said to have a 'natural talent' for it and similar work, men are relieved from doing it; society obtains free or cheap child care; and women are handicapped from competing with men" (p. 147).

If nurturing and caring are "skills" that are rewarded inside the profession of child care, they are also devalued outside the profession. Sugg (1978) has suggested that American education, teaching in particular, has been systematically feminized and has lost status as a result. Because others outside early childhood education, including teachers at other levels, see our requisite skilled behaviors as "natural," or as feminine predispositions, they may not feel compelled to reward those competencies with appropriate compensation. Or, since child-care job skills are acquired prior to their execution at the worksite, the skills themselves are not seen as job specific. Again, economic reward is unnecessary.

Reskin's (1991) arguments relative to gender typing and sex segregated work are also helpful in understanding men's small numbers for reasons other than compensation for work. Reskin proposes that dominant groups (men) maintain their economic advantages by differentiating work, and that they support this through physical segregation and behavior differentiation. Because "difference" is a necessary presupposition for dominance, physically segregating men and women is necessary. Reskin proposes that men actively keep men and women in different working contexts because working as equals minimizes perceived differences and threatens to reduce the dominance of men. Social task differentiation by gender also preserves males' hegemonic positions.

Reskin suggests that when women and men do work in the same physical and psychological space, equal pay for equal work is a more plausible outcome. Of course, women who teach are rewarded more equitably in relation to men who teach. However, when salary schedules for public school teachers are differentiated by grade levels, elementary teachers make less money than most other teachers. So, although primary teachers do better than women's sixty cents to each dollar of men's pay, they may still be a "good buy" for the culture.

Allowing men to participate in elementary culture may cause a shift in prestige and salary for both men *and women* in primary and preschool contexts (Seifert, 1988b). To reduce the likelihood of that possibility, the social construction of "primary teacher" has been loaded with features that surround the constructs of "female" and "mother." The relationship between social constructs for primary teacher and mother are nearly isomorphic in the minds of the culture. Given the implicit fear of "the feminine" and misogynistic responses to that fear, men will be dissuaded from primary teaching.

When a man does choose to break the social tabu of working *with* women, there are serious consequences to be paid. *Primary male* (or male primary teacher) has been so crafted that it implicitly includes negative, low prestige features, such as "feminine," "homosexual," and "pedophile." These cultural and semantic loadings on the concept of "male primary teacher" are, in my opinion, why the voices of these professionals are muted. And with silence, we lose the chance to interrogate those unspoken accusations. I am suggesting that these associations, construed negatively by the culture, are being used to control the number of men who choose to enter primary education and to manipulate those men who do teach young children. Further, it is apparent that the appropriation of the constructs of "feminine," "homosexual," and "pedophile" reveals much about the misogyny and heterosexism implicit in these devaluing comparisons.

TEACHERS' SEXUALITY

Primary teaching has been considered "women's work." In addition to cost control for child care, the professional persona for that work has also been influenced by patriarchal constructions of "women who work" (with children). Until the 1930s, women teachers in many areas were expected to be virgins. They were often required to be single and were not allowed to date. When they married, they left teaching. Later, when marriages were allowed, pregnant women were forced out of teaching. Essentially, only chaste women were allowed to teach. To teach, women were required to lack sexuality. Through the Victorian mores of sexual repression, women teachers were expected to represent themselves as having no sexuality. This repression is related to Western Victorian morality, which essentially split caring from sexuality. One could not be nuturing and sexual, since Eros was the feared demon that, if unconstrained, would overwhelm the goodness of a caring relationship with base, evil sex.

To return to the issue of gay men teaching children, one can see the problem in combining the categories of "gay" and "teacher." In popular culture, gay men are defined by sexual difference. By extension of that perceived difference, we are often construed as oversexed or as sexually not properly restrained, or as sexually turned bad or evil. In this sense, a gay man may be seen as the opposite of the chaste woman American culture wanted (wants?) teaching its children. In the 1930s Waller wrote: "the real danger is that [a homosexual man] may, by presenting himself as a love object to certain members of his own sex at a time when their sex attitudes have not been deeply canalized, develop in them attitudes similar to his own. For nothing seems more certain than that homosexuality is contagious" (1932, pp. 147–148).

Waller's belief that one's sexual orientation is subject to conditioning is now largely discredited in the medical and psychological communities. Yet teachers still deal with the tenacious fallout from earlier times.

THE COSTS OF CARING COVERTLY

A common perception of men who teach in primary grades and preschools is that these men are homosexuals. Another common perception is that homosexual males are effeminate. The effect of these largely inaccurate mappings between homosexuality, teaching, and gendered behavior has had disastrous effects on teachers. As a closeted, gay primary teacher, I constantly monitored my behaviors around my children. I was anxious about how other teachers, parents, and principals would interpret my interactions and relationships with my students. The paradox that my self-monitoring engendered is complex. As a strong child advocate, I valued the concern that I and other adults have for children. Therefore, like others around me, I was and am careful about the influences that prevail on the children I teach. But, because I was aware that others believed that social contact with homosexuals was harmful for children, I monitored myself carefully and particularly.

I remember deciding what to say to other teachers, who I should sit with at lunch, how "artistic" I could be with my classroom decor, and how I would justify so many plants in my classroom. Self-monitoring was also a ubiquitous part of making a self-representation with my students. When I saw any of my students in Kmart with their families, I was often embarrassed. I felt my face flush and had the sensation of being trapped. I now understand that my own homophobia had much to do with my fear that the parents had "figured me out." In monitoring my embarrassment and checking to see if I had let anything slip, I found the data for my own self-hatred. So, although I support the need to be scrupulous about who influences our children, I think that the automatic suspicion of gay men is something quite different.

Rofes (1985) presents a compelling portrait of his struggles as a closeted gay teacher. He goes through successive stages of self-representation, with the constant struggle of trying to have an integrated life. He ultimately leaves teaching, frustrated that he cannot be simultaneously gay and a teacher. But his decision to leave teaching is not based on any conflicts between his sexual desires and his behavior toward his students. Rather, his departure is based on his frustrations about fragmenting his life, his personal guilt about dishonesty, and fear that his self-representation as a gay man would reduce his teaching effectiveness. Nais's (1989) description of "feeling like a [primary] teacher" hinges on themes of "being yourself," "being whole," "being natural," and "establishing relationships with children" (pp. 181–186). Likewise, Noddings's (1984) analysis that teachers "be totally and *nonselectively* [emphasis mine] present to the student" (p. 180) is arguably *the* conflict. I do not read Noddings as saying, nor am I arguing for, teachers' (gay and straight) "rights" to be sexual with children. Rather, the argument is for teachers' rights to represent themselves, including their sexual orientation. Nor does my argument suggest that gay and lesbian teachers should discuss their private lives in ways different from heterosexual teachers. The important point about gay teachers' freedom for self-representation is a release of internalized paranoia and self-loathing that can preempt us from "being there" for children. Of course, these characterizations are very difficult when gay teachers feel threatened to be themselves.

Feeling paranoid about our sexual orientation, gay and lesbian teachers have adopted coping strategies that, in my opinion, reduce our effectiveness as teachers. In an interview study of British gay and lesbian teachers, Squirrel (1989) describes closeted gay teachers trying "to pass" as nongay teachers. With students, the teachers ducked answers to questions that had any relation to their gay lives. They were also secretive about their lives outside of school. They made themselves physically and psychologically distant from their students in an effort to conceal their sexual orientations.

Working from a cultural assumption that homosexuality is inappropriate, the teachers in Squirrels's study struggled with the "inappropriateness of revealing their own sexuality . . ." Lesbian teachers chose not to speak up, with the understanding that when speaking as lesbians their words would discredit the cause for which they spoke. The self-criticism inherent in such positioning is both painful and understandable. Gay men reported creating a facade of heterosexuality. They frequently had special women friends who would pose as partners. At this writing, my partner, Rick, and I are going on a "date" with a lesbian couple, Brenda and Dianne, who teach together at a local high school. We will be going to their faculty party as two "straight" couples. Our covering is not a perfect or simple solution. We are caring about our friends (and perpetuating mythology).

Although some would argue that teachers, in general, should separate home and school lives, my own perception is that such separation is difficult, taxing, and fragmenting. Separation, distance, and lack of self-disclosure are the conditions in teaching that Noddings (1992, 1984) has argued against. These conditions are certainly unlike what Nais (1989) has described as typical for primary teachers. And a further consideration is the issue of choice as to whether or not a teacher will choose to segregate home and school. Homosexuals usually do not choose to be closeted. And, to suggest that *only* gay and lesbian teachers should conceal lives outside of school is an example of the discrimination that gay and lesbian teachers are working to reveal and overturn.

Squirrel (1989) suggests that an underlying homophobic assumption in the culture is that lesbian teachers will "neuter" young boys and "recruit" young girls to lesbian lifestyles. Very serious costs are to be paid in living with the "recruitment argument." My internalized awareness of "recruitment" influences my relationships with students. A colleague who observed my teaching for a semester noted that I avoided classroom interactions with a "handsome" male undergraduate. There are countless examples of self-monitoring and self-censoring of sexual orientation that actually preempt caring relationships with students.

GAY MALE TEACHERS AND WORK DIFFERENTIATION

I do not intend to claim that teachers, certain teachers, percentages of teachers, or types of teachers are or are not gay or lesbian. That is their personal and professional business. However, the fact that sexual orientation is an issue at all in teaching is related to a cultural and economic use of "homosexuality." Homosexuality as a construct is relatively new. It is a social construction from the twentieth century created for political and economic control of people, especially men. Following the arguments of Foucault (1978) and Sedgwick (1985), Owens (1992) reasons that homophobia is a ritualized mechanism of social control. Owens suggests that there is great utility in viewing homosexual men as outsiders or others. Then, given the public perception that all men are, or should be, heterosexual, they can be blackmailed with accusations of homosexuality. The success of appropriating sexual orientation as a lever for social control depends on creating and intensifying the criminality as well as the feminization of homosexuality. Although such homophobic practices are most certainly oppressive to women and gay men, Owens suggests their more pervasive influence is in regulating the behavior of all men. "The imputing of homosexual motive to every male relationship is thus 'an immensely potent tool . . . for manipulation of every form of power that [is] refracted through the gender system— that is, in European society, of virtually every form of power' (Sedgwick, 1985, pp. 88–89)" (Owens, 1992, p. 221). I would also reinforce the obvious but no less significant point that homophobic social control invests heavily in misogynistic practice by "feminizing" homosexuality in order to devalue it.

The same arguments can be mapped onto the gatekeeping that restricts men's participation in primary education. These hegemonic moves appropriate women's cultural space (i.e., primary education) with the intent to devalue both homosexuality and primary males. Both moves preserve men's dominance. In addition, the gatekeeping that occurs at the entrance to primary teaching also appropriates the cultural space of homosexual men. The hidden message to men who choose to teach primary grades is that "those teachers are usually homosexual." And given the undesirability of homosexuality, men may be dissuaded.

GAY TEACHERS AND ACCUSATIONS
OF IMPROPER CARING

Men who teach young children within Noddings's and Nais's ideologies of teaching as care may be at risk. Anderson's (1966) powerful narrative "Hands" details the costs of a man who cares for children in teaching contexts. By the end of the story Wing, the teacher, is a ruined man. In writing about Wing's years as a teacher, Anderson describes him as "meant by nature to be a teacher of youth. He was one of those rare, little men who rule by a power so gentle that it passes as a lovable weakness" (p. 31).

Later in the story, Anderson creates in his character, Wing, the power to teach, care, and change lives through touch.

Here and there went his hands, caressing the shoulders of the
boys, playing about the tousled heads. As he talked his voice became soft and musical. There was a caress in that also. In the way
the voice and the hands, the soft stroking of the shoulders and
the touching of the hair were parts of the schoolmaster's efforts to
carry a dream into the young minds. By the caress that was in his
fingers he expressed himself. He was one of those men in whom
the force that creates life is diffused, not centralized. Under the
caress of his hands, doubt went out of the minds of the boys and
they began also to dream . . . (pp. 31–32).

But Wing's touching of the students is understood differently by the
townspeople. Through the character of the saloon keeper, who beats and
kicks him, Wing is warned, "I'll *teach you* to put your hands on my boy,
you beast" (p. 32, emphasis mine) and "Keep your hands to yourself"
(p. 33). Wing is driven from the town and endures his shamed hands by
keeping them out of sight and himself away from others. He becomes a
recluse. I am intrigued by the choice of Anderson's words "I'll teach you"
spoken by the attacker. Physical abuse of children in school contexts has
historically been tolerated to a greater degree than has caring touch.

In "Hands," Anderson uses the character of Wing to teach readers
about the injustices of misinterpreting touch and misunderstanding teachers' caring. Wing is victimized by the misinterpretation that was was born
of bigotry and fear. Yet, when I was reading the previously quoted para-
graph, I recoiled at the words "caress" and "stroking." These intimate physical acts of caring made me uncomfortable when I read them and now when
I write them. I thought about how I use my hands as a teacher. I have told
myself that touch is a productive and ethical teaching move. I have conditioned my hands that they touch my students only on their shoulders,
arms, and upper backs. I have further instructed my hands that touch
means quick "pats" and not massage. I have constructed a cage of permis-
sible touch.

I think my rules of touching in classrooms are good ones. I do not
mean to suggest that I think that I or other teachers should touch in ways
that are different from my rules. But it is important to interrogate how it is
that caring touching is so suspect a behavior, and punitive touching is not. I
think this says much about our culture's values regarding children's rights
and simultaneously a resistance to interrogate our own motives for touch
and paddling.

SOME FINAL THOUGHTS

At this economic moment, families are straining to accommodate to the related demands of two-career and single-parent households. Socially, we celebrate women's increased options that allow all of us to claim our rights to professional and work lives. But the stress these rights have placed on child rearing is palpable. Classrooms that are imbued with caring teaching are a likely support for troubled families. In fact, men have much to contribute to a caring gap in children's development. And gay men, with feet on both sides of the chasm of gender politics, may provide nurturing and caring in ways that are especially productive for young children. If we want teaching that is based on caring for our young children, and we want male role models for them as well, then it makes sense to keep our options for healthy diversity open. Bullying and excluding gay men (based on homophobic bigotry) is clearly inappropriate, especially in contexts that intend to be caring ones.

Teachers can be either committed or uncommitted in their caring for children. Their construction of teaching as caring is based on their own philosophies about learning and about children. Sexual orientation has little to do with whether or not men are or can be effective as primary teachers. Rather, others' use of their own perceptions of caring and their automatic suspicions about men's acts of caring are the real problem with men in primary teaching. My social construction of "teacher" and "one-caring" is constantly under revision, and it is that complex, multilayered understanding about gendered behavior, professional role expectations, and intention behind acts of caring that are in need of continuous investigation. Caring for children in our teaching is something that we constantly build, monitor, and reshape, based on the evolving relationship between the one-caring and the cared-for. At this time, part of that construction for men who do chose to teach young children is awareness of what others make of us and our caring.

REFERENCES

Anderson, S. (1966). *Winesberg, Ohio*. New York: Viking Press.
Belenky, M., Clinchy, B., Goldberger, N., and Tarule, J. (1986). *Women's Ways of Knowing*. New York: Basic Books.
Foucault, M. (1978). *The History of Sexuality*, Vol. 1. New York: Random House.

Gilligan, C. (1982). *In a Different Voice*. Cambridge, MA: Harvard University Press.

Nais, J. (1989). *Primary Teachers Talking*. New York: Routledge.

National Association for the Education of Young Children. (1985). *In Whose Hands?* (Report #760). Washington, DC: author.

Noddings, N. (1984). *Caring: A Feminine Approach to Ethics and Moral Education*. Berkeley: University of California Press.

———. (1992). *The Challenge to Care in Schools: An Alternative Approach to Education*. New York: Teachers College Press.

Owens, C. (1992). "Outlaws: Gay Men in Feminism." In S. Bryson, B. Kruger, and J. Weinstock, eds., Beyond Recognition: Representation, Power, and Culture, pp. 218–255. Berkeley: University of California Press.

Reskin, B. (1991). "Bring the men back in: Sex differentiation and the devaluation of women's work." In J. Larber and S. Farrell, eds., *The Social Construction of Gender*, pp. 141–161. Beverly Hills, CA: Sage Publications.

Rofes, E. (1985). *Socrates, Plato, and Guys Like Me: Confessions of a Gay Schoolteacher*. Boston: Alyson.

Roscoe, W. (1988). *Living the Spirit: A Gay American Indian Anthology*. New York: St. Martin's Press.

Sedgwick, E. (1985). *Between Men: English Literature and Male Homosocial Desire*. New York: Columbia University Press.

Seifert, K. (1983). "Suitability and Competence of Men Who Teach Young Children." Paper presented at American Educational Research Association, Montreal.

———. (1988a). "Men in Early Childhood Education." In B. Spodek, O. Sarancho, and D. Peters, eds., *Professionalism and the Early Childhood Practitioner*, pp. 105–116. New York: Teachers College Press.

———. (1988b). The Culture of Early Education and the Preparation of Male Teachers." *Early Childhood Development and Care* 38:69–80.

Squirrel, G. (1989). "In Passing: Teachers and Sexual Orientation." In S. Acker ed., *Teachers, Gender and Careers*, pp. 87–106. New York: Falmer Press.

Sugg, R. (1978). *Motherteacher: The Feminization of American Education*. Charlotte: University Press of Virginia.

Waller, W. (1932). *The Sociology of Teaching*. New York: Russell and Russell.

CHAPTER 4

FORBIDDEN TO CARE

Gay and Lesbian Teachers

RITA M. KISSEN

INTRODUCTION

My relationship with lesbian and gay teachers began with my experience as the mother of a lesbian daughter just beginning her teaching career. Watching a beloved family member negotiate the intricate maze of coming out, dealing with societal homophobia, and establishing an authentic identity as a teacher while protecting her own safety is probably the closest a heterosexual educator can come to knowing the rewards and the dangers that lesbian, gay, and bisexual teachers face every day of their working lives.

As a university supervisor of graduate interns, I work regularly with middle and secondary school teachers. Most are people I know only through our limited professional relationship, yet over the years, a steady progression of them have come out to me. Sometimes the disclosure took place in their classrooms, momentarily emptied of students. Sometimes it was at a conference or a diversity workshop. Although my public involvement in Parents, Families, and Friends of Lesbians and Gays (P-FLAG) and in local gay politics had identified me as an ally, the teachers and I were fully conscious that they were taking a tremendous risk in revealing their sexual orientation within a professional setting. Ellen, one of the first teachers I talked with, told me later: "When I told you that, it was really kind of a shocker to me, but you were identified immediately as safe. . . . I have such a hard time reaching the line between where I feel a person is safe and where I can actually take the risk that they might not be trustworthy or reliable with information."

They knew, and I knew, that self-revelation is a dangerous undertaking for any gay teacher. Gay men and lesbians may be growing more visible in many areas of society, but in the average American school, coming out of the closet still means risking ostracism, dismissal, and physical violence.

Philosophers and educators who have explored the meaning of caring remind us that care begins with authenticity. To be the person whom Nel Noddings calls the *one-caring*, one must be willing to present himself or herself honestly and openly—in Martin Buber's words, to "really be there," for the "cared-for" (Buber, 1965, p. 98; Noddings, 1984, p. 4). The "cared-for," too, must commit to "the willing and unconscious revealing of self" (Noddings, 1984, p. 73). Only when all parties present themselves honestly can there be an authentic relationship, the foundation of the moral imperative to care.

The gay and lesbian teachers who speak in these pages are deeply committed to caring. Though few have read the academic literature on the subject, most express ideals very close to those in such works as Nel Noddings's *Caring* (1984), and *The Challenge to Care in Schools* (1992). Yet as I listen to their voices, I realize that Noddings's discussion of caring is inadequate to the dilemmas they face. First of all, the honesty and openness central to her notion of care is simply impossible for most gay teachers. Few of the teachers I interviewed would argue with Noddings's assertion that the caring teacher must be "*present* in her [sic] acts of caring." (A discussion of the issues of essentialism and social construction raised by Noddings's consistent use of the feminine pronoun to describe the one-caring falls outside the parameters of this study; I am concerned with the considerations left out of the caring equation for gay teachers, whether they are men or women.) Yet Noddings does not consider what such "presence" might mean for people who are forced to hide a significant part of themselves. For teachers who must constantly guard against the discovery of their true identity, being "open" and "receptive" could invite serious danger.

These limitations are equally apparent in Noddings's more recent work on caring, The Challenge to Care in Schools. Here, Noddings expands on her earlier definition by outlining four elements in moral education (that is, education based on an ethic of caring). Two of these components, "modeling" and "dialogue," are especially problematical for gay teachers. By "modeling," Noddings means "show[ing] how to care in our own relations with cared-fors." Modeling is indeed an issue for most gay teachers, but for them it is not a path toward moral education, but a choice they are not free to make. Because they cannot present themselves authentically, they can neither serve as positive role "models" nor "model" caring by responding to the needs of students, especially gay students.

Dialogue, Noddings' second component, is another painful issue: "Dialogue is open-ended; that is, in a genuine dialogue, neither party knows at the outset what the outcome or decision will be" (p. 23). But gay teachers cannot risk such openness, for it involves giving up control over how much of their identity they will reveal. If they fall short of Noddings's ethical ideal, it is not because they are "jealous, or small-minded, or greedy" (p.109), but because they must hide to avoid harassment and physical danger.

Much of the discussion in the interviews that follow involves self-care, the maintenance of physical and emotional health in the one-caring. Here again, Noddings's advice that the caregiver care for herself fails to address the plight of gay teachers, for whom the barriers to self-care involve more than long workdays and hectic schedules. From childhood onward, gay people are bombarded with messages that they are evil, sick, or laughable—messages emanating from images in the media, pronouncements by public figures, and the behavior of the people around them. Furthermore, the need to hide their true identity forces them to live under the double burden of oppression and invisibility and prevents them from forming close relationships with colleagues. These impediments have little to do with Noddings's vision of the one-caring who "properly but considerately withdraws for repairs" (1984, p. 105).

Like Noddings, most of the teachers I interviewed associated self-disclosure with personal honesty and considered authenticity a prerequisite to caring. Hiding a significant part of their identity put them under a tremendous strain and made it almost impossible to establish relationships with students. Steve explained, "Every single day you go into the school you have to decide how much . . . room am I gonna give them [students]. I mean how close am I gonna let them get and how far away will I have to push them."

Yet despite the risks, and in many cases the impossibility, of coming out in the usual sense, most of these teachers were struggling to present themselves authentically. Though they were painfully aware that homophobia prevented them from caring fully for themselves or their students, they were developing strategies for self-care and for establishing just and humane classroom communities. Often, their own life experiences as a hated minority had sensitized them to the plight not only of gay students, but of all those who were victimized.

Pam spoke for many when she said: "Because of my understanding of the world, I see things, I think, in a broader perspective than a lot of other people. I can understand a lot of other people's pain." Pam's comment recalls Charlotte Haddock Siegfried's observation that "any systematically oppressed group will experience the world differently from those not oppressed" (Siegfried, 1989, p. 67). It also suggests that although their oppression inhibits gay teachers from caring openly for their students, it may deepen their commitment to creating a just community where all students feel safe. Such an environment may protect students from victimization; yet it does not take the place of the personal, one-to-one relationship that is at the center of caring and that is forbidden to gay teachers because homophobia—the fear and hatred of gay people—forces them to live with the constant threat of discovery.

THE PROCESS

This study is based on interviews with twenty-two people, all of whom self-identified as gay, lesbian, or bisexual and all of whom have worked as teachers, counselors, or librarians in grades K–12. We met through personal contacts and through advertisements I placed in several lesbian and gay newspapers. Seventeen were women and five were men; all were white; two described their families of origin as poor, two as working class, and the rest as middle or upper middle class. (Since these interviews were conducted, I have begun interviewing gay and lesbian teachers of color and learning how race and racism intersect with homophobia in their lives at school. Their stories will be an important dimension of my future work.)

Sixteen of the teachers interviewed for the present study currently teach in New England, two in the South, one in the Midwest, and three on the West Coast. Five were in their forties, eleven in their thirties, three in their twenties, and three were fifty or older. Nine were teaching in public high schools (grades 9–12), nine in junior high schools or elementary schools (grades pre-K–8), one in a private day school (K–12), and one in a Catholic parochial school. One woman was a consultant who worked out of her home, and one, a former elementary school teacher, was currently working as a children's book buyer.

Because this project is narrative and qualitative, the interviews were informal and open ended. Each lasted about an hour, but in some cases the exchange went on long after we turned off the tape recorder. Each teacher was invited to define the question "What is life like for you as a lesbian or gay educator?" according to his or her particular experience. In addition, I included several specific questions about their self-definition as lesbian or gay, their survival strategies for self-care in a homophobic environment, and their vision of a world where homophobia had disappeared from schools and they would be free to present themselves authentically.

BECOMING A TEACHER: "THE CENTER OF MYSELF"

Most of our interviews began with a discussion of "how I became a teacher." Along with a love of literature, science, or history, the twin concepts of identity and relationship figured prominently in their responses:

> I always saw teaching as an extension of other things that are really at the center of myself. (Peggy)
>
> I think that I always felt so comfortable in the teaching profession because it was woman dominated and I felt a safeness and a comfort and sort of a nurturance that I did not feel . . . in the corporate office environment. (Ruth)

Like their heterosexual peers, some were attracted to teaching because of a special relationship with an admired teacher. Whether they were of the same sex or opposite sex, these "crushes" embodied the personal connection they hoped to bring to their own classrooms.

> When I was a freshman in high school I was in love with my English teacher, so that passion sort of set the stage for my own being an English teacher. He probably knew I had this huge crush on him, but he was just wonderful. . . . I still see him every couple of years. (Dianne)
>
> I had a really fantastic biology teacher in high school and just adored her. . . . I was in kind of the college track but even with the kids who weren't . . . everybody loved her. 'Cause she really cared. (Steve)

THE GLASS CLOSET AND THE HALL OF MIRRORS

When I began talking to lesbian and gay teachers, I expected to find a few exceptional people who were out in their schools and a great many others who lived life in the closet. What I found instead was a process, a continually evolving dynamic in which teachers struggle for authenticity while protecting their jobs, their physical safety, and their emotional well being.

> It's like walking a fine line. Am I safe, am I not safe? . . .
> The "where is it safe?" question comes up all the time. (Dianne)
> Really it's not a secret, it's just limited discussion. I refer to
> it as like living in a glass closet. (Jean)
> I don't go around with an *L* on my chest or anything but I
> wouldn't say that I am really closeted. I have a hard time picturing how I am. (Linda)

Linda's comment shows how the need to hide and the simultaneous desire for authenticity can produce a cognitive dissonance, in which a teacher is never quite sure how he or she appears to the rest of the world. Caught in this double bind, teachers draw fine distinctions among different kinds of hiding and different kinds of disclosure. They may distinguish between answering questions with part of the truth and telling an outright lie. Linda said: "I get questions like, 'Are you married?' Or, 'You don't have any kids?'. . . I say I have too many kids, I don't have time for my own. No, I'm not married."

Some still use the "Monday morning pronoun" in the teachers' room or staff lounge, blurring the gender identity of a partner or referring to him or her with an opposite-sex pronoun when talking about what they did over the weekend. Grace explained: "You know, when everyone else is talking about their husband and their spouse and you say 'a friend and I did this, a friend and and I did that, we did this,' with never a name, with never a gender. . . . Someone said something once about 'your boyfriend' and I [wanted] to correct it and say, 'No, no, no, my girlfriend.'

Others consider silence more authentic than referring to their partner as a member of the opposite sex:

> When people talk about their weekends I [don't] make up
> stories, I just don't say anything. That's not good, but it's better.
> (Mike)
> I have always felt my life was divided because either people
> didn't know I was gay or I couldn't talk about it. Like last spring,

I thought, I am tired of this, and put Sandy's picture on my desk. It's just stupid little things like that. (Rose)

For teachers like Rose, who are relatively open and assume that many of their colleagues already know they are gay, the "glass closet" is also a hall of mirrors, where people pretend not to see what others know they see and reflections turn into projections of everybody's fear and denial.

One of the most devastating consequences of the glass closet is that it prevents gay teachers from caring for themselves. Noddings tells us that the "receptive mode" associated with caring can be achieved only when the one-caring enjoys mental and emotional freedom: "We do not pass into it [the receptive mode] under stress, and . . . we must settle ourselves, clear our minds, reduce the racket around us in order to enter it" (1984, p. 94). Further, Noddings cautions, "the one-caring must be maintained, for she is the immediate source of caring. The one-caring . . . does not need to hatch out elaborate excuses to give herself rest, or to seek congenial companionship, or to find joy in personal work" (1984, p. 105). But for gay teachers, the physical and emotional cost of having to hide lend a bitter irony to this laudable advice:

> I got a bleeding ulcer last fall, I thought, this is crazy. I nearly quit my job because I thought, it isn't worth dying over, this is not worth ruining my health. (Karen)
>
> Among other things, I weigh 40 pounds more than I did . . . I don't drink, I don't do lots of other damaging things to myself, but obviously food has become a problem to me. Part of the reason I went into therapy was that I had this sense that I'd weigh 350 pounds if I didn't. (Peggy)
>
> I'm surprised I didn't get an ulcer . . . getting into the car at 3:00 on Friday when school was out and driving 5 hours . . . to find any kind of gay community support . . . and then on Sunday you drove back knowing that on Monday it would start all over. (Rebecca)
>
> On some days I just shut my door and cried and got myself back together because it was so painful. (Rose)

Gay teachers' loneliness and isolation was most clearly illustrated when they talked about how their lives might change if homophobia magically disappeared. Many thought first of how they might connect with friends and coworkers, connections essential to self-care in any working environment, but especially in schools, where teachers spend much of their time isolated in their individual classrooms.

> I could talk about my life totally openly like everybody else does. . . . When we are sitting around in the faculty lounge and John X says, "Well Judy and I went to this movie over the weekend," then I could say, "Oh, Jack and I saw that too." I can't imagine that. (Mike)
>
> That is so totally unimaginable that I need a couple of minutes. Yes, it would be a lot different. . . . Margie and I are partners and I would like to be treated as a couple. (Jean)
>
> I could take all of me to school. . . . I could really put Sandy's picture on my desk. (Rose)

Rose's response hints at the fragmentation involved in having to hide a significant part of one's identity. Whether they had already identified as lesbian or gay before becoming teachers or had discovered their true sexual identity while they were working in schools, teaching as a gay man or lesbian meant an excruciating split between two core elements at the heart of who they were: their professional and their personal-sexual identities.

> Sometimes you feel distant—kind of distanced from everyone . . . 'cause all the time you keep two separate worlds. (Steve)
>
> I'll talk about other teachers' husbands or other teachers' children. It's like I don't have this life outside school other than, you know, people know about my Victorian house, and people know I like to travel, and people know I like to cook or paint or, you know, those facts about myself—as if I have no other life. (Allan)

This balancing act means that gay teachers must suffer in silence at moments when a heterosexual teacher would find it natural to turn to a colleague for support. Michelle described arriving at school at the end of a two-week visit from her partner, who lives across the country.

> It was very early in the morning, and it wasn't until I was driving to work in my car that it suddenly hit me that she was gone and I wouldn't see her for a long time. I started crying on the way to work. It was just really sad, feeling all lost and missing her and wishing she was still here. And then I arrived at school and I parked in the parking lot and I had to completely clean

myself up, straighten myself up and act like nothing was wrong. I was still wiping my face, blowing my nose, and then a coworker pulled up next to me in the parking lot and as I got out of the car I had to act like nothing whatsoever was wrong. . . . I was afraid that if she noticed something was wrong that I would start crying all over again.

Q. So you went into school. How did you make it through the day?

A. I had to kind of hold it together. I snuck out at lunch and called [her lover] and left a message on her machine.

Q. Did anybody ask you what was the matter?

A. No. You become good at acting. I'm pretty good at covering it up.

Hiding prevents gay teachers from caring for their colleagues as well as themselves. Several of my subjects recalled moments when recently divorced or widowed teachers turned to them for comfort, and they were unable to reach out and share their own stories of loss and survival. The divorces in their lives had involved same-sex partners, and talking about a same-sex partner with a colleague to whom one was not out felt inherently unsafe.

Longing for the freedom to self-disclose did not necessarily mean wanting to come out to everyone, or even to anyone. Like Mary, a high school librarian, teachers might begin by imagining some sort of grand proclamation of their gay identity: "Oh, I'd just like to stand on a rooftop and shout it out sometime. It's always a balancing act of choosing when and where it's gonna be constructive to come out. . . . It's scary."

But what Mary and the others really wanted was not to make a declaration, but to live in a world where coming out would not be a dangerous act. To put it another way, they wanted the power to make their own choices about how and when to self-disclose.

Along with the freedom to make these choices, gay teachers wanted to be seen as whole people, whose gay identities were only a part of who they were. Though they did not want to hide their sexual identity from students, they sought to be defined by more than just that identity: "I would like to feel safe enough to have the kids know from me that yes I'm a lesbian. . . . [But] I want to be seen as Dianne Jones, language arts teacher, not Dianne Jones, queer language arts teacher."

Being out was also seen as a positive part of creating an environment where students would acquire a more humane vision of the world. As Mike put it, "It would be tremendously beneficial to students, all students, all kids, if they saw gay and lesbian people as just another variation of the range of people. That would be worth so much that I can hardly even imagine it."

Most painful of all were the limitations on teachers' ability to care for the lesbian and gay students in their schools, a group for whom Jane Roland Martin's "three C's" of care, concern, and connection are almost nonexistent (Martin, 1989, p. 185). Many of the teachers I interviewed were familiar with the literature describing the plight of gay youth in schools (Coleman and Ramafedi, 1989; Hetrick and Martin, 1987; Hunter and Schaecher, 1987; Kissen, 1993a, 1993b; Krysiak, 1987; Rofes, 1989; Sears, 1991, 1992). All of them realized, too, that lesbian and gay youth are likely to suffer even greater isolation than adolescents from racial or ethnic minorities, for unlike the members of those groups, who can return to a family or community, gay youth may go through their entire adolescence with no image of themselves other than the negative ones projected by mainstream American culture. Faced with such complete alienation, it is no wonder that the suicide rate for gay youth is three times the national average (*Report of the Secretary's Task Force*, 1983) or that so many fall victim to chemical addiction, unsafe sex, and exploitative relationships by untrustworthy adults.

These statistics were painfully familiar to gay teachers, especially those who had identified early as lesbian or gay and could recall their own isolation. Pam confided, "I think that's the toughest struggle, to see kids and not be able to reach out to them and say , 'Yes, I do know what you're going through.' . . . In my whole process of coming out . . . I didn't identify myself as a lesbian or being gay at all. If I put a label on it then I had to assume all the negative stereotypes that had been given to me and it took me a long time to sort out the difference."

Rebecca's description of a particular encounter with a student expresses poignantly the pain of wanting to care and needing to hide:

> A boy who I never had in class . . . came bopping into my room between classes, came over to my desk. The class was empty and the kids were getting ready to come in and he says, "Miss Smith, are you gay?" Very blunt question. I looked at him and my heart sank and I had a million and two thoughts going around in my mind: "Am I honest with this kid? I don't know this kid. Is he trying to out me? Could I lose my job? What's going to happen if I tell him the truth? What do I do? Is he gay?

Is he asking me for support? Does he need help?" All these questions went through my head, the kids started to come back into the classroom, and I said, "No." That was a dishonest answer to him from myself . . . Maybe he needed my help. He's not back at the school this year. I don't know what happened to him. But that haunts me to this day.

Rebecca's words reveal virtually all the tensions I have been discussing in this analysis of how the need to hide prevents teachers from caring for themselves, their colleagues, and their students. Her first response is fear for her own safety ("Is he trying to out me? Could I lose my job?") Yet side by side with her personal anxiety is her desire to care for the student ("Is he gay? Is he asking me for support? Does he need help?") What "haunts" Rebecca is not only the knowledge that she was unable to be "honest with this kid," but the thought that he might have needed her help and that she doesn't "know what happened to him." Coming out to this student would not have been gratuitous self-disclosure, but an act of caring. It would have told him that Rebecca was someone it was safe to come out to, if he chose to do so. Even more important, if he were indeed gay, Rebecca could have reassured him that he was not alone by answering "yes" to his question.

It is worth noting that Rebecca is one of the more "out" teachers I interviewed; her principal knows she is gay and supports her efforts to make her school more tolerant of diversity. Yet when she considered how she might respond to another similar encounter, Rebecca was not at all sure. Finding a safe space within her school has not freed her from having to make anxious moment-by-moment decisions about how to present herself to others; only the dismantling of homophobia and heterosexism in the wider society could do that.

"I HAVE NO CHOICE BUT NOT TO RENEW YOUR CONTRACT"

Conversations about the fears that prevent gay teachers from revealing an authentic identity lead to one overwhelming concern: the fear of being fired. It is not surprising then, that a good deal of our interview time was devoted to a discussion of worst-case "nightmare" scenarios.

Most of the scenarios were remarkably similar. Teachers guessed that the pressure to fire them would be more likely to come from parents than from students or the administration.

Parents are very picky in this community. . . . The kids, as vicious and cruel as they can be, they can roll with the punches pretty much. (Rebecca)

Kids don't care about anyone else. They are so totally narcissistic that they really don't care about anyone's life but their own. [I worry about] some . . . group of fundamentalist parents. (Jean)

In such cases, teachers feared that principals and school boards who were not themselves troubled by homosexuality might succumb to parental pressure.

If I were ever to be fired I imagine it to be happening because the school board comes under political pressure, and I don't think the school board has very much spine. (Peggy)

I can hear him saying to me, "You know that we value your teaching tremendously. I think you've made a great contribution to the school. I would like to see you stay here. I think the world stinks, and I think people are awful, but for the good of the school I have no choice but to not renew your contract."

These fears are not paranoia. Every teacher I interviewed knew of someone who had been fired solely because of his or her sexual orientation. One teacher, Lydia, had actually been dismissed from a teaching job, and several others had been threatened with dismissal. Their stories are revealing, not only because they demonstrate the reality of gay teachers' fears, but because they show how teachers may suffer for violating the twin prohibitions against self-disclosure and caring. In addition, the experiences of both Karen and Lydia illustrate that, for gay teachers, those two prohibitions are often related.

Karen's troubles began when she gave low grades to some eighth grade basketball players, and two of their parents, who decided she "hated boys," filed a complaint against her. "It seems to do with the fact that some people think you're a lesbian," the principal told her. Karen was able to silence her attackers with the help of two allies, an art teacher in her building and a parent who rallied support, but the incident returned to haunt her when another confrontation erupted later that spring. Several fifth grade girls confided to her that their teacher had a habit of "running his hands down a little girl's blouse." When her report to the principal brought no results, Karen threatened to call the state Child Protection Services.

Karen's efforts to protect the fifth grade girls were motivated by a sense of justice and a desire to care. She was outraged by the school's failure to punish a blatant abuse of power, and she sought to protect the physical and emotional safety of the fifth grade girls, who had turned to her for help, even though they were not her students. But, because she had been targeted as a lesbian, Karen's attempts to care and to secure justice became a damning piece of "evidence" against her: "This teacher was accused by me, the woman who hates men. The woman who wanted to get rid of all the men in the building, the woman who hates boys and is now the woman who hates men. . . . When I told [the principal] that I was going to report to the Department of Human Services, he said, 'Do you want to keep your job? Are you planning on staying here?' I said, 'Are you threatening me?' And he said, 'Oh, no, I thought you were saying you were getting another job.'"

Karen spent a horrendous year fighting efforts to fire her. Although her story had a happy ending, which I shall describe later on, it reveals how dangerous it can be for a lesbian or gay teacher to become visible, even when such visibility involves trying to care for students.

Lydia was the only teacher in the group who had actually lost her job because she was a lesbian. Like Karen, her attempt to care for a student was used against her by a homophobic parent. And, like Karen, she had previously made herself more vulnerable by antagonizing students who had broken the rules.

The events surrounding Lydia's dismissal were preceded by an incident, which, though it did not directly involve self-disclosure, certainly involved homophobia. Discovering that several of her students were cheating on a test, Lydia had informed them that they would receive zeros and sentenced them to stay after school. One of the students had previously heard Lydia criticize another student for making a homophobic remark: "One of the girls went home and in the process of telling her mother that she had flunked the test for me, I think [she] must have softened that blow with telling this story about how I liked queer people so I obviously must be one."

Although the girl's mother complained to the principal, he took no further action, and the incident seemed closed. At the end of her second year, Lydia received tenure. Meanwhile, the girl in question had gone to live with an aunt and uncle in another town. The following year, Lydia's third, the student returned to the local high school. At this point, Lydia made the mistake that cost her her job: "

I wrote the kid a note when she came back and gave it to a friend of hers to give it to her. 'I heard you were back. It would be great to see you. Drop by the school sometime, Hope you're doing all right.' The mother got that note. I don't think the girl ever knew I had written it. But the mother decided that . . . I was obviously trying to come on to her daughter and that I should be fired for that."

As pressure mounted over the summer, Lydia waited to find out if the school board would remove her from her job. Even her union representative blamed her for not being "cautious" enough. Isolated and demoralized, Lydia gave in: "I felt like my own ideal—which was, if I worked hard enough and did a really good job and was the best that I could possibly be, then people would like me and I would be fine—was an illusion. . . . So I quit. It was awful. I felt numb. I couldn't believe it had happened."

"I GUESS I'M SOMEBODY"

Working in an environment where fear makes trust difficult or impossible, it is not surprising that gay teachers are unable to care properly for themselves or their students. Yet despite the strains imposed upon them, the teachers I spoke with have developed strategies to help them survive. At the most basic level, they often work harder than anyone else and strive to maintain a professional image:

> If there is anything I do to compensate it is that I work very hard. It never hurts. . . . I dress like a teacher. I wear jumpers, blouses and skirts . . . the basic teacher uniform. (Jean)
>
> They could try to fire me but I have been really careful to build my base of support with my parents and my staff. (Rose)

Despite personal isolation in their schools, gay teachers build networks of loving families and friends. Some must turn to "families of choice" when their birth families reject them. Lydia recalled: "I was pretty estranged from my family at that point [after being fired]. I did not tell my mother, who still doesn't want to know that any of that happened, She still wants to believe . . . that my life is a lot easier than it is."

For some, who had married and divorced before coming out, their own children's rejection became part of the pain. Rose was one such parent: "The first two years of this, my kids all went to live with their father and didn't have anything to do with me for a short period. My nuclear family, my birth family, all rejected me."

Others, like Karen, found unexpected support from sons or daughters: "This treatment of her mother has galvanized Judy [Karen's daughter]. . . .

She graduated from junior high school this year. She was valedictorian, so she gave the 'V' address. It was about discussing differences and she said the word *homosexual* four times. . . . It brought tears to my eyes."

Some teachers find support in their spiritual communities. Jean, who at the start of our interview described herself as a "recovered" Catholic, mentioned that she had recently joined a Unitarian church because "they are very supportive to gays and lesbians." Allan is active in his synagogue, a large lesbian and gay congregation in California. Peggy referred to her church life as one of the cornerstones of her personal support system, though she was frustrated by the need to hide her sexual orientation at church, as well as at school, because of her partner's wishes. Ruth is an active member of Integrity, a gay Episcopal organization where she met her partner. Alan, whose life as a Quaker is central to his identity, expressed the most integrated view of teaching, sexual orientation, and religion: "I feel called to be a teacher. I feel called to be a Friend. And I feel called to be gay."

Many others echoed Alan's idea that there was something special about being gay that gave them spiritual and emotional support. Ruth explained: "Being gay for me has just been such a positive thing. It has allowed my mind to think in diverse, creative ways which I think is an important element in being a teacher."

Most important are the networks of people with whom gay teachers do not need to hide. "My big job in the last year has been getting to the place where I now no longer move to any place in my life where there isn't someone who sees me whole," Peggy reflected. "When I'm with my family, there's someone. When I'm in church, there's someone. She's the only one, but she's there."

Rebecca described the support she had received from a lesbian discussion group she attends regularly: "A lot of them are teachers. A professor from New Hampshire got [it] together. . . . We are both educators, we can support each other. Then you meet somebody else who is a biology teacher . . . then you meet somebody else who is a music teacher . . . and all of a sudden there are people [who] come up and give you a hug and say what a big step you are taking and that kind of stuff."

Sometimes the caring comes from unexpected places. Rose, a counselor who had been ostracized when some of her colleagues discovered she was a lesbian, recalled such a moment: "The person who did the nicest thing for me was a woman who worked in the kitchen at the school and whom I had dealt with as a parent. She called me up and said, 'I have to talk with you,' and drove down to my office and said, 'Rose, I just wanted you to know that whatever is going on in your life it doesn't matter. I still like you as a person.' That was wonderful. And nobody else could be so direct."

Finally, although the need to hide makes it difficult for them to find one another, gay teachers within a single school can support one another.

Q: You said there was one other gay teacher in the school. Are you friends with him?
Dianne: Yes, he's not out at all to anybody.
Q: Is he out to you?
Dianne: Yes. I guess I'm somebody.

For most gay teachers, maintaining a professional image and building supportive networks make hiding less painful. For a few, following the moral imperative to care has meant coming out of the closet into the dangerous world of full or partial self-disclosure. Their stories reflect the apparent paradox at the heart of the entire gay liberation movement: self-revelation—coming out of the closet—is the riskiest act imaginable for someone who is gay, lesbian, or bisexual. Yet as gay activists from Stonewall onward have shown us, coming out is also the strategy with the greatest potential for true liberation. And for some lesbian and gay teachers, coming out is the ultimate survival strategy, the only one that can truly empower them to care.

One teacher who found self-disclosure a liberating strategy was Lydia, who managed to start over in another teaching job after she was fired. Rather than forcing her further into the closet, Lydia's experiences convinced her that her survival depended on being more open about her identity, to the point where most of her students now know she is a lesbian. She is convinced that her openness has contributed to her success at her present school and enabled her to establish caring relationships with her students: "I have more of a sense of humor. I have more energy. I organized a field trip for the whole freshman class for a day. Nobody had ever done that till this past spring. But it's because I'm not having my energy drained off on a daily basis with terror. I joke around with the kids a lot."

Karen, too, found the refusal to hide a successful survival strategy. By the time I interviewed her, a new principal had taken over, and Karen had managed to get tenure, "much to everyone's surprise, I suspect." A year later I ran into her again and hardly recognized her. At the time of our interview she had been suffering from an ulcer, her face thin and drawn. Now she looked radiantly healthy, even serene. She told me that she was still teaching at the same school and that the new principal had proved a loyal ally. In fact, Karen was now tacitly out to the administration and staff and had experienced widespread support.

For some teachers, coming out to a principal or administrator represents a significant first step. Rebecca, the teacher who was haunted by her inability to respond to the student who asked her if she was gay, eventually took the risk of revealing herself to her principal. Her self-disclosure began when she arrived one Monday morning to find her file drawer stuffed with toilet paper: "Underneath the toilet paper was a paper cup. Written in bold black marker [was], 'We hate you, Miss Smith, dyke from hell,' and on my desk calendar blotter written across the top was 'DYKE.'"

After a soul-searching discussion with her partner, who urged her not to ignore the incident, Rebecca went to see her principal. As she had hoped, he was immediately sympathetic: "He said, 'I can't believe this, this upsets me so.' We discussed homosexuality among students, that there are definitely some at our school, and finally narrowing the gap to zero in on me, with him saying, 'You know, Rebecca, I don't know what your sexual preference is . . . but . . . it doesn't matter to me.' I said, "If you think I'm a lesbian, you're right." He said, 'I knew you were when I hired you.'"

Soon afterward, Rebecca's principal asked her to lead a diversity team planning a year-long series of workshops for students and teachers at her school. Like many gay teachers who have been able to come out, she was lucky to find a principal willing to confront homophobia in his building. But without the courage to disclose her sexual orientation, Rebecca would not have found the opportunity to lead the diversity team and help make her school a more just and caring community.

Terry's self-disclosure to his principal was prompted not by a homophobic incident but by the desire to be an ally for gay youth at his school: "The principal said, 'Homosexuality is not something I have had much experience in dealing with before. I don't know their situation. I don't know the faculty situation.' And there was a kind of pause and he said, 'I don't know your situation.' I said, 'I don't have a situation. I'm gay but that's not a situation for me.' I said, 'Maybe that's a situation for you that I'm gay.' And, you know, there was hardly hesitation. He said, 'The issues would be, are you a different person than the person I love[d] and respect[ed] when you walked into this office? Are you an excellent teacher that I've always known you to be?'"

Alan, who came out in a local newspaper interview while he was student teaching, found unexpected support from his colleagues and community.

> The first grade teacher . . . she's a very taciturn person and she got very friendly, talkative. She said, 'Did I tell you my son, a real estate agent, knows Miles [Alan's partner]?' Morgan—she was in the first grade—her mother came up to me and said, 'I'm going to save this interview until Morgan is old enough to read it. I want her to read it.'
> Q: Did you get any negative things?
> A: No.

In rare cases, the desire to care for gay and lesbian youth prompted a teacher to come out to a student. Nancy, a Deaf teacher who works at a school for the Deaf, was someone who took this brave step: "There is one senior boy. He's not sure if he's . . . gay or bisexual or straight. . . . So he went to the counselor and the counselor came up to me and said, 'Do you mind sharing . . . do you mind if I share about you?' And I said, 'That's fine.' I said, 'You know, he's Deaf and he needs a Deaf role model as a gay person.' . . . Now [the student] comes up to me often and we communicate and we talk about it. And he says, 'You're a lesbian. Wow.' . . . I told him, "You better not tell your friends, though, in the high school, because you know, they haven't been exposed to my teaching.'"

Teachers like these, who had begun to come out in their schools, saw self-revelation as empowerment. Rebecca spoke for many when she talked about the issue of control: "When you are behind those blinds, those shutters, you are hiding. You don't want anyone to see in and when they do, they can . . . control you. Once those [blinds] are open, now *you* can control that."

Yet even the most self-disclosing gay teachers acknowledged that their success depended on circumstances beyond their control. Lydia pointed out that the differences between her two teaching experiences were due partly to the differences between the two schools: one, a small junior high school in a conservative, rural, fundamentalist community; the other, a mid-size high school in a coastal town whose large tourist population made it relatively cosmopolitan. Karen was grateful for the advent of a new principal who was willing to be her ally. Rebecca and Terry were blessed with building administrators who believed in diversity and were willing to stand by their principles. Their stories suggest that teachers who come out successfully in their schools need to be both courageous and lucky.

Even then, stepping out of the closet does not come easily. Lydia left the country for a year after losing her first job, and managed to rebuild her resume only by pursuing a second teaching degree at a college where no one knew her history. Alan, who was not teaching at the time I interviewed him, worried about how to present himself in future interviews with administrators who might be an unknown quantity. And although being out may give a teacher more control, it can make him or her a target for all the free-floating gay baiting in the surrounding environment. "Sometimes there have been things written on my blackboard like 'DYKE,' 'LEZZIE'" admitted Lydia. But it's not always negative. I have comics on my door, and there's one where on the margin somebody wrote just this past spring, 'Cool Dyke.' And in another handwriting is written, 'Yeah.' I'm sure they knew I would see that they like me."

For gay teachers who are not blessed with such enlightened administrators, colleagues, or communities as Rebecca, Terry, or Alan, even partial self-disclosure is just not an option, and self-care may dictate staying in the closet for the time being. In such cases, teachers compensate for the one-to-one relationships they are unable to establish by creating safe spaces within their classrooms.

> Classroom rule: no putdowns of any minority groups, [no use of] the word *nigger* and the word *dyke*—and I do enforce that—[and] *faggots*. (Jean)

> Kids actually say, "You wouldn't get away with that in Miss Jackson's class," no matter what it is, whether it's any kind of slam. . . . Kids feel real safe and real clear about what the expectations are. (Pam)

Sometimes even semi-closeted teachers were able to teach important lessons about homophobia. Like Karen, they were taking responsibility for the language used in their classrooms. "I've got radar and I keep tabs on all the conversations and if I hear *fag* or something, it's like, 'Tony?' Then I hear, 'Sorry, Miss White!' . . . My kids know that in my room there are rules about how you treat other people. . . . I told them where the word *fag* comes from and their little jaws dropped." (Note: The word *fag* is generally thought to derive from the medieval custom of using homosexuals as human "faggots," to be set aflame and used to start the fires that burned witches and heretics.)

Implicit in these descriptions of the classroom community is the link between justice and care that Ann Higgins describes in her account of a just community program in the South Bronx: "Care is only known when justice is its context in the activity of human life" (Higgins, 1989, p. 197). Like the group leaders in Higgins's account, the gay teachers I interviewed often justified their classroom rules in terms of relationship and connection.

Dianne explained, "Somebody will call someone else a queer and I always say we should use another word, that is inappropriate. Sometimes I'll say to a person, 'What if that person is gay. How do you think it makes them feel?'"

Alice, who teaches at an alternative school for "problem" youth, neatly connected the idea of justice (doing the "right" thing) with the ethical ideal of caring for the feelings of others: "I try to work on discrimination with everybody, you know. I mean don't do it. It's just not right. How would you feel? And one kid has actually said . . . 'I'll never be a fag and I don't understand it, but I won't beat on anybody anymore because I know it's wrong.'"

Alan went a step further and responded to a homophobic remark by talking about his own feelings: "A fairly close friend of ours . . . died the day before school started. . . . The day after I came back from the memorial service, one of the second graders started making AIDS jokes, 'You've got AIDS!'—which was common. I took him aside and said, 'I had a friend who just died of AIDS, and I came back from his memorial service, and I really don't like that joke. You need to think about the fact that there may be people here who have family or friends with AIDS, and it's not a funny joke. Do you know what AIDS is?' 'No.' He knew, but he wasn't going to say it. I said, 'It's a disease that people get, and it's not just a gay thing.'"

As teachers talked about the risks they were beginning to take, it became clear that being interviewed was itself an act of self-disclosure. The question of how to name themselves prompted some interesting reflections on authenticity. When I first asked Dianne how she wanted to be identified, she said she would use her own first name. Later in the discussion, she said being referred to that way wouldn't feel safe. I suggested that we could change her name to a pseudonym, but she persisted with her original plan.

> I wouldn't feel safe. There are things I don't feel safe about but I do them anyway.
> *Q*: I see what you mean. I can just use your first name.
> *A*: Sure, that would be fine.
> *Q*: If you are comfortable with that, I don't have to use your last name or the name of your school.
> *A*: My first name would be fine, as long as you spell it right:: *D-I-A-N-N-E*.

These inner debates over self-identification offer one more poignant example of the tension between safety and authenticity—the need to hide and the desire to be out—that complicates the impulse toward caring for gay teachers.

CONCLUSION: "I AM HERE"

This chapter began with a reference to my own daughter, for whom I care very deeply. While I was in the midst of writing it, she called me from the West Coast, where she is in her first year of teaching. We were both watching a TV interview with the leader of a right-wing group that had just produced a video called "The Gay Agenda in Education." My daughter was torn between anger and guilt: anger at the lies being perpetrated in "The Gay Agenda" and guilt because she feels constrained to hide her identity— the core of who she is—from her colleagues and students. Through tears, she reminded me of the gay kids killing themselves in shocking numbers; of the homophobic remarks she cannot fully confront for fear some student might ask, "Are you a lesbian?"; of the terrible sense of dishonesty that conflicts with her self-concept as a caring teacher.

As I searched for an answer, I realized that I had no good advice to give my daughter. Should I counsel her to throw off the burden of hiding by coming out to her colleagues and students? I could not forget that as a first year teacher on a limited-term contract, she would be especially vulnerable to scrutiny or dismissal. Or, should I advise her to go slowly, build a portfolio of good evaluations, and continue to keep her identity a secret until she had tenure? I could not deny the indignity and self-betrayal this would mean for her daily life in the meantime. In short, there was nothing I could tell my daughter that could enable her to care fully for herself or for her students; such caring could exist only in a world without homophobia. Thinking about our conversation later on, I remembered my interview with Pam, who described the experience of empathy that is at the heart of all caring: "Someone was talking about some guy . . . who came to him and said that he loved him, and he said, 'Do you know my pain?' And he said, 'No I don't know what pains you,' and he said, 'You can't love me until you know what hurts me, what my pain is.'"

During the past two years, I have met and talked with dozens of lesbian and gay teachers, but at that moment, as I tried to comfort my daughter, I felt their pain truly for the first time.

Yet even as I feel that pain, anger and sadness, I cannot think of the gay teachers I have met without great admiration. Despite the dangers they were facing and the stresses they endured, most of them spoke of moving further out of the closet in the future. Some, like Mike, saw self-disclosure as a way of building bridges to other gay teachers: "One of the things I may end up doing is I might try to do some kind of speakers bureau thing, either myself or some other people going around to schools talking to kids about all these issues. . . . I'm going to play it by ear with my colleagues, and in an unthinkable world it could be that a couple of them will come up to me . . . and say, 'Hey, you know what? I'm a lesbian.' Who knows?"

Others, like Dianne, hoped that becoming more visible, even if only to raise the issue of homophobia, would help the self-esteem of gay youth at her school: "One thing I just do, I keep taking tiny little steps. This past week we were working on a program . . . on personal self-discovery and self-esteem issues. . . . I mentioned to the team that there is nowhere in here that mentions a kid questioning their sexual identity. And the fact that kids who perceive themselves as homosexual have a horrible time with self-esteem and identity and who they are and who they are going to be."

Many teachers saw their struggles against homophobia as part of a larger battle against injustice. Like Alice, they found this larger struggle both "scary" and exhilarating: "When I look at the big picture—I think of the world as . . . a balloon and . . . it's like we're all inside this balloon punching it and if somebody was on the outside looking at it, they'd see just people: 'Come on, now. Let's get straight here. Let's get a grip. Start concentrating on what's important instead of these stupid piddling prejudices and wars and all that crap. If you look at the big picture, you've got to grow up.' So I'm just waiting for it. I want to be a part of it, but I'm a little scared, you know."

As Alice's remarks remind us, homophobia is a sickness that blights the lives of all students and teachers, not only those who are lesbian or gay. The idea that gay teachers themselves should have to take responsibility for ending homophobia is outrageous, to say the least. But there is a deeper meaning to these tales of "stupid little things" and "tiny baby steps." The teachers I interviewed, and others I have met, are beginning to see that risk taking and disclosure are essential for their their own self-worth and can ultimately enable them to care more fully for all their students. Every photo on the desk, every refusal to use the "Monday morning pronoun," every challenge of the slur overheard in the hallway is a way of saying, "I am here. I am lesbian or gay. I am a teacher. I am a whole person." Thinking about these things, I realize that though I have no good advice to give my daughter, I can continue to care for her by supporting her as she develops her own strategies for survival. Like many gay teachers, she may decide to conceal her identity for the time being to ensure her own safety. Or like some others, she may conclude that the costs of hiding are greater than the risks of disclosure and take the brave step of coming out in her school. Whatever decision she, and all the teachers like her, may make about revealing themselves, it is up to the heterosexual teachers, parents, administrators, and students who consider ourselves allies to end homophobia in school and society. Only when gay teachers and students are free to stop hiding will schools become places where all teachers and students can care and be cared for in safety.

RERERENCES

Buber, M. (1965). *Between Man and Man*. New York: Macmillan Publishing Company.

Coleman, E., and Ramafedi, G. (1989). "Gay, Lesbian and Bisexual Adolescents; A Critical Challenge to Counselors." *Journal of Counseling and Development* 68, no. 1, 36–40.

Hetrick, E., and Martin, A. (1987). "Developmental Issues and Their Resolution for Gay and Lesbian Adolescents." *Journal of Homosexuality* 14, nos. 1–2: 25–43.

Higgins, A. (1989). "The Just Community Educational Program: The Development of Moral Role-Taking as the Expression of Justice and Care. In M. Brabeck, ed., *Who Cares: Theory, Research and Educational Implications of the Ethic of Care*. New York: Praeger.

Hunter, J., & Schaecher, R. (1987). "Stresses on Lesbian and Gay Adolescents in Schools." *Social Work in Education* 9, no. 3: 180–190.

Kissen, R. (1993a). "Listening to Gay and Lesbian Teenagers." *Teaching Education* 5, no. 2: 57–67.

———. (1993b). "Gay Culture and Straight Jackets: Teaching and Action at a Midwestern University." *Radical Teacher* 43: 40–43.

Krysiak, G. (1987). "A Very Silent and Gay Minority." *School Counselor* 24, no. 4: 304–307.

Martin, J. (1989). "Transforming Moral Education." In M. Brabeck, ed., *Who Cares: Theory, Research and Educational Implications of the Ethic of Care*. New York; Praeger.

Noddings, N. (1984). *Caring: A Feminine Approach to Ethics and Moral Education*. Berkeley: University of California Press.

————. (1992). *The Challenge to Care in Schools: An Alternative Approach to Education*. New York: Teachers College Press.

Report of the Secretary's Task Force on Youth Suicide. (1983). Washington, DC: U.S. Dept. of Health and Human Services.

Rofes, E. (1989). "Opening up the Classroom Closet: Responding to the Needs of Gay and Lesbian Youth." *Harvard Educational Review* 59, no. 4: 444–453.

Sears, J. (1991). *Growing up Gay in the South: Race, Gender and Journeys of the Spirit*. New York: Haworth Press.

————. (1992). "Educators, Homosexuality, and Homosexual Students." *Journal of Homosexuality*, 22, nos. 3–4: 29–80.

Siegfried, C. (1989). "Pragmatism, Feminism, and Sensitivity to Context." In M. Brabeck, ed., *Who Cares: Theory, Research and Educational Implications of the Ethic of Care*. New York: Praeger.

CHAPTER 5

Understanding Caring in Context

Negotiating Borders and Barriers

JACI WEBB-DEMPSEY, BRUCE WILSON, DICKSON CORBETT, AND RHONDA MORDECAI-PHILLIPS

Discussing the dilemma of negotiating a shared vision of education, Noddings (1992) reminds us of the words of John Dewey (1902, p. 3): "What the best and wisest parent wants for his own child, that must the community want for all its children. Any other ideal for our schools is narrow and unlovely; acted upon, it destroys our democracy." Both authors acknowledge that the "best and wisest parents" would want a different education for each child, an education that addresses individual needs and maximizes a child's capabilities. Noddings adds that caring is the defining characteristic of "the best and wisest parent"; however, she (1992, p. 44) cautions that: "caring cannot be achieved by formula. It requires address and response; it requires different behaviors from situation to situation and person to person." But, in the midst of such attention to context, variability, and responsiveness, what defines the best interests of the cared-for?

Many groups have a stake in educating the children in any given school community—teachers, parents, community members, administrators, and students themselves. As we have talked with members of the "stakeholding" groups involved with the school we are currently studying, several perspectives on what is in the best interests of these children are beginning to emerge. Although all stakeholders share the goal that children deserve an education that furthers their chances for a successful future, they differ on the means of achieving that goal. For example, teachers enact their beliefs about "best interests" and care for their students in ways that vary from emphasizing the ability of children to make their own educational choices to implementing traditional instructional and disciplinary practices in their classrooms; parents and guardians stress the importance of traditional values and harken back to the days of corporal punishment and a focus on compliance; community volunteers and teaching assistants, who are also community residents, express their beliefs about "best interests" in their personal interactions with individual students and their basic caregiving behaviors; and students themselves describe the value of social relationships at school and at home in addition to the value of learning basic skills, while at the same time acting out aggressively toward one another and disrupting instruction.

We have seen these perspectives come into direct conflict with one another and that conflict tends to occur around "borders" that define the cultural and political terrain within and around which these groups operate. Mapping that terrain, locating groups and their interests, and identifying those borders is a necessary (and in some instances unavoidable) first step to understanding caring in context. What follows is our attempt to share the stories of our own "first steps" into unfamiliar cultural and political territory, moving toward an understanding of the meanings of caring held by the people who live and work in a school community. This is a progress report, as our journey is far from over and members of the school community are just beginning to think about coming together to move in the same direction.

In this chapter we describe the different ways in which parents, teachers, teaching assistants, students, and the researchers studying the interactions of these groups are beginning to define what *caring* means to them and illustrate how "caring acts" may or may not be interpreted as such by those being cared for. It is easy to make these distinctions retrospectively, but in real time the definitional borders are not so visible. Tempered by issues like race and class, the checkpoints that separate one group's views of caring from another's are subtle but entrenched. This entrenchment of discrete views may represent major barriers to the construction of shared meaning and action in a school setting.

We begin by describing an experience we had in which our attempt "to care" was not well-received by one stakeholding group in an urban elementary school community. From this, we move to a description of the school, the research we are doing, and the way in which we are beginning to think about caring. We then discuss caring in the context of four groups—teachers, parents, teaching assistants, and students—using observational and interview data from the first year of an ongoing ethnography.

BEGINNING WITH BORDERS

In February 1992 we wrote a report, *Connections in Caring* (Applied Research Project, 1992). The lead article in the report described our work in Northeast Elementary School (a pseudonym), set in the context of an "objective, just the cold, hard facts" description of its urban neighborhood. Shortly after we made the report available to the faculty and parents, we had several tense telephone conversations with community members that made it clear that they had not received the article well. Matters came to a head when the president of the Home and School Association called a meeting between community members and our research team. Ten women (two of whom were Hispanic; eight were African-American) attended, all long-time residents of the neighborhood, to represent their views about the "reality" of their community. Indicative of the place the school held in the history of the community, two of the younger African-American women were former Northeast students whose daughters now attended the school and whose mothers were also present in the room. A long-time African-American faculty member who was an ardent proponent of parental involvement also attended to lend her support to this group.

The meeting took place in the school's conference room, a long, multipurpose room on the building's first floor. Used constantly throughout the day as an adult lunchroom, a pretzel salesroom, a place to check in tardy students, and a meeting spot, the room was remarkably free of all usual activity; there seemed to be a general awareness of our meeting and of the seriousness of its purpose. We, the members of the Applied Research Project (AR) at Research for Better Schools (RBS), sat in pairs, facing one another across the middle of the table. There were four of us; two were white men with over 30 years of educational research experience between them, much of it in sites similar to Northeast, and two were women, one white and the other African-American. The former had done research in an urban school, whereas the latter was involved in her first study. However, this last member of the team was more intimately familiar with neighborhoods like Northeast's since she grew up not too far away. At the center of the controversy were five sentences that we had written in the report to describe the community setting. These sentences told about Northeast's students living in a neighborhood in which the average home price is $7,500, in which a nearby intersection is an acknowledged drug-trafficking center, in which a growing number of the children attending the school live in single-parent homes—most often supported by a female head of household—or with an extended family, in which 95 percent of the children qualify for Chapter 1 funds, in which unemployment—particularly of young African-American men— is on the rise, and in which the fragile employment market is such that well- paid, unskilled work opportunities are rapidly disappearing and, to work at all, people "must know more to earn less" (Nicolau and Ramos, 1990). These "facts" were drawn from newspaper articles and school reports. In light of the statistics we had relied on, this was indeed a neighborhood troubled by the drug trade, plummeting housing values, and family instability. We had "balanced" that picture with a description of the participants' commitment to creating a caring environment that supports successful learning.

If we had anticipated any reaction at all from the school community it would have been a positive one. We thought we were acting as advocates for the community, painting a picture of committed parents and teachers trying hard to act in the best interests of children against what seemed like overwhelming odds. Instead they viewed us with the same mistrust with which they greeted the efforts of other well-intended members of social agencies, reacting this way: "We're working to get it together; you have to work with the children and the community. We're exploited by the system because we're lower class." And the message to us was that our attempt at advocacy had been viewed as exploitation.

As the discussion progressed it became clear that several of these women had never read beyond those first few damaging sentences. In the words of one participant, "I really took offense; I took it personal, it was unfair." There was little hesitation as, one by one, participants took advantage of this opportunity to tell us just why they found the article so offensive, insensitive, and unrepresentative.

We had described the neighborhood as "one of the most notorious drug-trafficking centers in the city," and two of the women spit out the label *notorious* with disgust. One of the grandmothers, herself now a student at a nearby university, shared emotionally: "It pissed me off! Drugs are all over the city, they're in the white houses in the suburbs, too. You just don't see it, the rich can afford to hide it." We were taken aback.

The tone of the meeting changed only when the African-American member of our team spoke up, affirming their right to be concerned, acknowledging our "sins," and offering to give them an equal opportunity to be heard in a subsequent report. From this point the confrontation became a discussion. However, although they acknowledged the growing drug problem and cited their own concern with the growing number of young parents, whom they described as little more than children themselves, these neighborhood residents made it clear in no uncertain terms that they were unwilling to have us portray those problems.

Being called on the carpet is never a pleasant experience. Being called on the carpet when you have more than a sneaking suspicion that you are wrong is decidedly unpleasant. What happened was like having your passport and baggage scrutinized as you enter a foreign country. It is difficult, under penetrating glares, not to wonder if you are in fact unsuspectingly smuggling in something that is offensive in the eyes of the host country. We immediately became acutely aware that cultural baggage made us assume that our actions would have been readily recognized as well-intentioned and in the best interests of others. It was extremely discomforting to have those assumptions "checked" as we foundered at an unfamiliar border.

Looking back, we realize the community members were defending a past, a history that they felt in many ways was integral to understanding the present condition of the neighborhood and imperative for understanding what was positive in the school. They grounded their concerns in an historical description of the changing nature of the community: "It used to be quiet here, you could put your children out to play, the whole block was like a family and we left our doors open. . . ."; "The homeowners have bought elsewhere, the houses have become rented . . ."; "There used to be some industries, some factories, there was a lot of businesses, like the Apex Laundry, and a lot of working class people . . ."

They also described the changes they perceived in the way the school served their community: "Northeast was like a big family, that's how we talked about the school—a family. Years ago children were taught these things, 'Respect yourselves and others.' It was a motto of the school about ten years ago. Now things are too lenient. Children walk the halls a lot. These things aren't being taught because we have new teachers who aren't familiar with the procedures and we get the teachers who don't want to be here, they are 'dumped' here and they don't care."

Thus, they were making the point that not only has the neighborhood changed, but so too has the school's relationship to the community. This context is integral to a full understanding of the social conditions we described.

At this point in the meeting, the older community members present began telling stories about their children attending Northeast. Then, those children, the two parents of students currently attending the school, told their side of those same stories. In the process they shared their vision of what they believed is acting in the best interests of their children. That vision focused on strong, assertive discipline and high expectations for behavior. Those women bemoaned the passing of corporal punishment, describing how previous principals "kept kids in line" with the threat of "a whipping." They shared stories of their own children "knowing that if they got one (a paddling) at school, they would get another one at home, a worse one." They expressed their respect for faculty members who could "make kids mind" and "teach them how to behave." When they described former students who were now considered successful by the community, they implied that their success stemmed from having learned "their place" in school. For example, one woman told about her son, Buddy, who had been "in the principal's office every day" and who had finally gotten the message and "straightened up." Buddy went on to finish high school and then to pursue technical training to "do all right now, he's a good boy."

As they told those stories, they claimed their right to portray their neighborhood as they saw it, not as other participants saw it. At the same time they shared cultural values about schooling that we could see coming into conflict with the values and practices that some of the teachers, teaching assistants, and we were more comfortable with. Finally, these community members, by their very presence if nothing else, shared their willingness to invest in the school and participate in a dialogue about how to benefit their children.

This discussion made us realize that tapping into that history, and respecting its place in the community's image of itself, would be an important step as the faculty members and we build a more reciprocal relationship with community members, one grounded in an understanding of what role the community feels the school should play in the community and of how they have come to define *caring*. We also realized that we needed to look beyond our naive attempt at empathy and to embrace reciprocal communication across cultural borders. We learned the hard way that no matter how hard you "try to care, if the caring is not received, the claim 'they don't care' has some validity" (Noddings, 1992, p. 15).

GETTING TO NORTHEAST

To reach Northeast Elementary School—a 10 minute trip—we must drive through the increasingly gentrified surroundings of our office building and travel through a recognizably middle-class, multicultural neighborhood of well-tended row houses with off-the-street parking and front porches, and then we cross a major thoroughfare and enter the neighborhood that is served by the school. The rest of the trip is uncomfortably and involuntarily like "sightseeing." We look out of our car windows at unfamiliar and unsettling sights: burned out buildings, automobiles that have been torched or stripped and abandoned on the side of the street, and the facades of homes and churches covered with graffiti. While here and there are buildings that show evidence of recent renovations, doors freshly painted, and vegetable and flower gardens being cultivated behind fences surrounding once vacant lots, these signs are overwhelmed by much more commonplace sights such as the car sitting at the bottom of the cracked, peeling, and litter-strewn community swimming pool. Then there are the closed and sometimes hostile faces of the people on the street, mostly African-American and Hispanic males, many of whom look to be of the age that we would expect them to be in school rather than congregating around the doorways and stoops of empty buildings or on the corners. They look back at us as we travel through their neighborhood in such a way as to make us feel our difference.

This somehow threatening landscape has been dubbed by one of our participants as "The Land of Lots," and we feel the emptiness implied in that adage. Whereas the physical evidence of decay is disturbing and most readily apparent, it is the look on passing faces that remains with us as we leave the car and enter the school—and makes us consider borders and barriers that are every bit as real and jarring as the geographic markers we encounter on our way to the school.

With approximately 700 students, 75 percent of whom are African-American and 25 percent of whom are Hispanic, Northeast serves one of the most impoverished and disadvantaged populations in the city of Philadelphia. The school itself is one of the system's older physical plants still in operation. Many of the "savage inequalities" (Kozol, 1991) so evident in inner city schools are apparent at Northeast: a general lack of resources, including an inadequately equipped library and resource center, the lack of up-to-date curriculum materials and classroom supplies, and few funds for extras such as field trips. Although some of those deficits are filled by the pursuit of special grants, by creative management of their schoolwide use of Chapter 1 funds, or by the efforts of the Home and School Association, others are much more difficult to address. Teacher turnover is high and vacancies often remain unfilled long into the school year—not only denying students a sense of continuity, but also services such as those of a counselor, often for months at a time.

Thus, holes in the fabric of a viable, vibrant academic environment are readily apparent; and children appear to be falling through those holes, "slipping through the cracks" in the words of one participant, as indicated by the data the state and the district used to qualify Northeast as a Schoolwide Project school. Having been identified as needing to improve attendance, achievement test scores, and grades, Schoolwide Project schools have been given discretion over their Chapter 1 allocations and can use these funds to benefit all students, rather than just those who are technically eligible (Winfield, 1991a). Although some improvement appears to have been made, allowing Northeast to continue in this program, the scores still reveal large percentages of the student population in the lowest quartile on these measures. These improvements do not begin to compare to state or national averages—evidence that perhaps these children are not merely failing in "the system," but rather, when all is taken into account, that "the system" is failing to serve them. Participants on the faculty at Northeast express their belief that the school district has "turned its back on them, and forgotten Northeast," and community members explain that the larger, more faceless "system" would like to pretend that their problems are all their own and not society's.

GETTING TO CARING

The list of what the school, its community, and its students do not have was seemingly endless and tragic in our eyes when we first began visiting the school. Along with our ideological assumptions, we carried a concern with caring in education, and we believe, with Noddings (1992), that caring is nurtured in continuity of purpose, place, and people. The cultural and political borders we sensed on our visits represent barriers to that continuity and to the conditions that would make it possible to put caring at the center of efforts to educate children. We wanted to help this school help its students become successful learners, and we wanted those successful learners to be caring, but we did not initially integrate these purposes. Our work with the school and its community did that for us.

That work began early in the fall of 1991 when one of us was invited to address a group of Philadelphia administrators concerning the issue of defining successful learning and aligning school improvement efforts with that definition. After the meeting, one of the principals extended an invitation to speak with her leadership team about the same issue. This meeting subsequently led to another with the entire faculty at Northeast. The leadership team was preparing to revise its annual school improvement plan and expressed their desire to get the faculty thinking along the lines that had been laid out during the two initial contacts; namely, that significant reform should begin with a shared understanding among participants of a successful learner and then should work backward from that understanding to create supportive experiences that encourage those characteristics in all children.

The faculty meeting opened with a discussion of the characteristics students needed to become successful learners. The list generated by the teachers and administrators included: "positive attitude, involved in the community, good job performance, happy relationships, a sense of responsibility, discipline, self-esteem, hard working, trustworthy, determined, self-motivated, ambitious, and values." Our team member facilitating the meeting sorted the characteristics into the broad categories proposed by a review of the research on successful learning (Jones and Fennimore, 1990). The review proposes a broad definition of successful learning that goes beyond acquisition of subject matter to include being knowledgeable (able to locate and produce needed information), empathetic (able to appreciate and adopt multiple perspectives from which to view the world), self-determined (able to initiate, direct, and evaluate one's own learning), and strategic (able to solve problems creatively). No one took issue with the categorization, and the meeting ended with a request for us to enter into a long-term research and assistance relationship to help inform the school's reform efforts and frame their work around appropriate experiences for their students. Our interest in pursuing the relationship was to take advantage of an opportunity to not only track reform but also to observe how participants adopt a broader definition of successful learning.

Our first step in building a shared understanding of a *successful learner* was to interview nearly every adult ($N = 61$) connected with the daily lives of the students at Northeast (including teachers, teaching assistants, administrators, support staff) about the characteristics these children would need to be successful learners. In addition, we probed their assessment of the school's ability to focus on these characteristics, as well as their identification of the obstacles they face and the resources available to support their work.

The view of a successful learner that emerged from the interviews was also easily categorized into knowledgeable, empathetic, self-determined, and strategic; however, something else that emerged was a strong concern with caring and the social relationships of students. Teachers, assistants, and other adults at the school cited the need for "parents who care," "adults here who care for them," "caring teachers," and "environments where they feel comfortable caring and sharing." In addition, participants cited "concern for others," the ability to "think first and then act," "to be responsible," and "to act in the best interests of others," as major concerns. These beliefs implied that the social context of learning needed to be addressed as well as the development of individual characteristics.

Our first inclination was to fit their concern with caring into the "empathetic" domain, but empathy can be a singularly individual characteristic carrying no responsibility to act. We thought of the many cases in which a "successful learner," someone who was knowledgeable, strategic, self-determined, and empathetic, had acted to the detriment of others. Although "successful" in the individual sense and able to exercise empathy in such a way as to gain an understanding of the weaknesses of others and use that understanding to their own advantage, these individuals lacked the element that addresses the social context of learning and its application—caring. Our understanding of successful learning grew beyond empathy, beyond the possession of individual qualities, to include a moral dimension that would compel an individual to invoke those qualities to benefit others in a responsive and responsible manner. Successful learning then requires attending to the social relationships in which actions are constructed and meaning is negotiated. "Empathy," in our thinking, could no longer contain "caring," and our understanding of the relationship between caring and successful learning began to move beyond the rhetorical.

Our interactions with participants at Northeast Elementary made real for us the distinction Noddings (1984, p. 30) makes between empathy and caring: "The Oxford Universal Dictionary defines empathy as 'The power of projecting one's personality into, and so fully understanding, the object of contemplation.' This is . . . 'feeling with.' The notion of 'feeling with' . . . does not involve projection but reception I have called it 'engrossment.' I do not 'put myself in the other's shoes,' so to speak, by analyzing his reality as objective data and then asking, 'How would I feel in such a situation?' On the contrary, I set aside my temptation to analyze and to plan. I do not project; I receive the other into myself, and I see and feel with the other." From this perspective, caring requires action, going well beyond empathy— or the ability to see the world through the eyes of others—to accepting the responsibility to act (or refrain from action) based on what you see. Caring is a value, but more than that it is a moral imperative. Caring moves self-determination into social responsibility, and employs knowledge and strategic thinking to decide how to act in the best interests of others. Caring binds individuals to society, to their communities, and to each other. Caring for us then cannot be an "add-on" to a model of successful learning, but the shelter under which the other characteristics are enacted and developed.

GROUPS, BORDERS, AND CARING

We were not the only group operating in the school with an undeveloped understanding of how others look at acting in the best interests of others. Our misguided assumptions were embarrassing, but were ultimately not of much significance for what happened with students. However, the implications of teachers', parents', other staff members', and students' interactions at the borders that separate how they view caring are much more grave. We now turn to the ways in which these various groups defined *caring*, with the idea that this will enable us (and them) to begin to see where these borders are and to begin to negotiate travel across them.

Each of the following sections attends to a distinct group. This may seem odd, given that caring is a reciprocal act; but, at the moment, this is in fact the way that participants view their situation. They speak of how they are "isolated" from one another and how their perspectives are largely uninformed by meaningful contact with people in other groups. We draw on primarily our interviews with members of these groups to represent how they describe what acting in the best interest of others means and to hint at the issues of role, class, race, and age that reinforce the borders that hinder the construction of shared meaning.

Teachers

The teachers shared their beliefs about the characteristics of successful learners with us and about "the best interests" of their students during our initial interviews with them. When we began preparing to pilot test a directed survey with the students, we conducted observations in a number of classrooms to get a sense of the children and how they interacted with one another and their teachers. What we really came away with from those observations was an understanding of the ways the teachers believed they were acting to support their personal definitions of "best interests" in their classroom practices. Between the interviews, the observations, and numerous informal interactions throughout the school year, we pieced together pictures of how several teachers tried to "practice what they preached."

None of the teachers whose beliefs and practices we describe here lived in the Northeast school community and not all of them chose to work there. Although they shared an occupation and they were all women, they cut across lines of race and professional orientation. Cathy, a white fourth grade teacher, made the decision to teach at Northeast consciously. She had previously been at a select private school, but expressed a personal need to work with "disadvantaged students." In her words, Cathy wanted these students to become "empowered, recognizing their responsibility for their lives" and for them to develop "a sense of self" that centered around their cultural heritage and personal expression. A "facility with words and numbers" was a skill she saw as necessary to the development of that empowerment and sense of self, but underlying everything that happened with these children were their needs for "security in the home" and to be "fed and clothed."

Cathy's view of acting in the best interests of her students was embedded in the value she placed on empowerment and self-actualization. She emphasized the importance of written communication skills as a means to these ends, even though that focus was sometimes carried out at the expense of classroom order. Cathy freely admitted that, in her search to have students explore their writing skills independently, the ones who were not directly supervised took advantage of the freedom to do things other than their work. Yet, she steadfastly attended to individual and small group instruction.

Mary, a young, white, female kindergarten teacher, added to our growing awareness of the variability of meanings of caring or "best interests." Mary came to Northeast because she was "interested in working with kids that have not a lot going for them, kids that deserve a better chance." Her efforts with her students illustrated her belief that "a lot of good can be done—it's not their fault yet; it might be some day." Mary phrased her vision of appropriate student outcomes as encompassing a broad "checklist of skills, rather than tests—we have to show children they know this; they need to see their successes in school more."

Mary felt that she serves the best interests of her students by encouraging them to be self-directed and self-controlled. Thus, students' taking responsibility for their actions was an important goal in Mary's eyes. She began each working period by asking the children to choose from a number of activities they would like to do. They negotiated their choices with Mary. Using her knowledge of their needs and capabilities, Mary either encouraged them to try new activities or practice familiar ones until she was sure they had mastered them. Mary determined the range of "choices" and decided when "this is not a choice" for her students. She also defined what was "acceptable" behavior and expressed a commitment to helping students acquire social skills that will help them succeed in school and later in life. She was concerned, however, that these skills, so important in school, were not receiving reinforcement in the homes of many of her students.

JoAnna, a Hispanic teacher in her first year, came to Northeast by luck of the draw in the lottery that used seniority to assign teachers to schools. She felt that Northeast's children needed "self-reliance" first and foremost and then "self-confidence and knowledge, which will come after self-reliance." The final characteristic she wanted children at Northeast to develop was "respect for others and others' property." JoAnna believed that sharing her expectations with the parents of her culturally diverse group of students was one way she acted in their best interests—often at a sacrifice of personal time. She contacted parents first through a written contract detailing her expectations and, then, maintained that contact by sending a daily work diary home with her students. Short notes in the diaries required parents to respond regularly. These diaries were sent home to a parent population in which adult literacy was an acknowledged problem.

Arlene, an African-American intermediate teacher, came to Northeast straight out of college four years ago. She explained that she had a "no-nonsense" attitude and believed it was important to set high expectations for student behavior and achievement. While very aware of the personal circumstances of her students and adamant that compassion ("to care about what others feel, having understanding for others' background who are less fortunate") should be a characteristic students should develop, she also shared her perspective that "Northeast makes too many excuses." Other characteristics she believed these seventeen students will need to acquire to be successful learners included "ambition, responsibility, and willingness to be hard working." She stated her concern that "it doesn't seem like they are striving for the future, only to get to the next grade," and the bottom line was that "they are the only ones responsible for their future and their actions." She shared her belief that "teachers who push their kids" were acting in their best interests and communicated her disgust that "other teachers don't push and the kids don't expect to be pushed; it's not consistent."

Arlene's willingness "to push" was evident in her communication of her expectations in her classroom, both for behavior and for academics. She believed that consistency in those expectations exhibited her focus on the future of her students—that they be able to see that future and take advantage of it. Her disdain for teachers who "don't push" was consistent with the values expressed by the African-American parents and community members we encountered in the meeting recounted earlier.

As our familiarity with the beliefs and practices of teachers at Northeast grew, we came to understand that we needed to get beyond our "successful learning" definition of *caring*, which was broad enough to encompass nearly everyone's rhetorical understandings to give the surface impression of agreement between groups and individuals. It was clear that these four teachers had very different ways of defining and enacting *caring* in their classrooms, and these ways of caring could easily contradict those espoused by different groups in the community. For example, teachers who were willing to sacrifice order and control, who saw the children as somehow deficient socially, who expected communications that might be intimidating or impossible (in the case of parents who were unable to read) might not be as easily accepted by the community as teachers who enforced strict discipline and expected kids to conform.

We also had the sense that something was missing in the pictures of *caring* we carried from teachers. Although their commitment to their students was clear, teachers' views of the community were often unidimensional, constructed from the press of clearly visible social problems—unemployment, drugs, alienation from greater society, increased violent crime, family instability—and not at all from what the parents, community members, and students cited as positive defining features of their lives. Their willingness to care, then, did not always extend beyond their classroom doors and certainly was not negotiated across the various cultural and political borders that marked the social terrain of the neighborhood.

Parents

One group that felt welcomed were the Hispanic parents actively involved with the school. Parental involvement from this group was high at Northeast, due to the efforts of a core group led by the Home-School Coordinator, who is a long-term resident of the community. These parents were very visible in the school, making up the better part of the audience at special events and filling the buses to help chaperone field trips. Although Hispanic students accounted for only 25 percent of the student body, their parents held two of the four office positions in the Home and School Association. Hispanic parents shared that they were very comfortable participating in the school and those who volunteered on a regular basis felt appreciated. As this parent shared, "The school people express the way they feel [about me] and that makes me feel good."

However, this involvement took place within the confines of a culturally delineated territory. For example, the two Hispanic parents who attended the meeting described previously sat together in silence at the foot of the table, every once in a while exchanging commentary in Spanish, but never contributing to the public discussion. Their presence indicated their interest in the issue of the report, but their behavior indicated their separation from the other participants, all of whom were African-American. In fact, they later shared they felt the tone of the meeting was posturing on the part of the others. Just as the Hispanic parents at our community meeting sat silent, so did the majority of Hispanic parents remain isolated from the mainstream of the school. It was most like a school-within-a-school arrangement, with Hispanic children and parents beginning their experiences at Northeast segregated from the African-American population. The majority of Hispanic kindergarten students were placed with the Hispanic kindergarten teacher and English as a Second Language (ESL) students are served in a separate class, once again with an Hispanic teacher. There were also bilingual teachers at every grade level, with a combination class to serve the fourth and fifth grades.

Many of the recommendations drawn from research on increasing parental involvement (Epstein, 1990) were evident, including home visits by bilingual staff, regular communications concerning children's progress, Spanish translations of school notices, the use of Hispanic parents to reach other parents whenever possible, and parent education workshops. The Home-School Coordinator, Mrs. Hernandez, had instituted all of these, some formally, others informally. Mrs. Hernandez conducted home visits to update parents on their children and to make informal inquiries into their personal and academic progress. She also connected parents, both Hispanic and African-American, to community resources, such as bus token distribution sites, employment opportunities, and health services.

Positive though this involvement may have been, much of it further separated the Hispanic and African-American populations, compounding an existing barrier to negotiation in the school. Hispanic teachers described "their parents" as involved and supportive, as opposed to "the other parents," and the Home-School Coordinator shared her frustration that when a discipline problem occurs, "if it is an Hispanic student, they always bring it to me and they come down hard on them; the others they just let get away with it." A Hispanic parent claimed that an important characteristic for children at the school to develop would be racial tolerance, "not prejudiced." She further stated that this was a problem that develops over time and that "in the upper grades the kids are disrespectful of each other, and the black kids don't get along with Hispanics." This parent hoped that in the process of changing to provide the children with a better education, the school community could "be like a family—not two, separated along racial lines." Her statement brought the reminisces of the long-time African-American parents to mind and their comment, "Northeast was a family, it was the Northeast family," at a time in the history of the school community when there had been the greatest homogeneity of community and faculty. When the Hispanic parent went on to describe her community's experiences within the school, she underlined the power of cultural connection, describing the Pan American Day assembly, organized by the ESL teacher, supported by the parents, and performed by all the students to celebrate the Latino heritage of some of them. Experiences like these meant to her that "The teachers and the parents are working together . . . it's kind of like a family."

The family, however, had readily apparent divisions that surfaced in different institutional treatment among groups of parents, guardians and students believe exist. The institutionalized school practices that benefited the Hispanic community, such as bilingual instruction, were questioned by some members of the African-American community. As one parent noted, "Many of those children were born here and they speak English fine." Further they discuss the impact of this underlying tension, as an African-American grandmother working at the school as a crossing guard described Mrs. Hernandez as "scared" to communicate with African-American community members and her own role as one of easing relations for Mrs. Hernandez by acting as "a go-between between the school and the parents."

African-American parents also perceived and challenged powerful negative stereotypes that they felt were held by the faculty and that they believed had an impact on their children's educational experiences. As one African-American grandmother shared, "They say our children are not prepared for school, don't have books, don't read, but many do." A mother targeted what she believed was the source of some of the pigeonholing of students themselves, saying, "Don't decide a kid ain't going to do nothing; sometimes kids are left out because of their behavior." The African-American community in particular raised the issue of "being left out," describing that "some teachers talk down to parents." On the other side of that perception some faculty members shared their belief that "the parents don't back us up" and "the parents don't value education." The African-American parents and community members we spoke with expressed that they did indeed value education, that they felt it was important to be involved in their children's school experiences, and that they felt such involvement benefited their children's learning.

Teaching Assistants

When we sat down with the teaching assistants at Northeast to ask their advice concerning how we might "get into" the community to interview parents and community members, we recognized another group whose definition of caring might vary from the ones held by others in the school community. This group of participants had not had access to any of the other feedback sessions we had conducted with the faculty concerning our interviews with adults. Their workday ended at noon, long before afternoon faculty meetings were scheduled. We might have anticipated a reaction similar to that of the community members, taking offense at our representation of their community since the majority of the teaching assistants at Northeast were also long-term African-American residents of the community. However, the only question they raised was in response to an anonymous teacher's comment about the neighborhood: "What did they [the teachers] mean by 'college doesn't prepare you for this'?" In the ensuing discussion, their view emerged that college cannot prepare you to care for children; such preparation comes only in genuine relationships.

This group saw themselves as role models for the children, providing some of the parenting they see lacking in their community. They felt the children "look for love and caring" from them, that they, "need to be touched, patted on the back, and told they did a good job." They expressed their caring for these children by "when we see a child not looking the way he should, we'll wash his face and hands, put a little skin lotion on," or "when they need discipline, we'll say, 'Listen, let me tell you something, I know your mother'." They got that caring back in "hugs," and "flowers," and in the knowledge that "they don't forget you." When asked, "What do the children see that is caring?" the assistants responded: "That we take time with them. Each individual is different; each kid has a different personality; you can't deal with them all the same"; "Kindness"; "How you show love"; "How you talk to them."

These women also perceived that they provided a positive vision of what was possible for these children, that they give children "a chance to see their own community people going out to work, to see that life isn't all about standing on a corner."

The assistants stood behind a border of their own, between their connection to the community and their role in the school. They saw the impact of the separation of the Hispanic and African-American populations in acknowledging that the Home-School Coordinator was responsible for making official home contacts and that she was "scared of the black families, and so we back [her] up a lot." They also saw the separation of the faculty from the community, illustrated in their accounts of classroom interactions. One assistant related: "This little boy is so pitiful; this one child hits my heart. The teacher picked his hair in front of the class, I told her, 'You don't do that. You don't do it in front of the kids.' He was so embarrassed." Another shared that she had noticed the way one child dressed to come to school and that he always seemed hungry, so she nurtured a relationship with him and finally: "He wrote a letter to tell me his mother was on drugs. Because he came to me, the teacher yelled. I said, "[Teacher] excuse me, you don't see it the way we do here."

This sort of teacher behavior, viewed by the assistants as insensitive and uncaring, was seen as the result of the fact that the teachers "get in their cars and they're gone—we're still here." Yet the assistants' marginal status in the school, not credentialed enough to gain professional standing, in their view meant that their expert knowledge of the community context was not afforded the respect they felt it should have received. In fact, when asked if their efforts to connect the school and the community were recognized, one assistant retorted, "by the kids, yes, but not by the echelons. In fact we're sometimes seen as interfering, as not quote-unquote 'professionals'." The dilemma for the assistants was that the "professionals" valued the clerical work they did while the children valued the relationships they established.

The assistants were also in a unique position to see the impact of the changing character of their neighborhood on students' experiences. As an assistant noted, "I think it has changed, since the drugs took over the families. Three of us have been at the school since 1971; we've seen tremendous change. Children always had their little ways, but you could talk to them. But now, you go in the classrooms and they don't even hear you."

They were concerned that their relationships with the children and their connection to the school community may not be enough to keep them in a strong position to address the rising tide of instability in students' lives and that they may lose their ability to make caring connections with them.

Students

The adults, both in the school and the community, indicated a concern with caring for children. However, if the students do not perceive themselves as being cared for, the necessary basis for both encouraging the development of caring and enabling children to learn successfully would not be strong enough to make a difference in their lives.

Students at Northeast crossed borders every day, moving from interactions with teachers and teaching assistants behind classroom doors, with each other in the schoolyard and the cafeteria, and with community adults in the streets and houses. They had to negotiate those very borders that separated the adults in their lives from one another. Understanding how they perceive the actions of adults around them, what meaning the community holds for them, and what they believe is in their best interests is a necessary piece to negotiating any vision of how they might best be served.

Just as the school was preparing to close for the summer we began talking with the children in six classrooms, grades K–5, (N = 125), using a survey we were developing for use with the entire student body. What we heard was often dramatic and nearly unbelievable to at least some of our ears. Nearly half of the children described shootouts and drug sales as "something scary that happens in my neighborhood" or as "something that happens all the time in my neighborhood." Several students described either seeing a shooting or hearing gunshots, and one little boy described finding a gun after a shootout and how he coped with it by finding an adult and warning other younger children not to touch it. For those of us commuting in from the suburbs each day, it was compelling to listen to these concrete descriptions of the existence of such conditions in the daily lives of children—particularly in light of the absence of such conditions for our own children. The drama of this contrast captured our attention early in the interviews, but as we continued talking with students, we began to hear the other side of these stories.

Although the teachers offered a unidimensional perspective of the community, the parents and community members offered up a more positive perspective that they wanted portrayed. Somewhere in between, the children shared a balanced perspective of their neighborhood and their place in it. Their responses did not deny the existence of the conditions in which they live as described by the faculty—living in the basement of a drug shooting gallery, constantly exposed to violence in the form of shootouts and fights, never having enough food at home and frequently coming to school hungry, and many days coming to school not quite sure where they will be spending the night—but they were also quick to describe the positive aspects of their lives in this school community. They talked freely of looking forward to afterschool activities such as swimming, playing basketball, jumping rope with friends, and riding their bikes. They talked about special traditions like block parties or neighbors baking a cake in celebration of a little girl's birthday; and they focused on celebrations of Christmas and Halloween that were familiar to us. Their responses exemplified what Winfield (1991b) describes as "resilience," the ability to survive and thrive under the adverse conditions that often lead to the categorization of these children as "at-risk," a category this community finds offensive.

When we asked students to talk about school, they described their images of both "good" and "bad" teachers. What emerged was a very consistent set of responses that, on the positive side, reflected a healthy respect and concern on the part of teachers for the well-being of children. For the students, a good teacher is one who puts the best interests of kids first. The most frequent adjectives used by far were *nice* and *kind*. What they described was a teacher who could relate to them as individuals and loved them for who they were. Patience is an important virtue in that formula, as acknowledged by students who stressed the importance of teachers "not getting angry." Younger children talked about good teachers being "nice";

bad ones engaged in "hollering," "yelling," and "hitting." The older students were divided concerning whether or not schoolwork was in their best interests—whether "good" teachers were those that gave work or did not give it—and they echoed the younger ones that "screaming" and "being mean" were "bad" behaviors.

The most remarkable feature of the students' perspectives was that only a few of the things they mentioned had to do with instruction, such as "teaches," "knows how to teach," "gives us math," "helps me with my work." Children appear to view teachers as adults, rather than instructors, and value caring and interpersonal relationships with them. From this perspective, a bad teacher was one who was more concerned about rules and orderliness than individuals. The most common responses to "a bad teacher is one who . . ." included "screams and yells," "hits kids," and is generally "mean to us." There is no denying that these students are active and that in large groups young children present some discipline problems, and children expressed their concern with personal safety and with interruptions during instructional time. However, the obvious answer from the students' perspective is not to respond with force—violating their trust that adults will "take care" of them. Responses that remove the children from social interaction and classroom activity are also associated with "bad" teachers. Teachers who deny children social connections by "making us put our heads down," "making you sit by yourself," and not allowing students to "play," also violate their understandings of what is in their best interests.

Children also value learning, making connections between school and their ability to "get ahead." One of the kindergarteners was a little girl who described another child being sent to the principal's office to be disciplined and subsequently being expelled. Her concern was that "if you get sent home, you can't learn; I want to stay in school and learn; I want to be a doctor." While many of their responses are not nearly as sophisticated in their logic as this, a number of students expressed their desire to learn. One student even described a "bad" teacher as one who "didn't teach us to learn." However, their images of "getting ahead" were often unrealistic or limited. While this may in part have been due to their age, the limited vision expressed by the majority of the students—little boys wanting to be either a policeman or a fireman, and little girls who aspired to be nurses, or in the case of one who wanted to "grow up and be somebody's girlfriend"— echoed the view expressed by the faculty.

When the students themselves described what they meant by caring, they acknowledged the tacit nature of many caring interactions, explaining that they knew when someone cared for them because "I know when I know" or "I can see it in their eyes." There was also an instrumental, tangible, materialistic side to caring, with children explaining that "they buy me things"; "they give me things"; and "they feed me." While many of them acknowledged this caring that is associated with material expression, an even larger proportion used language that reflected important adult relational actions. For example, the most frequent response to questions about how children know when the adults in their lives care for them was "they help me." Students revealed the importance of trust in their recognition of caring, sharing, "If I ask for help, I know they will help me." While these more subtle understandings were important, simple, direct verbal expressions of caring were also necessary, as indicated by children who explained that their caring relationships with important adults in their lives, both at home and at school, were affirmed when "tell me they love me," and reciprocated, "they know I care because I tell them."

These children's responses illustrate the centrality of their need to be cared for, expressed as follows by Noddings (1992, p. xi): "To care and be cared for are fundamental human needs. We all need to be cared for by other human beings. In infancy, illness, or old age, the need is urgent and pervasive; we need caregiving, and we need the special attitude of caring that accompanies the best caregiving if we are to survive and be whole. But at every stage we need to be cared for in the sense that we need to be understood, received, respected, recognized."

Although the other borders we have described will certainly be difficult to address, this final one is most compelling. How do we include children in negotiation, how do we ensure that their voices have a place and a worth in that process? A hopeful note was sounded at a feedback session just prior to the start of the 1992–93 school year. We shared student responses to questions from the survey with the faculty, focusing on student descriptions of good and bad teachers and what they reported "they hear their teachers say a lot." Upon hearing that the most frequent responses to the question "something my teacher says all the time is . . ." were "be quiet," "sit down and do your work," and "shut up!" one teacher commented, "That says something doesn't it?" Another queried, "Is that what we really want them to be hearing?" This is a compelling question that, for us, raises questions that "say something" to the school's efforts and the isolation of beliefs and values that currently impede those efforts.

CONCLUSIONS

People come to particular situations, behaviors, and decisions with feelings, concerns, aspirations, and a history of personally lived experiences, as well as a deeply human need for a sense of well-being. Human relationships based on respect for human dignity reveal sensitivity to these in both everyday relationships and conflict resolution. To care about others means that we attempt to see beyond the "desirability" (in our terms) of particular feelings or aspirations and to understand how particular people came to want what they want, to be who they are, and to behave as they do. It also means that we are concerned about their sense of well-being and our part in maintaining or improving it. When we care about others, we do not simply act for people (on their behalf) as "objects" of our care, but also with them as mutual "subjects" in the human experience. (Beane, 1990, p. 62)

Social borders separate teachers from their assistants, the community from the school, one set of parents from another, and the children from the adults. They all care, but these groups—influenced by personal biographies and cultural histories—do not necessarily see the caring in each others' actions. Instead of experiencing the security and comfort of being within a "family," they feel the mistrust and suspicion that comes from looking from the outside in. Caring, thus, is decontextualized, with each group defining acting in the best interests of others without consideration of the others' perspectives and circumstances. It is no one's, and everyone's, fault. It is no one's fault in that group borders are buttressed by cultural supports: class, race, gender, and age. It is everyone's fault in that such supports can be weakened only by direct negotiation. Someone has to be willing to venture into uncharted territory, someone has to actually walk in the terrain of others perceptions.

There are some signs of progress. Many more parents, guardians, and community members are coming to the school for events such as Back to School Night and workshops on parenting skills and academic assistance than have in the recent past. In addition, there are more individual acts of outreach on the part of faculty members, particularly from the newer faculty members, who are making home visits at report card time and are willing to visit the neighborhood on a Sunday afternoon to walk the streets and knock on doors inviting people to come to a school event. Caring means nothing unless it means something to both, or all, parties involved in the action. Thus, negotiating borders will have to become customary before all of the well-intentioned energy at Northeast can be channeled into promoting the best interests of the students.

How do schools and their communities come to consensus around a common vision of education for all children? And if caring is to be part of that vision, how do we begin to negotiate a common definition of just what it means to "care"? Finally, how do we come to know the borders that can and should be crossed in pursuit of the answers to those questions and those that should remain sacrosanct in the negotiation process? In the ensuing dialogue we hope that the meaning of *the best interests of children*, the basis of caring, holds for each group in the school community will be open both to question and to justification.

ACKNOWLEDGMENT

The preparation of this document was supported by funds from the U.S. Department of Education, Office of Educational Research and Improvement (OERI). The opinions expressed do not necessarily reflect the position of OERI, and no official endorsement should be inferred.

REFERENCES

Applied Research Project. (1992). *Connections in Caring*. Philadelphia: Research for Better Schools.

Beane, J. A. (1990). *Affect in the Curriculum: Toward Democracy, Dignity, and Diversity*. New York: Teachers College Press.

Dewey, J. (1902). *The School and Society*. Chicago: University of Chicago Press.

Epstein, J. (1990). "School and Family Connections: Theory, Research, and Implications for Integrating Sociologies of Education and Family." In D. G. Unger and M. B. Sussman, eds., *Families in Community Settings: Interdisciplinary Perspectives*. New York: Haworth Press.

Jones, B., and Fennimore, T. (1990). *The New Definition of Learning: The First Step of School Reform*. Oakbrook, IL: North Central Regional Educational Laboratory.

Kozol, J. (1991). *Savage Inequalities: Children in America's Schools*. New York: Crown.

Nicolau, S., and Ramos, C. L. (1990). *Together is Better: Building Strong Relationships Between Schools and Hispanic Parents*. New York: Hispanic Policy Development Project.

Noddings, N. (1984). *Caring: A Feminine Approach to Ethics and Moral Education*. Berkeley: University of California Press.

————. (1992). *The Challenge to Care in Schools*. New York: Teachers College Press.

Winfield, L. F. (1991a). "Lessons from the Field: Case Studies of Evolving Schoolwide Projects." *Educational Evaluation and Policy Analysis* 13, no. 4: 253–262.

————. (1991b). "Resilience, Schooling, and Development in African-American Youth." *Education and Urban Society* 24, no. 1: 5–14.

Part Two

DILEMMAS OF CREATING SCHOOLS AS CENTERS OF CARE

CHAPTER 6

CARING AND CONTINUITY

The Demise of Caring in an African-American Community,
One Consequence of School Desegregation

VAN DEMPSEY AND GEORGE NOBLIT

Many people are beginning to question the premise of thinking about the problems of schools in instrumental terms. Typically, we define the goal of schooling as learning that can be defined by standardized tests, and the guiding logic of educational policy and educational reform for most of this century has been to design technical strategies to enforce that narrow definition of learning. However, it is not clear that these policies actually improve either learning or schools. Indeed, the lesson of the now waning reform movement is that the more we think and act in instrumental ways, the more poorly our children achieve. There were times in the not too distant past, however, when schools were seen to be successful. In these times, schools were less instrumental and more moral in their reasoning. They were embedded in communities in such ways that schools were seen as moral agents of communities; schools cared about students and community, and vice versa (McClellan, 1985).

Nowhere was this more true than in African-American schools and communities. Although these schools were stigmatized as undesirable educational settings by the political process that surrounded school desegregation, and as a result were disproportionately closed as part of that process, it is now clear that we did not understand what those schools provided for African-American children. Nor did we understand the ethos created in those schools. The stigmatization was due, in most cases, to the consequences of political, fiscal, and social neglect and not to the meanings and hopes that those communities attached to schools.

But in a sense, the original desegregation issue of equality of educational opportunity has become a legacy where African-American schools are thought to have lacked quality because they were underfunded, understaffed, and neglected in many other ways by the political structure and society in which they were embedded. In the African-American school we will describe here, that neglect was manifested, as it was throughout the South, in many ways. Teachers were paid at rates significantly below those of their white counterparts. Students were issued secondhand and hand-me-down textbooks that had been used originally at white schools. Overcrowded classrooms in the 1930s and 1940s required splitting the school day so that half the children came to class in the morning and the other half in the afternoon. The point is not to dismiss the destruction to African-American school through such social injustice but to move the conversation, for a moment, from what was bad about them to what was good about them by examining what made one African-American school good to its patrons. For this community, desegregation changed the rule from good as defined by embeddedness in community to a definition based in constitutional requirements and local political needs. Desegregation was a power issue as much as anything, and the community we will describe lost because of the terms of power. Understanding how this school created a context of caring may teach us much about what African-American children need to be successful and, as important, may be able to teach us how to think in a different way about education for all children. We think that this will require our revaluing caring and relearning what it means to care, nurture, and sustain children.

Noddings (1984) and Gilligan (1982) have emphasized the relational, personal and situational aspects of caring. People construct caring in relationships even as they construct their definition of what it is to care. It is our argument that caring is contextual also. Any phenomena is grounded in social and cultural constructs and processes, and an understanding of the context of African-American education and caring therein should enhance our ability to revalue and relearn much about caring that may be applied to our current schools. In these communities, education was valued because of its historic link to emancipation and the struggle for equality in America.

Education was explicitly moral. You went to school to learn, but more important you went to school because it was symbolic of your commitment to your people (Rose, 1964). Religion was also closely linked with both emancipation and education, making any separation of church and state ludicrous to consider. Finally, these schools did not seem to pit learning content as being separate from having a relationship with the child. Caring about a child meant that teachers taught valued information *and* nurtured and sustained the child.

Irvine and Irvine (1983) have suggested that a search for the lessons on schools and communities might uncover several contexts that were critical in the education of African-Americans, including interpersonal contexts, institutional contexts (schools themselves), and community contexts. In their assessment of the role of these contexts in the education of African-Americans, Irvine and Irvine argue that education cannot be discussed outside of the "contextual significance of the broader socio-cultural and historic roots of blacks, as a people . . ." (1983, p. 412). Such an argument lends credibility to the need to examine the relationships that helped make schooling successful in African-American schools and the role that caring relationships played in that.

Irvine and Irvine incorporate the roles, experiences, and functions of people and institutions found in those relationships into a notion of community in the education of African-Americans in the pre-desegregation era. They argue not only the institutional and personal collectivity within African-American communities, but the importance of community for establishing norms, values, and meanings as well. They define *community* as "the sum total of institutions" and regard community as "spatially specific and geographically bounded" (1983, pp. 418–419). Irvine and Irvine further explain the relationship between their notions of community and schooling: "Understanding the black community involves understanding its basis for solidarity, its implied sense of control, its values and its collective aspirations for its young. Moreover, it involves understanding how its institutional resources and other means are arranged to meet the ends. In short, it involves the totality of what is to be understood by the term community" (1983, p. 419).

And: "There is, as it were, a collective stake in the educational process of the youth in the community. In its turn, the family, the school, and the community contribute to the overall production of educational achievements of black youth. This suggests that each of these sources supports or otherwise contributes to the education outcome" (p. 419).

Irvine (1990) has expanded this discussion of influences on the education of African-American children to encompass a broader range of institutions and effects. She includes in that range considerations of societal context, institutional context, interpersonal contexts of both teachers and students, and the expectations of both teachers and students.

Referring to the nature of the interaction of these different contexts, Irvine argues that the opportunity for success in the education of African-Americans as a marginalized group is a matter of the "cultural synchronization" of the cultures of children with the cultures of teachers and the schools in which they are being educated. Cultural synchronization occurs when "teachers and black students are in tune culturally" and "it can be expected that communication is enhanced, instruction is effective, and positive affect is maximized" (Irvine, 1990, p. xx). Irvine's idea of student achievement as being enhanced when cultures are "in sync" is especially interesting when considered in light of the definition of *culture* she draws from Ogbu (1988): "shared knowledge, customs, emotions, rituals, traditions, values and norms that are embodied in a set of behaviors designed for survival in a particular environment" (Irvine, 1990, p. 22). We will describe how one African-American community engaged many of the components cited by Ogbu in constructing the caring relationships vital to the education of their children.

Lightfoot (1980) reinforces the significance of the relationships between school, family, community, and the culture constructed therein when she claims that, "The family teaches what matters most, and the learnings are deeply ingrained in personal and cultural history" (p. 8). She further warns that disruption of that syncrony, such as that which we think occurred during desegregation in the school and community which we will describe, eroded the ability of African-American families to influence the education of African-American children. Lightfoot argues that to examine the education of African-American children solely from the confines of the schoolhouse is limited in that it reveals only part of the story about the education of children and maybe not even the most significant part. Examinations of the education of African-American children need to include the roles played by several institutions, including the school, the family, and other "social and institutional settings" (p. 7).

Both Irvine and Lightfoot are clear that community is central to education. Yet it is less clear what and how the community provided for African-American students on a day-to-day basis. We believe that Noddings (1992) helps us understand what community provides. The community not only cares about its children by ensuring that they learn some content, it also cares by instilling in children that they are part of something much larger than just themselves. Noddings sees this as one definition of caring in education. Caring provides for a sense of continuity of which the cared-for is a part. African-American schools and communities seemed to understand well how to provide for the continuities Noddings sees as essential—continuities of purpose, place, people, and curriculum. We think that, by examining closely how such schools constructed caring and continuity, we may better understand what our schools need today to be regarded as valuable by our citizenry. We will look at how the continuities that Noddings identified were constructed in one African-American elementary school, from about the turn of the century until the early 1970s when it was closed as part of a district desegregation plan. We will not discuss continuity of curriculum since we were unable to uncover records about curricula and our interviewees did not remember much about it.

RECONSTRUCTING A COMMUNITY'S SENSE OF ITSELF

In the fall of 1987, we were given the opportunity to examine the continuities of which Noddings speaks by constructing the history of Rougemont, an historically African-American elementary school closed during the desegregation era. Originally we were invited into a neighboring, historically white elementary school we called Liberty Hill. The principal, who was new to the school that fall, asked us to help him build a sense of "unity" among his faculty. Based on his concern with the amount of tension that existed within the faculty, both among themselves and between the school and its communities, we suggested that the faculty and the researchers produce a "history" of the school as a cohesion building project. In the process of researching the history of this school, we found that, to capture a more complete understanding of the story at Liberty Hill, we had to take into consideration the history of Rougemont. Rougemont, which had been closed in 1975, became linked to Liberty Hill when the children of the Rougemont community were redistricted into Liberty Hill School, where many of the community's elementary students attend school today. Ironically, it was only through our studies of a white school that we were able to discover the significance of Rougemont.

We spent three years, from the fall of 1987 through the summer of 1990, attempting to come to an understanding of the Rougemont community and education within it. Bringing to our study an oral history perspective (Thompson, 1978), we interviewed forty-one people who had in some way been associated with Rougemont School through its history. That list included current members of the community—some who have lived in Rougemont since the 1910s—who have remained even though the community has deteriorated around them in the last fifteen years. We also interviewed former community members who have moved to other parts of the city. We interviewed former students, including those who attended the school as far back as the 1920s up through those who attended the school as late as the 1960s. We talked with teachers and principals of the school, seven of whom who were still employed by the district as teachers or administrators as of 1990. Of particular note is one former teacher who taught at the school from 1926 through 1966. We talked with her not only about her own tenure at Rougemont School, but about her mother's tenure there as well—from 1898 through 1950. We located these people through personal references, through board of education records, and through the assistance of churches in the Rougemont community.

Oral history is best understood as a way for people to reclaim their past and relocate themselves in the present (Halbwachs, 1980). Unlike interviewing that seeks to document, oral histories ask people to reconstruct their culture and, in doing so, place it in the present and the future. In many ways, this chapter represents a story that this community wishes to be carried forward. Indeed, oral history is an ideal way to address the issues raised by Irvine and Irvine, Lightfoot, and Noddings as they relate to the Rougemont community and their school—what was good about their school on their terms, and reclaiming the power to say so.

Though much of the documentary evidence pertaining to the history of the school is no longer extant, we were able to find useful, and sometimes rich, information in school board minutes and documents from two school districts of which Rougemont Elementary School was a part during its history. We also had access to archival data in the public libraries and the personal and institutional collections of churches within the Rougemont community.

Treyburn is currently a city of about 120,000 people, located in the piedmont section of a southeastern state. In recent years it has become noted for a substantial number of medical facilities, giving it the nickname "the city of medicine." It is the home of two major universities in the state, one public and one private, the public one being predominately African-American. Treyburn is interesting to our study in the fact that it has a significant and powerful middle and upper middle class African-American population, with two of the largest African-American owned businesses in the country centered in the city. Rougemont, though, was not part of that community and is socially and geographically isolated from it. The Treyburn City School district has one of the more successful educational histories in the state, but in the last twenty years has become more noted for ranking last in SAT scores and first in the dropout rate in the state.

CONTINUITY OF PLACE

The origins of the Rougemont community are based in the relocation of Randolph College to the city of Treyburn in the late 1800s. The small, private liberal arts college had been located in another town about 100 miles to the west of Treyburn, and moved to Treyburn under the wishes of one of its benefactors, a wealthy member of the tobacco industry of the state. Charles Walters, a janitor with Randolph College, relocated as well and built his first home in a wood adjacent to the new home of the college. His home was the first in what would become Rougemont, and the path he wore to the college would become Rougemont's first street.

Rougemont eventually became a thriving community of lower middle and lower class citizens as Treyburn grew around the tobacco industry. Most of the citizens of the community either worked as skilled labor in Treyburn factories, in service jobs with Randolph College, or in the homes of adjacent white neighborhoods. As the city grew around it, Rougemont became geographically bounded by the college on one side and the development of white neighborhoods on the other three. Rougemont was also isolated from what would eventually become a thriving middle class African-American community on the opposite side of Treyburn and isolated as well from the African-American political structure, and politics in general, of the city. Rougemont developed its own businesses, its own shops and stores, its own churches, and eventually its own school. To meet the demands of the fledgling community, the citizens also constructed a political organization unique to Rougemont needs, and elected a citizen of the community as the "Bronze Mayor," the symbolic political leader of the area. The Bronze Mayor and the "Rougemont Council" organized the community around projects such as the creation of a community park, voter registration drives in the 1960s, and the attainment and support of Rougemont School.

CONTINUITY OF PURPOSE

For most of its history, Rougemont was a place where people were able to construct and maintain a continuity of purpose. Due in part to its insularity and its ability to focus on community ventures such as the education of its children through Rougemont School, the community developed an atmosphere residents described as "close-knit." They described the closeness and the relationships of support in Rougemont as "one big family." Rougemont was a community where everyone knew everyone, and where everyone helped everyone. One resident commented that: "I used to joke, especially when I started driving . . . I would have like to have two hands just to wave as I went by and have my third hand on the wheel. But walking or riding or whatever, you knew everybody."

The closeness and family atmosphere that existed in Rougemont was instilled in children early and in some cases took on more than a symbolic role. *Family* meant not just emotional and psychological concern for each other and each other's children, it also signified community license in the disciplining of children. Such a network meant that children would many times suffer from punitive "double jeopardy," or as a person who was reared in the community described it: "It would not bother your parents at the time if someone took you in their house and gave you a spanking if they saw you doing something wrong. And when you got home you got another one. There was that kind of closeness."

"Ma Franklin" represented the most notable presence of the community's concern with the shared rearing—and disciplining—of children. She was described by a woman who was reared in Rougemont as "everybody's mom" and was a cherished symbol of the close-knit of the Rougemont community. One person remembered from her childhood that: "There was a lady there all the kids called Ma Franklin. She's still living, she's about ninety years old now. We still call her Ma Franklin." She continued: "If she caught you doing something wrong or fighting she might spank you and then take you home."

Teachers at Rougemont School were allowed to make full use of the family atmosphere of the community, and the idea that disciplining children was a shared responsibility. As a former principal of the school stated: "Folks helped each other. Relatives lived a couple of blocks away, so there was extended family in the area. There was a grandmother or uncle nearby. I was just as free to talk to them as to the parents. Whatever you said would get back to the parents verbatim, and in some instances the relatives would just handle it."

Part of the strength of this network was the awareness among the children that school and community were in a close partnership in the educational process. What was news in school was almost simultaneously news at home, and, as a student remembered: "If your were disobedient, oh yeah, the call was made that very day and you didn't want your parents to know that you had misbehaved because the rule was if you got it at school, you got it again when you got home."

Rougemont as a community represented more than just the shared tasks of disciplining children, looking in on elderly neighbors, and mutual concern for each other. Rougemont children provided a collective focus for the community through Rougemont School. The attention and affection went both ways, and care that the parents and community felt for the school was reciprocated. A former teacher commented that, "It was a community school and everybody seemed like they loved it." Another former teacher described the relationship between the school and community this way: "It was a wonderful community that people stick together, that cared about each other, that loved each other. It was just great. They were fully involved in the school. Whatever went on they were there."

Rougemont parents viewed their involvement with the school on a daily basis as integral to the students' education, as did the teachers. One teacher described this relationship as "special," and continued:

They would come to the school. You didn't particularly have to go to them. They would come to you to want to help to do. For parents that is good, you know. They'd want to know how they could help. What can they do? If you had a problem at school, or maybe if you needed something and you would say, "Oh I need such and such a thing" they would try to get it for you. If there was a problem with a child they would do that. If we would say, OK, we're having some particular thing at school, whether it included the total school, whatever was needed they would get it. Would help to try anyway.

A former principal commented from his vantage point on the support the parents gave the school: "The parents liked the school. The community enjoyed their school. The community would come in to visit and to eat with the kids. It wasn't like pulling eye teeth to get people in."

As much as parents and the community were welcome in the school, teachers were equally welcome to visit in the homes. Teachers knew that part of their support system was access to their children's homes and families. One teacher commented: "And I guess the parents, as I said, was right there whenever there was a problem. I had a little thing where I would walk home. At 2:30 if I had a problem with a kid that day then they knew, 'I'll walk home with you today.' And I guess this was one thing that kept the children from having so many problems."

With parents at the fingertips of teachers and the school, problems could be solved quickly. Parents could walk to school with their children, and they had ample opportunity to converse with teachers: "Primarily if [teachers] would visit in the afternoon after school it was because of a problem that was going on and they would try to get with the parents before it got out of hand, which again I think is really important. And I think that personal touch really showed the concern, the interest."

The closeness of community in terms of people, place, and purpose was evident in community rituals such as the Spring Carnival held for the students at the end of each school year. A symbol of the strong relationship between community and school, the parents planned the carnival and held it in Rougemont Park across the street from the school. The parents organized the carnival in part as a fund raiser for the school and set up games and activities for the children to play and be entertained. The local businesses in the community provided materials and supplies for the carnival, and profits were given to the school. For one former student, the carnival was "the biggest event at our school." She recalled the carnival in this way: "You might pull up a baby doll on a fishing pole, or some spectacular gift, not a little spider or things like we do now. But the parents in the neighborhood went way out, because that was the main event of the year at our school. Like people have baby dolls and stuff. They clean it up at home and make new clothes for it. And if you were lucky you'd pull up a baby doll or a yo-yo, which was big thing then, or a bat and ball, you know, little things. And you might pull up a booby prize, but you know, you're lucky to pull a good prize."

A former teacher, remembering the support of the parents, and the willingness of the community to support Rougemont School, described the spring celebration this way:

> We had, I remember the parents there. They always planned the social gathering in the spring over at the park. That was beauti-

ful. It reminded you of a family type of situation. This was in the spring. This is where the parents would, like in the olden days, I guess. I'm from the country where people would pack picnic lunches, go to church and spread. Well, they would do these things in the park for the kids. They would grill food and things of that sort. That was a very good relationship. It was other things. You could almost feel, how you know people care. You could just feel the warmth.

CONTINUITY OF PEOPLE

Though education in Rougemont was a multi-institutional concern carried out by parents, community business, the churches, and others, ultimately the greatest share of the burden and responsibility fell on the school's teachers. The parents and the community placed high expectations, as well as their collective hopes for their children, on the faculty of their school. The Rougemont community defined the teachers' educational roles broadly, expecting the teachers to be present "every time there was something at the school." A reflection of the strength and importance of churches in the community, teachers were also expected to periodically attend services with the Rougemont families. The services, though, served as an opportunity for the community to accord its respect, treating teachers with homage usually reserved for the ministers. According to one parent and former student in the community: "You have to remember, too, that for many years . . . and this was certainly true when I was a child . . . for many black people, for most black people, the teacher was *the* person in the community. That was because primarily [teaching] was the profession that most blacks went in if they wanted to get ahead and so forth. So, when the teachers came to church then everybody took a back seat and they were always allowed to speak. . . . It was a really a big thing when they would come [to church]." And another former student recalled, "There was prestige. My parents thought preachers were good, but teachers were great!"

Rougemont teachers accepted the expectations of parents and community as their purpose and passed those on to the students whom they taught. Students in turn, if not always fulfilling, at least understood the expectations that had been constructed for them. As one former student said: "You knew when you went to school that morning that you will be doing whatever you were told to do and you were going to stay there until you finished it. That was another thing . . . you didn't finish your work, you didn't go home when the other kids went home." Students heard consistently from their teachers that they were expected to learn, to do well, to excel, and to compete with anyone. As another student said, "They [teachers] didn't take excuses lightly."

Teachers expected more than just a mastery of subject matter that was delivered in Rougemont School. Teachers expected students to learn lessons about their own lives and what they should expect from themselves. A former principal explained: "The teachers wanted their kids to be proud of themselves. They wanted their kids to have an understanding of their culture and history, and what they were doing . . . , what they were needing to do." To that end the Rougemont teachers not only displayed the works of their own students in the hallways and public areas of the school, they also made public reminders of the African-American story writ large, and members of the broader national community who served as role models and symbols of the heritage and hope of African-Americans.

These recollections, however, do not convey the true significance the Rougemont community attached to the teachers. The preceding are generalizations that were offered us, yet in our interviews many parents and former students—and former colleagues as well--told stories about particular teachers, teachers whose lives became emblematic of the culture of Rougemont school, and the importance of continuity of people. This continuity was manifested in the relationships teachers had with the children and adults of Rougemont. While many teachers were discussed in this light, two were of special importance in the memories about Rougemont and to the history of Rougemont school and the community: Cora T. Russell and her daughter Cleo Russell.

Much of the beginning and history of Rougemont School is centered around Cora T. Russell. She appears in the Treyburn County Board of Education records as far back as 1920, having accumulated twenty-one years of experience then, and her teaching spanned the decades into the early 1950s. Although she is remembered to have first taught at a neighboring school, for Rougemont residents the story of Rougemont School and Cora Russell are synonymous for almost half of this century.

Except for brief periods, Cora Russell was the principal and main teacher at the school. When there were enough teachers for each grade level, Mrs. Russell took over the sixth grade with the expressed purpose of ensuring that students were ready for secondary school. Cora Russell was described by former students as a tough teacher, but a "good tough," as one student put it. Her job according to a parent, was "to get them out of Rougemont School's sixth grade and send them on to high school." As one of her students recalled: "We didn't leave Rougemont School to go to high school unless we knew something. She kept you there until you were ready." She added: "Mrs. Cora Russell would keep somebody in the sixth grade until they were twenty years old before she'd let them go down to Southside [Junior High School] and not know nothing in the seventh grade and say they've come from Rougemont School."

A parent recalled: "One year a class graduated and a girl was in the class and Mrs. Winston who was at the junior high school in the seventh grade . . . , she got this girl and she said 'Goull,' you know, instead of *girl*. 'Goull, where you from?' She said she was from Rougemont. [Mrs. Winston] said, 'Did Cora Russell teach you?' And she said yes. [Mrs. Winston] said, 'I've got to talk to her. I've got to tell her she's slipping because she ain't never sent nobody from Rougemont like you.'"

Mrs. Russell was legendary in Rougemont, reputed by her students to be able to write on a blackboard as easily as others could write with paper and pencil. Children believed "She had eyes behind her head," as a former student described her. She did not have to witness a disruption to know who was responsible. According to her former students with whom we talked, she would go to the children having difficulty, sit with them, and work out the problem. As a result, students were not afraid to ask questions or to seek help.

Cleo Russell, Cora's daughter, reinforced her mother's powerful presence in Rougemont School by joining the faculty in 1926 as a first grade teacher. Cleo Russell continued teaching until 1966, giving the school some forty-six years of continuity in style and beliefs. We were fortunate in our study to not only have descriptions of her from former students and parents, we talked with Cleo Russell herself about her role as teacher at Rougemont School.

One of Cleo Russell's favorite methods of teaching, according to her and her former students, was to get down on the floor with the children first thing in the morning and ask, "What are we going to do today?" The children, who were well imbued with the routines of her classroom, recounted as adults that they would then recite the activities that would normally be part of their day—except reading. The children would leave out reading because, according to Ms. Russell, it was hard for them, and because it was Cleo Russell's priority.

Cleo Russell taught reading from charts and pictures she placed around the room. She expected first graders to complete a preprimer, a primer, and two readers. *Dick and Jane* was always the last reader, according to Ms. Russell. Although the children tended to like everything about first grade but reading, she remembered "getting the job done," and her children learned to read.

The first grade children did prefer physical education according to Ms. Russell, because, like so many children, they liked to play outdoors. She remembered, as did her students, that they liked to sing, especially to her accompaniment on the piano in her classroom. Some of the standards for her class she recalled were: "My Country 'Tis of Thee," Lullaby Baby," "Way Down Upon the Swanee River," and "Weep No More, My Lady."

Cleo Russell taught some subjects sitting on the floor with the children, and drawing was one such subject. She would say, "We're going to draw. I'm going to draw my apple, and I want yours to be prettier than mine!" In drawing and in all the subjects, Cleo Russell described her job to be to "get it out of them." She wanted the children to do the best they could, and worked hard to "get it out of them." This was a consistent purpose of Rougemont School, championed for over forty-five years by the Russells. And for almost a quarter of a century, the purpose would initially be met in the first grade and reinforced in the sixth grade by a Russell.

In many ways, Rougemont defined itself via these two teachers. Their names were used to symbolize what was good about the school. The narratives of their lives were lynchpins of all stories about Rougemont School. The people, the purpose, and the place are all intertwined and all central to the meaning of Rougemont School.

SUMMARY AND CONCLUSIONS

In the spring of 1975, Rougemont School was closed in an effort to meet the mandates of court ordered desegregation. In the decision, four schools of the district were slated as possible sites to be closed; two traditionally African-American and two traditionally white. The two white schools were left open and still operate; the two African-American schools were closed, Rougemont being one of them. In the eyes of many in the Rougemont community, their school was a "good" school, and desegregation eliminated not just their school, but their good school. In this case, *good* was defined as being embedded in the community and caring for the children and the community. But *good* in this sense was not good enough when the school in question was an African-American school. Desegregation established new rules for Rougemont about what *good* meant and established new power to define those rules. The legal remedy of desegregation defined *good* as that which permitted racial mixing and on the terms of white school boards (Foster, 1990). African-American schools were disproportionately closed. African-American teachers lost their jobs. What was also lost by the closing of the schools was continuity of people, place, and purpose. Without such continuities, discourse, relationship, and community lose their center. Rougemont lost, in their school, the key institutional base for the continuities that make community possible. The definition of *good* itself is lost.

We have shown how one school and its community constructed caring via continuities of place, purpose, and people. The closing of this school signaled disruption in those continuities and the demise of the Rougemont both educationally and as a community. It still exists as an identifiable neighborhood geographically, but the close-knit relationships are all but gone. The churches have helped keep vestiges of community, but being seven in number these divide as well as unify the people. People now report increased crime and a decreased sense of safety. This is indeed a tragic fate for the school and community we discussed. However, this case can indicate how essential caring is to schools. Caring seems to work on at least three levels. First and foremost, caring seems to nurture and sustain students. Rougemont students interpreted themselves as being developed via the school and classrooms. Second, caring builds the interconnective tissue of community by promoting and valuing relationships. The citizens of Rougemont had both identities and social networking develop via the school. Third, caring gave each person more than an identity and a set of relationships. It also gave a sense of continuity. Identity was more than just a sense of one's self, it defined one as a part of a larger cultural and historic movement.

It is clear that we cannot recreate Rougemont today. However, we can learn from African-American schools how essential caring, continuity, and community are to education. A provocative lesson for our thinking about education is that schools must be part of communities to be successful. Our efforts to consolidate schools in the name of cost efficiency and curricular programming may have also contributed to the problem because these efforts replace continuity and caring with a technical logic. Rationality replaces morality and consequently undercuts the embeddedness of schools in communities. Learning these lessons, however, can occur when researchers facilitate these communities in the reclamation of their culture and heritage. As we do this, we reconstruct the contribution of African-American education to the wider discourse about schooling. We also better understand how educational policy is an exercise of power that allows the rules defining the meaning of *good* schools and privileges the discourse of power over the voices of connection.

REFERENCES

Foster, M. (1990). "The Politics of Race: Through the Eyes of African-American Teachers." *Journal of Education* 172, no. 3: 123–141.

Gilligan, C. (1982). *In a Different Voice: Psychological Theory and Women's development*. Cambridge, MA: Harvard University Press.

Halbwachs, M. (1980). *The Collective Memory*. New York: Harper and Row.

Irvine, J. (1990). *Black Students and School Failure: Policies, Practices, and Prescriptions*. Westport, CT: Greenwood Press.

Irvine, R. W., and Irvine, J. J. (1983). "The Impact of the Desegregation Process on the Education of Black Students: Key Variables." *Journal of Negro Education* 52, no. 4: 410–422.

Lightfoot (1980). "Families as Educators: The Forgotten People of Brown." In D. Bell, ed., *Shades of Brown: New Perspectives on School Desegregation*, pp. 2–19. New York: Teachers College Press.

McClellan, B. (1985). "Public Education and Social Harmony." *Educational Theory*, 32, no. 1: 33–42.

Noddings, N. (1984). *Caring: A Feminine Approach to Ethics and Moral Education*. Berkeley: University of California Press.

———. (1992) *The Challenge to Care in Schools*. New York: Teachers College Press.

Ogbu, J. (1988). "Cultural Diversity and Human Development." In D.T. Slaughter, ed., *Black Children and Poverty: A Developmental Perspective*, pp. 11–28. San Francisco: Jossey-Bass.

Rose, W. (1964). *Rehearsal for Reconstruction*. Indianapolis: Bobbs-Merrill.

Thompson, P. (1978). *The Voice of the Past: Oral History*. Oxford: Oxford University Press.

CHAPTER 7

INTERPERSONAL CARING IN THE "GOOD" SEGREGATED
SCHOOLING OF AFRICAN-AMERICAN CHILDREN

Evidence from the Case of Caswell County Training School

EMILIE V. SIDDLE WALKER

Increasingly researchers have begun to reexamine the nature of the historically segregated schooling of African-American children (Foster, 1990,
1991; Irvine and Irvine, 1983; Jones, 1981; Sowell, 1976; Walker, 1993).
This research extends the dominant paradigm, which has focused almost
exclusively on the inequities existing in segregated schools, and begins to
consider the elements that may have been "good," or valued, by the participants in those environments. In general, the studies suggest that the retrospective recounting will restore voice to those educators who successfully
schooled African-American children in the past and perhaps provide important contextual information to assist in understanding the lack of success
many African-American children are experiencing in schools today (Foster,
1990; Walker, 1993).

Excerpted in part from Walker, E.V.S. (1996). *Their Highest Potential: A Case Study of African-American Schooling in the Segregated South*. Chapel Hill, NC: UNC Press. (Forthcoming)

129

One of the findings that has emerged consistently in this research base on good segregated schools is the importance of caring relationships within the educational environment. In the earliest comprehensive work, Jones (1981) likened the segregated Dunbar High School to "one's home away from home where students were taught, nurtured, supported, corrected, encouraged, and punished" (p. 2). Her findings confirmed the description of six "excellent historically black" high schools and two elementary schools provided by Sowell (1976). In his review, the "commitment of principal and teachers" to students and a "school atmosphere characterized by support [and] encouragement" were two of eight common themes listed which explained the excellence of his chosen schools. According to Sowell, great variety existed in the teachers and principal and their methods. The "only common dominators [were] faith in education, commitment to children, and faith in what it was possible to achieve" (p. 53).

Subsequent studies have confirmed and extended the early findings on the dominance of the caring relationship. Using ethnographic interviews with excellent African-American teachers, Foster (1990, 1991) has provided insight into the nature of the relationship between students and teachers. Quoting one teacher as he describes the type of interaction he may have had with students prior to integration, she writes: "The big difference was that I can see we were able to do more with the Black students. In other words, if I wanted to come in this morning, have my kids put their books under the desk or on top of the desk and I'd get up on top of my desk and sit down and just talk to them. 'Why are you here? Are you here just to make out another day? Or are you here because the law says you must go to school? Are you here to try to better yourself?' This kind of thing I could talk to them about" (p. 133).

The teacher laments his inability to talk to current African-American students in this way. He and other teachers in her study describe the valuing of children that was part of their segregated teaching experience and bemoan the lack of direction and high expectations, which they believe are no longer part of the day-to-day experiences of most African-American children in school. Their assertion is supported by the work of Irvine and Irvine (1984), who posit that teacher-pupil relationships changed from a two-way interaction in the segregated school (pupil ability and social class) to a three-way interaction in the integrated school (pupil ability, social class, and race). The result of the inclusion of race as a variable, they argue, is that African-American children are not exposed to the same motivation and success expectation as they were in the segregated schools, thus "the deeper psychological and sociological needs" (p. 416) previously part of their educational system are currently lacking.

Taken together, these studies provide the powerful assertion that within segregated school environments an attribute called *caring* was a dominant factor in defining the goodness of the school. This "caring" seems to have been associated with the creation of a "homelike environment" where "support and encouragement" were primary characteristics and where teachers and students interacted in a personal, familial way. In particular, teachers were committed to helping children excel and expressed confidence in their ability to succeed.

Yet, in spite of the documented certainty of the presence of caring relationships, the literature base on segregated schools lacks a comprehensive understanding of the ways in which caring manifested itself and of its influence on African-American students within the context of a particular school environment. Moreover, although more specialized, nonsegregation focused studies have demonstrated the importance of caring teachers in enhancing student achievement (e.g., Ashbury, 1984; Gilbert and Gay, 1985; Noddings, 1984, 1986; Simpson and Galbo, 1986; Wheeler, 1988), these studies as well have neglected to explore the significance of interpersonal caring in the successful schooling of African-American students. In using the term *interpersonal caring*, I refer to the direct attention an individual gives to meet the psychological, sociological, and academic needs of another individual or individuals. This type of caring may be contrasted with "institutional caring," which also seeks to attend to the psychological, sociological, and academic needs, but provides for those needs to be met directly or indirectly through explicit school policies. In general, institutional caring focuses on the good of the group.

This chapter's purpose is to address the omission of a contextual analysis of the presence of interpersonal caring in the literature by focusing on an explanation of how this type of caring functioned successfully for African-American students in one "good" segregated school. Although caring in this school environment has been identified to encompass both institutional policy and interpersonal interactions, the analysis in this chapter will center on caring only as it relates to the interpersonal component. Specifically, the chapter will (1) overview the type of daily interactions that have been identified as part of the school environment; (2) discuss the response of students to the interpersonal caring they received; and (3) explore the significance of interpersonal caring in the historical context and in implications for current school reform.

SETTING AND METHODOLOGY

The data to answer these questions will draw on a larger study that has been using historical ethnography to understand the nature of schooling in one school for African-American children identified by the community as a "good" school. The intent of this work has been to understand, from the perspective of the participants, the factors that made the school valued by the community and to understand the interactive effects within the school environment that might have made it a better school for some students than for others. Currently, this data base exceeds 100 interviews and includes a document collection that covers principals' reports, newspaper clippings, school board minutes, letters, yearbooks, miscellaneous papers, and pictures dating from the school's beginning as a high school in 1933 to its closing as a segregated school in 1969.

The focus of research has been on the Caswell County Training School, a structure described by the local newspaper in 1951 after the building of the new school as "modern in every way." Although in its earliest years it experienced poor and overcrowded conditions, with the building of the new school, it became the first educational structure in the county to be housed on three levels and to contain as part of its facility a two-level auditorium. The new structure was also equipped with a public address system, full stage lights, a cafeteria, and in later years a gymnasium. In addition, it was the only school in the county to be accredited by the Southern Association of Schools and Colleges when integration occurred.

The effort to uncover the themes that were significant about this school to those who were participants in the environment has involved three "cycles" of data collection. The first began with open-ended ethnographic interviews (Spradley, 1979) with former students, teachers, administrators, and parents. Each subsequent cycle has narrowed in focus to allow more intense data collection on the emergent themes. Methods of analysis have relied primarily on Miles and Huberman (1984) and Glasser and Strauss (1967). In the latter instance, the document base has been triangulated with interviews from participants who represent a variety of backgrounds and a range of relationships to the school. In this way, an effort is made to reduce the influence of nostalgia and ensure the emergence of an accurate representation of the nature of schooling in the environment.

INTERPERSONAL CARING IN DAILY PRACTICE

When teachers of the former Caswell County Training School talk about the students and their day-to-day interactions with them, they frequently describe how important they felt it was "not to sit high and look low on children" and of how they wanted "to make children believe that they were somebody." In general, they used interpersonal relationships to express a caring that assumed full responsibility to "push children" to learn in their classes and to make an effort to be sure that each child would become the "best that they could be."

The extent to which teachers independently held these views and the extent to which they were influenced by the very persuasive personality of their principal is unclear. What is clear is that Mr. Dillard, the well-respected leader who was instrumental in beginning the high school shortly after he first moved to the county in 1930, also espoused and frequently reinforced similar views. Remembering his comments in faculty meetings, a teacher of the 1960s recalls his adamant admonishment that they "were teaching human beings, not just a subject." And: "'If you can't care about the children, then you don't need to be here.' He always stressed that they were human and should be treated right."

This philosophy was stressed even before new teachers were hired. R. L. Fleming, the assistant principal who closed out the 1968–69 school year after Dillard's death in February of that year, recalls that, at his interview, he was asked by the principal whether or not he liked young people. After relating his experiences with them, Fleming listened to the principal provide his own insights: " What you have to remember is that your sole concern is for our boys and girls. Let them know that you care. This is the basis of good teaching—concern and caring for a child regardless of who he is. If that child knows that you love him and that you are giving him the attention, regardless of the social-economic condition he comes out, he will arise above that . . ."

The validity of this teacher and others reflections on Dillard's belief about children is verified in the "Comment on the Kid" section of the 1967 teacher's handbook distributed to the faculty. In it he reminds his readers of an English woman 300 years ago who expressed dismay over the "liberties [young people] take to themselves" and shares her belief that they probably "appear very much worse than they are." In the text Dillard utilizes the quote to convey his hope that the understanding this woman expressed toward children would not exceed the understanding his teachers would extend to children. He admonishes against the "puritanical attitude" that, he says, "has, at time, grasped our land" and he solicits teacher understanding, rather than judgment, of students.

This effort to understand and "push" students that formed the basis of the beliefs of principal and teachers manifested itself in several identifiable ways in the school. One of these can be seen in the response of many teachers to poor performance in class. Of a child who seemed disengaged and listless in his or her approach to work, Mrs. Lucille Richmond remembers: "I might take him aside and say 'what's wrong with you this morning? You don't seem too happy. Is there anything I can do?' Or, sometimes I might say, 'Why are you so evil and snappy today? We've all got to live in this classroom and we all have to get along with each other. If I can help you, let me know.'"

Of this approach, she reports that students would usually tell her what was wrong and would then be better able to function within the class. Her view is corroborated by other teachers who say students were indeed willing to explain the source of their difficulties if they were asked.

What was key in understanding and overcoming classroom difficulties, however, is the phrase *if they were asked*. Mrs. Janie Richmond explains: "Sometimes they had a bad day at home. Sometimes they may not have had breakfast. Sometimes their parents had a fight. You never know. But when I'd ask them, not harshly saying 'you'd better do such and such,' but just tell them I wanted to know why they weren't performing, they'd tell me. Sometimes they'd cry and I'd have to say, 'Don't cry. Tell me what happened.' There were other times when I'd have to pull out of them what was wrong, but when they went back into the classroom, their attitude improved."

The teachers saw this getting at the source of the problem and improving the student's attitude as an important task to keep the child receptive to learning. "If a child comes in upset," adds Mrs. Lucille Richmond, "it doesn't take anything to throw him off."

Far from being confined to elementary teachers as in the case of the preceding examples, this provision of personal attention within the classroom when student difficulties arose also permeated the high school environment. Like their elementary counterparts, high school teachers also made efforts to be sure that students did not disengage from learning course material because they were discouraged, did not understand the material, or were being lazy. Sherman Pickard, a graduate of the last preintegration class and now head of the local lodge of Masonic Brothers, remembers several of his high school teachers calling students aside when they felt someone wasn't "trying" hard enough. Referring to one of his English teachers, he remembers her summoning him to a conference by saying: "Sherman stop by before you leave." When he "stopped by", he was told: "You know we did this yesterday. Now why did you do something like this? You know you can do better. I know you can do better than that."

In essence, he was not allowed to perform poorly on assignments. They "made me work," he remembers. "Not only me," he adds, "but anybody who gave up."

Likewise, in a retrospective recounting of how she might handle a student who had performed poorly on a paper, another of the English teachers, Mrs. Chattie Boston, explained to the researcher:

> *Boston*: If your grammar wasn't good throughout, you'd have to write it over before you got a grade in my class.
> *Researcher*:Let's say I had given you a composition that wasn't too good—neither my grammar nor my paragraphing—how would you tell me what I needed to fix?
> *Boston*: Well, baby, I would just tell you the truth. . . . I would rather call you up to my desk. If I wrote it on your paper, somebody else would see it and I wouldn't want to embarrass you. . . . I would just tell you, "Vanessa, your grammar isn't too good nor your paragraphing. I think you can do better, so I'm letting you take this back and do it over."

Consistently, a component in the interpersonal interactions with students in the classroom who were having difficulty is the desire not to embarrass them. This is evidenced in their frequent calling of students outside the classroom door or talking with them outside of class. Remembers the band director, Mr. Tillman: "You can't deal with all students the same. They all have different personalities so you've just got to treat them all differently."

In addition to the individual efforts to eliminate barriers in the classroom that might inhibit learning, teachers and principal also assumed responsibility for motivating students to excel in areas in which they thought that student had potential. Alean Allen, now former president of the state teacher's association, was one such student. Remembering how she loved to talk, she explains how the teachers in high school helped her focus this trait: "My homeroom teachers, Miss Brown and Miss Price, automatically assigned me to the debating team. [They said] I had the ability to do this and that [I would] do well over there."

The record indicates that the teachers' assessments were correct since the debating team she was on won the championship for three years. Yet, the story she tells of ways in which she was encouraged and directed in the school environment is not unusual. For example, the same teacher who admonished Sherman Pickard to work harder in English was also the one who gave him the honor of being a junior marshall. When he told her he would prefer not to, she said, "Sherman, we picked you . . . are you saying that you are not going to do it?" By the end of the conversation, Sherman, as might be expected, was one of the marshalls that year.

This encouragement, in many instances, took the form of a broad-based counseling role that the teachers and principal assumed for students outside of class. Far from just being delegated to a counseling office, participants in the school remember that all faculty were available to students to discuss school-related or personal problems as was necessary. The "Evaluative Criteria" teachers filled out in 1953 in preparation for their first formal accreditation visit by the Southern Association of Colleges and Schools confirms this finding. "[Guidance] is considered as a cooperative undertaking," is the statement recorded in the manuel to answer the question: What are the best elements or characteristics of the guidance services? "Both teachers and guidance personnel attempt to assist students in the solution of their problems."

These counseling sessions sometimes went on before school, sometimes after school, and sometimes during study periods when students would seek out teachers who were having planning periods. In fact, they might occur at any time a student perceived a teacher or the principal to be available. Recalls veteran teacher Rev. Wiley: "They felt free to come to you. They would talk about more than just class. They would talk about personal problems." On the nature of those impromptu conferences, one student (Patricia Pickard) reminisces: "During our study period, we would go out of the study hall and go to some teacher's room that didn't have classes at the time. . . . They'd sit down a long time and talk to you, in general about life, how tough it was once you graduated. . . . They would always, someone would tell us, you can't get anywhere in the world, in life, unless you have a good education. And when you go out of here, you had better know some stuff. . . . He kept saying, you are going to graduate one day and you won't be able to turn the clock hands back, so you better get it right now."

Far from being an activity performed only by the teachers, the students likewise had equal access to their principal for similar conversations. Donald Coletrain adds: "You did not have to worry your teacher to see the principal because you would see him some time during the day. He took time to talk to you. You did not have to set up appointments."

Adds another student: "If he saw us in the hall, he would hold a conversation." Peggy Parker concurs: "He talked to everybody."

Sometimes these conversations involved unsolicited advice from the principal on their dating choices. "[You need to] stay away from [that] boy," one female student remembers being told. In many other cases, students were being pushed to stay in school or reminded of the importance of their being "better than just good" if they were going to "make it" in life.

When one student, now herself a high school teacher, reported that she was going to quit school, Mrs. Boston responded vehemently. "Quit school? Quit school for what?" On being told that the student had been discouraged by family members, she advised: "Honey, don't you let anybody tell you that you aren't going to be anything. That's left up to you. You can be anything you want to be. You've just got to want it bad enough."

But perhaps most striking is not just the amount of personal attention that students were given about school problems or classroom concerns. Students also report the personal encouragements they received and, in several known cases, the assistance provided by teachers and principal to help them secure funds, * that enabled them to attend college. Now a French teacher at the integrated high school, Mrs. Mary Graves remembers Mr. Dillard approaching her as she was working at her student job in the cafeteria and asking her what she planned to do the next year. She responded that she planned to work. Two days later he reappeared.

---

* Most often Dillard used personal contacts with college administrators to help get scholarships for students who could not otherwise attend school. However, there are also cases where he provided personal money for students who needed it, both to go to school and to help them stay in school. No familial or other connection explains his actions. Rather, he seems to have been committed to seeing that students who had the potential to excel had the opportunity to do so, in spite of any lack of resources.

He asked me when my study hall was and told me to tell the teacher that he wanted to see me. When I reached the office, he said, "I looked at your grades. You've got real good grades. Don't you think it would be a waste to work in the mill or keep somebody's children?"

I told him I couldn't go to college, that I didn't have any money and that my mother and father couldn't afford to send me to school.

"Would you go if you could?" he asked me. When I said yes, he told me to go talk to Mrs. Boston.

Mrs. Boston told me about scholarships. She said that Professor Dillard had a lot of faith in me, that he really wanted me to go to college. "These papers," she told me, "won't send you for four years. But, we're behind you."

Then she sent me back to Mr. Dillard. He told me if I let him down, he was "through" with me. And, he made me promise to call him if I ever got in need.

Dr. Lacheta Hall a self-described "show off and tomboy" in school who frequently got sent to the principal tells a similar story. Recounting how a homeroom teacher "convinced [her] without any pressure that [a particular school] would be a good school," she describes how the teacher provided her with assistance on the application. "She did things that teachers just don't have time for now. She took me through the financial aid application even though we had counselors."

Equally compelling is that the stories are not just of assistance provided to students for college. In addition to nourishing those academically inclined, numerous examples exist of the principal giving jobs to and helping students get jobs who were unable to go to college. Former student Bushnell describes Dillard contacting him in an area town to let him know that the local mill was preparing to hire its first black. At Dillard's suggestion, he took the job because "[he] said I could handle it."

Mildred Hughes, likewise, recalls Dillard contacting her when he found out she was not furthering her education. "Girl, you have too much potential," she remembers him saying. He then offered her a secretarial job at the school. "I won't be able to pay you much, but we are going to get you started." Today she has been employed by the county Mental Health Center for the past fifteen years.

Other students recall more simple forms of assistance, but ones that were equally significant to them. These include the principal being sure they had lunch, providing them with the means to get items they needed for school, and, in some cases, supplying items that were needed. Bobbie Taylor, now the owner of a local florist shop in the town, remembers: "Those were some rough times for me and if it was not for Dillard I would not have finished high school. I did not have the money and I felt that a lot of my classmates were better off than me. . . . I did not have the money to buy my senior supplies. He gave me a job in the cafeteria. That helped with the supplies."

Another student remembers the librarian giving her gloves for Christmas after she had to come to school on cold days without any. Elementary teacher Mrs. Benjamin, a teacher who taught at the school throughout Dillard's tenure, adds that they frequently provided clothes for children, especially during the early years. Significantly, all these forms of assistance were the result of direct relationships with the students involved.

On whatever level and whether in class, in school, or out, there appears to have been a dominant theme of commitment to interpersonal relationships that sought to understand and address the needs of students. This was one of the ways they, in the words of Mrs. Hattie Brown, "made the children believe they were somebody." Moreover, a close review of the data indicates that even with the increase in numbers of students and teachers over the years, the type of interactions students who were graduates of the earliest classes describe with teachers is the much the same as those which were present at the school's closing.

THE RESPONSE OF STUDENTS TO THE CLASSROOM AND SCHOOL ENVIRONMENT

Conversations with former students—including those who did not complete school, those who did receive their high school diploma, and those who went on to some form of higher education—confirm the individual help and personal inspiration they received from teachers and principal and verify the availability of the staff to them. Indeed, as evidenced by their unsolicited reflections during interviews, for the students the personal interactions they had with the staff are paramount in their memories of the school.

This individual attention apparently communicated several messages to students. One of these was that the principal and teachers cared very much about them as individuals. Dr. Hall, the student who previously described described herself as a "show off," remembers that she had "lots of interaction" with the principal because was often a "smart mouth." For the most part she describes the talks, rather than spankings, she got from the principal when she was sent to the office. "He would shake his head and say ëone day, you will be all right.' From this interaction," she explains, "I sensed caring. He wanted to see that [I] got more than a book education." Mrs. Erie Graves, a student two decades earlier, also associates the word *caring* in her description of the interest teachers took in individual students. Contrasting her teachers with ones now whom she says "do not care as much for the children," she remembers of her own experience. "They used to be sure that you learned. They would not let you act up in school. The teachers took an interest in every student."

This caring for them that students perceived to be at the root of their interactions with teachers and principal made them feel they could relate to the teachers, made them want to be like their teachers, and made them believe what the teachers told them about their success potential. Students, for example, recall being able to joke with the teachers, even though they respected them highly and knew they "didn't play" in the classroom. They also speak of wanting to be like their teachers and of how much they believed what teachers told them about themselves. Of the latter point, Mrs. Alice Byrd recalls the influence of Rev. Wiley: "He used to praise me and tell me I had a memory like an elephant. Anytime we had a chapel program and they had a lot to be memorized, he'd say 'get Withers to do it. She's got a memory like an elephant.'"

In response, she says, she started to believe that she was really good at memorizing long scripts. Likewise, in college she majored in history because the same teacher had convinced her "she was good at it."

More than the particular response of students to specific interactions, the general attention individuals received in the environment seems to have contributed to their feeling that they were part of a family. Haley Totten says of Dillard and the school: "He loved us and treated us like his own children. We felt like we were at home." Others, as well, use the term *fatherlike* to describe their relationship with the principal. Similarly, students describe teachers who were "just like a mother." Interestingly, they are not all referring to the same teacher when applying this characterization.

Rather, a "motherlike" approach was the basis for many student-teacher interactions.

In evoking the image of a family, the students utilize the imagery that the principal himself used to describe the school. They were a "family," he often told his staff. As in a family where parents have the liberty to praise, prod, push, and punish their children, so in their interpersonal relationships with students, the school took on took on similar responsibilities. In so doing, the lines between teacher-principal-parent often became so merged that students responded to the school with the same type of response that is usually reserved for the parent role. Says one student who talks about getting in trouble for skipping class: "Everyone respected him. You would rather have your father see you do wrong than [Mr. Dillard]. If would have the same effect on you if he saw you do wrong."

In addition, like a family, students were motivated to excel in the environment because they did not want to disappoint those who were working so hard to ensure their success. Dillard, in fact, is credited with allaying many discipline problems simply because "nobody wanted to face him" recalls former school secretary and student Mrs. Novella Graves. This is not to suggest that his punishments were harsh. In fact, depending upon the violation and the student, "punishment" may simply have been the "good talking to" that students often describe. Thus, the reluctance to go to him appears to stem more from a desire not to let him be disappointed in them than from a fear of what his discipline might be. Even in matters of classroom learning, students demonstrate equal attention to not wanting to disappoint their teachers. Remembering when part of his homework on one occasion was to learn to spell *geography*, Perlie Totten Lea recalls: "I knew I could spell it, yet forgot when I was called on. The teacher looked so disappointed that I remembered. It just came back."

Perhaps most like a functional family, the students also report that they did not feel isolated or alone in the school experience. While attention had to be divided among the host of them, students believed that, even if they were "quiet," they would not get "lost" in the school. Mention is frequently made of how well the principal knew the students, even in the last years when the student body without the elementary department numbered over 800. According to Harley Totten, Dillard knew each of his students well. "You could have your back to him," he recalls, "and Mr. Dillard could call your name." Moreover, students felt comfortable and important because he did know them. "We really loved him because he was a person that was really interested in you. And it was amazing of all the students, he could call you by name. He knew us. That made you feel very special. Very special," says Nellie Williamson.

This sense that they were everybody's "children" and that they could count on the treatment equivalent to thoughtful parents in the school environment seems to contribute to the positive response of students to their principal and teachers.

THE SIGNIFICANCE OF INTERPERSONAL
CARING IN INTERACTIONS WITH STUDENTS:
DISCUSSION AND IMPLICATIONS

When the principal and teachers note their relationships between students and teachers as being "exceptionally good" in the 1953 self-study Evaluative Criteria they completed for the Southern Association of Schools and Colleges, the evidence suggests that this evaluation on the part of the school of itself was an accurate description of one of its strengths. Further, the written documentation denoting their positive evaluation of themselves in this area also provides corroboration that indicates that the recounting given by students of the school environment cannot be reduced to nostalgic reflection. Evidently, large segments of the student population experienced the "understanding" that Dillard admonished his teachers to have and that the teachers themselves embraced.

Yet, characterizing the interpersonal interactions almost uniformly in positive terms is not to suggest that in every case students were exposed to teachers with equal commitment or to imply that every student experienced total equality in the environment vis à vis the experiences of other students. Four interviews suggest that some students perceived differences existing with regard to proximity to town, skin color, academic competence, and familial relationships with teachers. However, although the importance of this variation is not discounted, the strength of the argument to change the overall characterization of the environment is diminished as in the text of their interviews these students too describe relationships in the school like those earlier depicted. Additional data need to be collected to establish the full impact of other components of the school environment that may have influenced student perception of equality of attention.

Of the nature of interpersonal caring in this environment, several points may be made. First, the presence of interpersonal relationships in the school environment seems to have enhanced students' feelings about school. As described earlier, their dominant memories in conversations about their former schooling usually speak first to the extent to which they felt cared about, by a teacher, teachers, or the principal. Dr. Hall described this as feeling as though she was getting "more than a book education." Her perception is confirmed by her peers who speak much more adamantly about the degree to which they felt cared about than they do about the particular teaching methods used by teachers. Such an emphasis is not to imply that the students perceived teaching methods as insignificant or that they did not believe that they learned; rather, the emphasis placed suggests that an important component of a successful school environment was inclusion of the interpersonal relationship with the students as individuals.

This strong presence of the variable of interpersonal caring in the segregated school environment corroborates the theoretical frame of Irvine and Irvine (1983), which posited that the segregated school attended to the deeper psychological and sociological needs of students. It also extends the work of Jones (1981) and Sowell (1976) by offering several suggestions as to exactly how the a school atmosphere "characterized by support" (Sowell, 1976) operated. For example, little disunity existed in this environment between the beliefs of the principal and the beliefs of the teachers about the importance of making each student feel as though he or she were special. Such uniformity means that students received few conflicting messages about their value in the environment, a consistency that may be speculated to have been a powerful influence on their psychological well-being as they grew to maturity in a segregated society. Likewise, the interpersonal relationship served as a mechanism to enhance student learning. By providing attention to the needs of the whole person, rather than confining their interaction to teaching subject matter, these teachers and principal created a response mechanism that made students more willing to engage in subject matter. Thus, the psychological and tangible attention revealed in the interpersonal relationships, according to students, were strong contributors to academic and life success.

This overview of the nature of interpersonal caring also provides additional support for the teacher in Foster's research who laments the disintegration of the importance of "relationship" in the education of African-American children since integration. Her teachers infer its importance as it has been described by Godwin (1991): "Our expectation of our youngsters largely determine how they will behave. If you believe they will never let you down, hold high expectations of them, and treat them with respect, they will perform. Show them you expect them to be thugs and they will never disappoint you" (p. 130).

This case lends additional support for both points and suggests that interpersonal caring may be a powerful component in influencing success. Unfortunately, to date the historical relationship between caring and the academic, psychological, and social achievement of African-American students has been seldom considered in the educational community as important context for school reform. Instead, reform leaders have focused on curricular initiatives (Hale-Benson, 1986; Heath, 1983), institutional practices (Braddock, In press; Fine, 1988; Hilliard, 1988), and cultural discontinuities (Gilbert and Gay, 1985; Hale-Benson, 1986) as ways of addressing the current lack of success of African-American students in integrated and de facto segregated schools. Although each of these initiatives is important for exploration, these data suggest that it is also important to consider the influence of caring relationships in discussions on how to increase the success of African-American students in integrated environments, especially given the teachers and principals who historically "cared" students into learning.

Of course, no effort is being made in this study to argue that the experiences in this school represent the experiences of all African-American students in segregated schools. Nor is a focus on some of the "good" relationships in this school's environment meant to be construed as a call for resegregation or as a way to dismiss the inequities that existed in this and other segregated schools in the South. However, the data presented here do suggest that the uniform image of segregated schools as being environments without merit is one that should be called into question. To the contrary, it may be possible that the African-American teachers and principals who taught students in oppressive circumstances may yet have much to teach as they remind current educators of the importance of building self-esteem, of placing high expectations, and of being willing to provide individual attention to students. These reminders of the past from teachers who successfully engaged African-American children in learning perhaps will facilitate dialogue on how to create integrated environments where African-American children can again be made to feel like they are "somebody."

ACKNOWLEDGMENTS

The author acknowledges early research support for this project from the University of Pennsylvania. Primary support has been supplied through a

Spencer post-doctoral fellowship from the National Academy of Education and two faculty development grants provided by the University Research Committee of Emory University. The author is also grateful for the assistance provided by research assistants Trudy Blackwell and Evelyn Lavizzo.

REFERENCES

Ashbury, F. (1984). "The Empathy Treatment." *Elementary School Guidance and Counseling* 18, no. 3: 181–187.

Braddock, J. (In press). "Tracking: Implications for African-American Students." In V. Gadsden and D. Wagner, eds., *Literacy Among Black Youth*. Norwood, NJ: Ablex.

Fine, M. (1988). "De-institutionalizing Educational Inequity." In *School Success for Students at Risk*. Orlando, FL: Harcourt Brace Jovanovich.

Foster, M. (1990). "The Politics of Race: Through the Eyes of African-American Teachers." *Journal of Education* 172, no. 3: 123–141.

———. (1991). "Reclaiming Silenced Voices: Connectedness and Constraints in the Lives and Careers of Black Teachers." Paper presented at the National Academy of Education, Stanford, California.

Gilbert, S., and Gay, G. (1985). "Improving the Success in School of Poor Black Children." *Phi Delta Kappan* (October): 133–137.

Glasser, B., and Strauss, A. (1967). *The Discovery of Grounded Theory*. New York: Aldine Publishing.

Goodwin, R. K. (1991). "Roots and Wings." *Journal of Negro Education* 60, no. 2.

Hale-Benson, J. (1986). *Black Children: Their Roots, Culture, and Learning Styles*. Baltimore: Johns Hopkins University Press.

Heath, S. (1983). *Ways with Words*. Cambridge: Cambridge University Press.

Hilliard, A. (1988). "Public Support for Successful Instructional Practices for At-risk Students." In *School Success for Students at Risk*. Orlando, FL: Harcourt Brace Jovanovich.

Irvine, R., and Irvine, J. (1983). "The Impact of the Desesegregation Process on the Education of Black Students: Key Variables." *Journal of Negro Education* 52, no. 4: 410–422.

Jones, F. (1981). *A Traditional Model of Educational Excellence*. Washington, D.C.: Howard University Press.

Miles, M., and Huberman, M. (1984). *Qualitative Data Analysis: A Sourcebook of New Methods*. California: Sage Publications.

Noddings, N. (1984). *Caring: A Feminine Approach to Ethics and Moral Education*. Berkeley: University of California Press.

———. (1986). "Fidelity in Teaching, Teacher Education, and Research for Teaching." *Harvard Educational Review* 56, no. 4: 496–510.

Simpson, R., and Galbo, J. (1986). "Interaction and Learning: Theorizing on the Art of Teaching." *Interchange* 17, no. 4: 37–51.

Sowell, T. (1976). "Patterns of Black Excellence." *The Public Interest* 43: 26–58.

Spradley, J. (1979). *The Ethnographic Interview*. New York: Holt, Rinehart and Winston.

Walker, E. (1993). "Caswell County Training School, 1933–1969: Relationships Between Community and School." *Harvard Educational Review* 63, no. 2: 161–182.

Wheeler, M. S. (1988). "Individual Psychology in the College Classroom." *Individual Psychology* 44, no. 2.

Wilson, J. (1987). *The Truly Disadvantaged: The Inner City, the Underclass, and Public Policy*. Chicago: University of Chicago Press.

CHAPTER 8

CARING IN COMMUNITY

The Limitations of Compassion in Facilitating Diversity

JANE A. VAN GALEN

In one of the courses that I teach, I sometimes ask students to write an essay about personal attributes that they would bring to their teaching that would contribute to their success as teachers. When I have made such assignments, many of the students, especially the women, explain that they will really *care* about students and that this caring more than any other professional or intellectual attribute will shape their work with their students. Several years ago, however, one young woman answered this question in a different way. She wrote, "I will, of course, care for my students, but I know that this is not enough. I also care deeply for my houseplants and they perish under my care."

In this chapter, I want to look closely at the caring that is manifested in a school I have been studying for several years. The broader focus of the study that I am conducting is the exploration of the dynamics of a school organized around explicit norms of "community." A growing body of research reports higher levels of academic achievement, fewer discipline problems, stronger parental support, and higher levels of professional satisfaction among teachers in schools in which relationships within the school and between the school and its environment are shaped by shared, explicitly

147

articulated relational norms and values as opposed to being governed solely by more bureaucratic administrative structures (Bryk and Driscoll, 1988; Bryk, Lee, and Smith, 1990; Chubb, 1988; Chubb and Moe, 1989, 1990; Coleman, 1985, 1990; Coleman and Hoffer, 1987; Everhart, 1988; Fyans and Maehr, 1990; Grant, 1988; Hill, Foster, and Gendler, 1990; Lee, Dedrick, and Smith, 1991; Lesko, 1988; Lightfoot, 1983; Marrett, 1990; Metz, 1986; Newmann, 1990; Newmann, Rutter, and Smith, 1989; Peshkin, 1986; Rutter et al., 1979; Salganik and Karweit, 1982; Wehlage et al., 1989). Yet this literature, most of which is based on causal modeling of discrete variables, is much less clear about how community norms are generated and sustained or how (or even whether) these organizational patterns might be replicated in schools that are now functioning within more traditional organizational patterns (Salagnik and Karweitt, 1982; Talbert, 1988). Many questions remain as to how teachers define *caring*; how administrators, students, and teachers come to identify their relationships with one another as being part of a more encompassing "community"; and how the relational facets of teaching and learning contribute to school success. More emic work is needed to better understand schools in which the norms of "caring" shape the planning of, reflection upon, and legitimation of school practices.

The school that I have been studying, St. Tarsisius High School,[*] is a Catholic high school located in a declining neighborhood in a medium-sized city in the Midwest. The school has traditionally served white, blue-collar Catholic families, but in the last ten to fifteen years, enrollment patterns have changed as the community has experienced severe economic decline, the school's neighborhood has undergone demographic transition, and many parents have become increasingly disillusioned with the local public school system. During this period, increasing numbers of middle class and upper middle class children (many them children of upwardly mobile alumni) and lower working class and poor children have enrolled. Although differing in important ways from one another, many of the St. Tarsisius parents believe that the school will offer their children strategic advantages in the competition for college admissions and employment. The student body in the 1987–88 academic year (the year during which most data collection took place) was 20 percent African-American and slightly more than 20 percent non-Catholic. As the school underwent diversification, it remained explicitly Catholic in its values orientation. Achievement

---

[*] All proper nouns are pseudonyms.

rates, as measured by standardized tests, remained relatively high. The school's staff, students, and parents oftened attributed the social, academic, and athletic accomplishments of the school to the pervasive sense of "caring" that shapes the life of the school.

Yet all was not well within the school. The school tracked it's English classes and offered honors sections of social studies classes and advanced course work in mathematics. Even though many African-American parents explained that they chose the school to give their children academic advantages, African-Americans were seriously underrepresented in honors and other advanced academic classes. In a school in which nearly one of five students was African-American, no African-American men were enrolled in any of the honors English classes during the period of the study, and none of the honors sections included more than two African-American women. The senior honors English class included no African-American students during the 1987–88 school year. African-American enrollment in the accelerated math program was slightly higher: Two African-American men were enrolled in freshmen honors algebra, and two African-American men and one African-American woman were enrolled in the calculus course—the highest math course the school offers. Only two African-American students were to be found in the junior-level honors history class.

Social class was also a subtle but pervasive concern within the school. Working class parents wondered aloud in interviews whether school staff could help but be deferential to parents who actively supported the school financially, and students sometimes reported in interviews that they believed that teachers and coaches showed favoritism to middle class students whose parents were often active alumni of the school. And although gender issues were less frequently brought up during interviews, the life of the school is seeped in a rich tradition of boys varsity sports that relegates young women to the role of observers to many of the calendrical rituals and community events that bind the parents, graduates, and current students of St. Tarsisius together in "community."

Thus, the question that I would like to address in this chapter is whether "caring" is enough for the students at schools such as St. Tarsisius High School or whether, as my student and her withering houseplants suggested, preparing students for uncertain economic, political, and social futures might require something much more. I would like to ask whether the staff's mindfulness of the relational facets of the school masks from the teachers', students', and parents' perceptions the possibility that their warm and nurturing school is, nonetheless, still an institution that collaborates in the socialization of students to social roles differentiated by race, social class, and gender. In an unjust world, caring defined along one's own cultural assumptions would seem not to be enough.

Nel Noddings (1984) has written:

> When my caring is directed to living things, I must consider their natures, ways of life, needs, and desires. And, although I can never accomplish it entirely, I try to apprehend the reality of the other.
>
> This is the fundamental aspect of caring from the inside. When I look at and think about how I am when I care, I realize that there is invariably this displacement of interest from my own reality to the reality of the other. (p. 14)

It would seem important for the staff of St. Tarsisius High School to consider how white, middle class teachers who are part of a school with a long history of serving a homogeneous population of white, working class students might come to "apprehend the reality" of students from backgrounds very different from their own. Noddings (1984) writes that the "one-caring desires the well-being of the cared-for" (p. 24), but what Noddings does not say is that such "caring" involves making judgments about what *is* in the best interests of others. The literature offers many examples of teachers who may have presumed that they were working in the best interests of their students but who misread situationally and culturally grounded behaviors of students of color (Au, 1980; Delpit, 1988; Fordham, 1988; Heath, 1982; Moll, 1992; Taylor and Dorsey-Gaines, 1988), poor children (Anyon, 1980; Bennett, 1991; Lareau, 1987, 1989; Rist, 1971), and female students (Sadker, Sadker, and Long, 1989; Shakeshaft, 1986). It cannot be taken for granted that even the most caring teachers know what is in the best interests of students. Nor can it be presumed that teachers can merely sidestep their own culturally bound perceptions of students, especially when students do not respond to schooling in ways that teachers have come to expect. The caring that Noddings describes would appear to require a careful reading of the cultural, economic, and social lives of students to appreciate the "reality of their lives" through which schooling is interpreted. Such caring seems also to call upon teachers to assume an active role in working toward a social world in which that which *is* in the best interest of students from every background can be realized. Without incorporating an understanding of the reality of students' economic, political, and social lives apart from the school and without working also toward conditions that affirm the value of diverse "natures, ways of life, needs, and desires," it would seem that caring might easily be frustrated (Higgens, 1989; Houston, 1989; Martin, 1989; Puka, 1989).

In this chapter, I will explore the ways that *caring* is defined at St. Tarsisius High School. Then, I will consider the consequences of these forms of caring for minority students and female students.

METHODS

The study employed the qualitative, sociological research methods of participant observation, intensive interviewing, and document analysis over an eighteen-month period. These methods were chosen because the research questions required that phenomenon be understood from the perspectives of the actors involved in the school (Becker and Geer, 1970; Blumer, 1969; Goetz and LeCompte, 1984). Further, these qualitative methods allowed for consideration of the context within which daily activities of St. Tarsisius take place, a perspective that is often lacking in the quantitative analyses of schools as "communities."

In the spring of 1987, I attended orientation sessions for incoming freshmen and their parents, observed in a random sampling of classes in most academic areas, and began interviewing the four school administrators. During the 1987–88 school year, I began more systematic observations and interviews. In addition to nearly 150 hours of classroom observation, I also observed other school activities, including orientation sessions for new students and their parents, graduation, awards ceremonies, liturgies, social functions, staff meetings, parent conferences, development committee meetings, and athletic and performing arts events. For the classroom observations, I followed the daily schedules of systematically sampled students from each of the three English tracks. Field notes were recorded at the end of each observation. Brief follow-up visits and classroom observations were also made during the fall of 1988.

Focus group and individual interviews were conducted with all but two of the teachers, forty-five students, and with a sample of twenty parents stratified by race, religion, and type of elementary school attended by their children. In addition to interviewing the students whose schedules I followed for the classroom observations, I also systematically sampled students from each of the four classes to represent Catholic and non-Catholics, white and African-Americans, students who were highly visible in the school and active in extracurricular activities and students who were generally uninvolved in the school beyond their classes, and students who had attended Catholic and public elementary schools. An announcement that I was interested in interviewing parents was placed in the school newsletter early in the fall of 1987, and approximately half of the parents that I interviewed were drawn from those volunteering in response to this announcement. I requested interviews with the rest of the parents at school events, through phone calls, and through contacts in settings outside of the school. As with student interviews, parents who were selected for interviews were chosen for their representativeness of the many types of parents that are part of the St. T.'s "community." Interviews were also conducted with administrators and alumnae who, although not parents of current students, remained active in the school's athletic or development programs. Student interviews generally took place within a single class period, and all student interviews were conducted at the school. Teacher interviews were conducted in school during teachers' planning periods and after school. Parent interviews, ranging in length from forty-five minutes to two hours, took place in the parents' homes and at the school. All interviews were audiotaped and later transcribed.

Historical records of the school were read and analyzed, as were student and teacher handbooks, course descriptions, newsletters, alumni publications, student disciplinary, attendance, and academic records, and internal memos and correspondence. These data were coded and analyzed using Glaser and Strauss's (1967) "constant comparative" method of ongoing and interwoven data collection and analysis.

Additionally, a parent questionnaire ($N = 96$) designed to elicit information about communication networks and participation in school activities was also administered to a random sample of parents stratified again by race, religion, and the type of elementary school attended by their children.

RESULTS: FORMS OF CARING AT ST. TARSISIUS

At the first formal gathering of freshmen students and their families—a covered dish dinner given for students and families of the freshmen class held early in the fall—Father Vincent, the school's principal, welcomed the school's newcomers to the caring community: "We truly are a community here. We have a spirit of caring that is deeply enhanced by your presence.

We are a community of believers, united by common values. We all need to rely on one another. I am looking forward to our relying on one another."

Such talk of the "caring" spirit of St. Tarsisius High School permeated public declarations of the school's goals and values and was pervasive in interviews with students, teachers, administrators, and parents. Teaching methods, evaluation policies, and disciplinary procedures were described in public settings and in interviews by the school's staff as evidence of the school's caring for the students. For example, Father Vincent at a faculty meeting presented several changes in the school's procedures in the ways that standardized tests were administered in terms of caring: "What this will do will be to give the students *you* in the testing—and that will give them more warmth and more caring. We believe that our students will benefit from this."

Administrators explained that teachers were hired based on the administrators' perceptions of their ability to "care," as explained in an interview with Mrs. O'Hern, the school's assistant principal: "We are looking for people who are willing to form relationships. So we're very interested in that aspect of their personalities—are they willing to go above and beyond the didactics and the pedagogy of the classroom. We try to slip that [into the interviews] in a lot of ways."

And in a group interview, two teachers discussed the "caring" atmosphere of the school as others in the group nodded their assent:

R_1: There are still hard core kids, but basically, it's a loving atmosphere. I think that here you get a lot of love from kids.

R_2: And the kids get a lot of love from the faculty.

R_1: Yes, and the kids get a lot of love from the faculty. A lot of love.

Parents noted that the caring of the teachers was one of the main factors that distinguished the school from others in the area. Parents and students described the school in interviews as having a "family atmosphere" that readily welcomed newcomers and where teachers were almost always ready to go the extra mile to help students with personal or academic problems.

I found such comments intriguing, and I looked more closely at my field notes, interview transcripts, and school documents to learn more about how such caring was manifested in the day-to-day life of the school. I found parents and students describing teachers who were willing to put forth extra effort on behalf of students' well-being. I found students describing the warmth and humor with which teachers conducted their classes. And, I found parents, students, and staff describing teachers who were deeply involved with the school through their personal involvement with the students' many extracurricular activities. I will explore each of these manifestations of caring in further detail.

Personalized Help

One of the main forms of caring that students, parents, and staff noted in interviews was the teachers' willingness to work individually with students. I observed and heard of compassionate expressions of help and support offered to students from school staff. A senior who had moved out of his parents' home because of intense conflicts there recounted in an interview how one of his teachers—"who didn't even particularly like me"—had called him to make sure that he was OK when he missed several days of school. When the mother of a junior was critically injured in an automobile accident, several teachers quietly gave him the use of their cars so that he could visit the hospital during study hall and lunch hours. A senior quietly told me of the help that she had been given the year before when she had become pregnant, even though the help that she was offered went beyond official diocesan policy.

Yet when most parents and students described the caring of their teachers, they were not talking about such incidents. Few individuals beyond those involved even know of their occurrences. Instead, the individual help and support that parents and students described as evidence of caring was defined primarily as assistance with assigned academic tasks. I heard in nearly every interview how willing teachers were to help students individually with their work. As one mother explained in her interview: "It astonishes me how willing they are to put themselves out instead of saying, 'Well, I quit. You know, school's out at 3:00. Bye.' You know they always say, 'Well, we're here till *whatever*,' and that impresses me."

In their group interview, sophomore Catholic students also discussed their perceptions of teachers' willingness to go an extra mile as a key strength of the school:

I: What are things that you like about the school?
R₁: I like the teachers. They really care. It's not like they are just teaching you and "we don't care if you fail." They do help you to work up to your potential.

I: What are some ways that they show you that they care?

R_2: They help you. If you have to you can talk to them and they might stay after school to help you or help you during study hall or something.

R_3: They'll give you a chance to bring up your grade through extra credit. They'll give special attention to you if you are having problems in class. They'll stop class to answer your problems. They won't go on until your problem is answered.

Indeed, on orientation days for freshmen and new students and on the opening days in other classes, teachers frequently told students that they would gladly help them through any problems that they were having with the course. On days before tests or on days on which tests were returned, teachers again reminded students to come for help during study halls or after school. And parents of incoming students attending an orientation session in the spring before their children enrolled were told by an administrator: "I can honestly say that I don't know of a single faculty member who would refuse to help your child. I can say with absolute certainty that they will be happy to work with your child."

Nearly every student readily explained in interviews that they knew that teachers were consistently willing to stay after school to help. They told of appreciating teachers' general invitations to stop by their rooms after school and specific invitations to specific students who had done poorly on assignments or exams or who had missed school. Yet, when asked about their own experiences receiving such help, relatively few students said that they had taken advantage of such offers. Many students rode buses to school, many others were involved in afterschool activities, and most students simply asked their friends for help when they had questions about homework. Yet students did frequently hear teachers offer their assistance, and some even knew of instances in which classmates had sought afterschool help. From this, many students and parents assumed that teachers were, in fact, spending much more of their own time working with students, and the perpetuation of this myth strengthened students' and parents' beliefs that teachers cared for students.

I did observe many occasions of students receiving individual attention *within* classes. While employing almost exclusively whole class, lecture, and recitation teaching styles, most of the teachers in the school approached their teaching in a somewhat informal style—they paced the instruction to match students' understanding, and they interrupted lectures frequently to ask students if they had questions. Typically, formal class activities ended several minutes before the bell rang to allow students time to request assistance when beginning assignments.

In reviewing my field notes of classroom observations, I found many instances of teachers spending considerable class time responding to students' questions. As is typical of high school classrooms, there were many instances of students giving single word or short answers in response to teacher questions and of teachers nodding their affirmation of students' answers or merely saying "right" after a student's response to a teacher question. But I looked more closely at instances of a more elaborated form in which in-class help was given—those instances in which several sequential exchanges between the teacher and an individual student followed a student's answer to a teacher's question or a student's request for clarification. An example of such an exchange would be when Mrs. Sorenson, a math teacher, elaborated upon the question raised by a student in a freshman honors algebra class.

The class was going over homework problems that had been completed the night before. A white female student asked to see a homework problem demonstrated. Mrs. Sorenson said, "OK, fractions." The student said, "I get fractions, but . . ." Mrs. Sorenson wrote the equation on the board and then cued the girl through the problem as the girl gave one and two word answers to her questions. The girl would give an answer for the particular step of the equation, and Mrs. Sorenson would say, "What then?" or "Then what?" After approximately two minutes of this, the girl said, "Oh, there it is. I was adding." Mrs. Sorenson continued explaining how such problems should be solved, directing her comments to the girl. She continued to prompt the girl through single word responses and did not call on other students who were raising their hands for a chance to answer the questions that she was posing to the girl. The entire demonstration and elaboration took approximately three to four minutes.

Such extended exchanges with individual students were not unusual in many classes. Students witnessed many instances of teachers taking class time to demonstrate a problem in response to a student request, to correct misinformation evidenced in a student response, or to guide a confused student to a correct answer, even when there was no indication that other students in the class shared the concerns or difficulties of the student to whom teachers directed this individualized help. What students did not tell me in interviews, because they apparently were not aware of it, is that teachers were more than twice as likely to engage white male students in these extended exchanges than they were to "stop the class to answer the problems" (in the words of the sophomore student quoted previously) of female students. Additionally, I was much more likely to observe these extended exchanges in the advanced and college-prep English, math, and science classes than in the basic English classes and social studies classes where African-American students were more likely to be enrolled. In the "basic" classes, and in the nontracked social studies classes, interaction between teachers and students was much more likely to be question and short answer sessions involving little extended engagement.

Uses of Humor

Students and parents noted in interviews the warmth and humor that teachers brought to their teaching as further evidence of the teachers' caring for students. As with individual help, I often observed teachers using jokes in classes to tease students into performing in class, to reprimand students, or to draw the class's attention to something the student had accomplished outside of the class. In analysis of my field notes, I noted whether the jokes were directed to the class as a whole or whether an individual student was singled out in the teachers' joking behavior. Most of the jokes and other uses of humor in the classroom fell into the latter category—that of a teacher singling out an individual student to joke with or about.

In looking more closely at these jokes that singled out an individual student for attention, I found that some of these jokes demonstrated a teacher's interest or familiarity with the student beyond the immediate classroom situation. Other jokes singled out a student for individual attention, but the content of these jokes was classroom specific. Still other jokes engaged students in banter and conversation through which the teacher drew information out of the student about the student's life outside of school.

An example of the first type of joke would be an English teacher's response when a student asked her to clarify a point about grammar that had come up in responding to a customer's question at work. The teacher answered the student's question about grammar, but not before laughing and saying , "Yeah, I can see it in the aisles of Lyndon Avenue Discount Drug." The teacher's response revealed that she knew where the student worked and further contained an element of teasing this student about the absurdity of him discussing grammar at work.

An example of the second type of joke—the classroom-specific joke—would be that of a business teacher giving a humorous illustration of a legal principle that used the names of two students as business owners facing bankruptcy.

Mr. Browner [the teacher] said, "let's consider the Carmello pizza business." Carmello was a white male student sitting near the back who Browner had previously admonished to be sure that he was ready for the football game that night. "We'll call it Sleepy Pizza in reference to his alertness in class. And he buys his flour and other supplies from Stephanie (an African-American female) who's a multimillionaire and regularly gives money to St. T.'s so I can keep my job."

The joke singled these two students out for attention that was apparently welcomed by the students, but the jokes in no way implied that the teacher knew anything about these students beyond the immediate situation.

Teachers' joking to demonstrate interest in learning about students' lives outside of the school is illustrated by an exchange that took place in a drafting class. The teacher, Mr. Collins, and Dean, a white male student, engaged in an extended session of teasing as other students, who were working on projects at individual desks, listened in. The session had begun when Mr. Collins noticed the student's numerous keys as he came up to the teacher's desk to borrow some equipment.

Collins asked Dean if he were working in a gas station with all of those keys. Dean said, "No, they're all for my cars." Collins asked how he could afford cars. Dean said that he had three and he worked for his Dad who had his own business. Collins asked Dean what his father's business was, and Dean said something nonspecific that I could not hear. One of the other students said, "Yeah, a Chop Shop." Collins said, "Yeah, a chop shop. They'll send out channel 27 news: 'This is Steven Snyder [a local newscaster] reporting from Dean's cellar and Chop Shop.' And there will be Dean with a snarling dog behind him." Other students, working at their desks, laughed.

Collins asked Dean if he were an enginehead. Dean said that he could just keep things running and named all the things that he could fix on a car. Collins then said that his battery had run down yesterday and when he took it in to be fixed, he felt suspicious because he did not know anything about cars. He said that he may have to hire Dean next time. He could pay him with either an F or five bucks, and as a bonus, he'd let Dean wear his Dan Merino Isotoner gloves. The class snickered and Dean went back to his table.

Although other uses of humor were also indicative of general good will and warmth between students and teachers, jokes that demonstrated the teachers' interest and familiarity with a student before the entire class seemed to be a more direct and tangible sign that teachers had involved themselves with students lives at some level beyond the immediate classroom tasks, a step toward "apprehending the reality of the other."

Such joking was not evenly distributed among all the St. T.'s students. During my classroom observations, white male students were the recipients of two thirds of the jokes that communicated a teachers' familiarity with a students. "Familiar" joking with white male students covered subjects ranging from the students' cars to their overall academic record to their plans for the future. African-American males were the partners in one quarter of the familiar jokes that I observed—a disproportionately high share of the jokes for a group that constituted approximately 10 percent of the school's population. However, the content of these jokes differed markedly from that of the jokes involving white males. Fully half of the jokes directed at African-American males were about their performances in a recent athletic event—performance that, although beyond the classroom, were still school-specific behavior. While the jokes involving white males communicated to the student and to the class at large that the teacher found interest in his life beyond the classroom, the jokes directed at African-American males rarely indicated any understanding of the student beyond the boundaries of the school.

As with individual help, gender differences were pronounced in the analysis of joking patterns in the classrooms of male and female teachers. I observed only three incidents of a teacher teasing or joking with a white female in which the content of the joke implied that the teacher knew something about the student beyond the immediate classroom situation, and one of these jokes was about the student's relationship with her boyfriend, not about her attributes or accomplishments. I observed only one instance of a African-American female as the partner in a teacher's joking, and in this incident, the teacher made mention in a lesson of a gift the student had given him several months earlier.

African-American students and girls were also rarely engaged in the public, inquisitive teasing in which the teacher solicited information about students' accomplishments or interests outside of school.

Women were, however, often the subjects of teachers' classroom-specific jokes, with nearly a third of such jokes being directed at female students, but the content of these jokes differed from those directed at men. When classroom-specific jokes were made about male students, they were likely to be gender-neutral jokes. Teachers sometimes joked with men about staying awake in class, for example, or drew attention to idiosyncratic behavior of particular students. An example of this type of joking was observed in a math class.

Mrs. Billings called on a white male to answer a question and he did so. She smiled and responded, "OK, let's try it this way. You know how Jimmy is—he's always trying to do things the opposite way." She laughed and then demonstrated the problem in the way that Jimmy had proposed.

In this exchange, Mrs. Billings communicated to the class her recognition and even her appreciation of Jimmy's unusual approaches to problem solving.

The situation-specific jokes directed at women by both male and female teachers much more frequently involved a sexist stereotype. Girls were more likely to be teased about worrying about their appearance, about spending class time talking about boys, or about generalized stereotypes of women. An example of such sexist joking is found in the following field note segment, also recorded in a math class.

Mr. Sims drew a figure on the board and asked for the formula for finding the missing measures. He called on a African-American female, who went through a string of calculations and then faltered. She was stuck when she got to the point of 18.5/2. Mr. Sims said to her, "if you have $18.50, what's half of it?" The girl answered correctly. Mr. Sims smiled broadly and said, "All you have to do with a woman is mention money."

The class, including this student, smiled at Mr. Sim's joke, and the atmosphere of the class remained unmistakably relaxed and warm. Yet embedded in such warmth are patterns of gender construction (Connell et al., 1982, p. 174) that do little to channel girls toward individual competence and strength.

Sexist joking was also observed in teaching situations beyond the regular classroom. At the daylong senior retreat held late in the spring of the year, for example, the keynote speaker began his remarks with jokes that contained several sexist references. After brief introductory comments, he said,

> God did I hate school. Now I like school. My sister thinks I'm crazy, but I like to study things that are not studied in the classroom, like the mysteries of life.
>
> Mysteries like why you can take a bite of a hamburger and a drink of pop and it tastes good but when you stick the hamburger in the pop it tastes terrible. Or why do old Italian women

chew constantly? My grandmother was always chewing, and I asked her what she had in there and she never had anything. And why are waitresses so dumb? They say, "can I get you anything?" No kidding. I just came in to sit down. I say, "I'll have black coffee" and they'll ask if I want cream.

And another mystery that I can't understand is why high school girls have to bend something to say hello. Boys just come up to you and say [in a deep voice as he is squaring his shoulders] "hi." Girls do this [he scrunched over, waved only his fingers and said in a cutesy, high voice, "hi!"]

The gathered seniors, and especially the boys, laughed loudly at these remarks and at the mocking imitation of girls.

Earlier in the year, at the sophomore retreat, the keynote speaker told a joke that students also apparently found hilarious in which the punch line implied that a frightful punishment involved being sentenced to walking around heaven with an old, ugly woman instead of Vanna White. Later in the day of this same retreat, the students laughed uproariously at a student skit (intended to call attention to the stereotypes boys and girls hold of one another) in which girls, dressed as boys, talked about "getting a piece off the babes at a party that night." Numerous boys in the audience, stood and gave one another high-fives at these remarks, and their behavior was not challenged by teachers or other students.

Warmth and humor pervade the days at St. Tarsisius High School, and this contributes to the students' sense of being cared for in the school. Yet through the warmth and humor employed in the school, male and female students and white and African-American students—all of whom told me about the "caring" atmosphere of the school—were learning different relational norms.

Being Involved

A final way that students perceived that teachers demonstrated their caring for their students was their extensive involvement in the school's offering of extracurricular activities. In interviews, teachers explained that their school days extended well beyond the classroom time, and parents recounted meeting and talking with many teachers at athletic events and other public activities. In classes, teachers often mentioned a student's performance at an athletic event in informal conversation. One mother explained in an interview: "There are usually teachers at all the activities, showing their support for the kids, and the kids just love it when the teachers make a comment to them about their activities or their games."

While teachers were frequently reminded at staff meetings or in memos of upcoming events, the administrators did not require teachers' presence at the myriad of meetings, games, plays, or class dinners that occurred monthly. Specific teachers such as class advisors might have been reminded that "their presence would be most welcome" at a particular event, but the extensive involvement was largely voluntary. In a group interview, the heads of other teachers nodded in agreement as one teacher, who had previously worked in a public school where "no one ever appreciated anything," proudly explained the extent of her commitment to her work with her students: "You can't do it all. You could be here twenty-four hours a day. I've already been up here two nights this week. Monday was a speaker, last night was the class dinner, Friday will be the game, and then there's the freshmen football game and I have so many freshmen. I just can't go. My mother said 'We never see you anymore.' Of course they don't see me any more. I have children of my own. Luckily, one of them is here, but the other one has his own life. I have a husband and God forbid that he ever ask me to accompany him in his life because he comes to this game, he comes to the plays, he helps out with the plays, he's understanding. He'll make dinner so I can sew costumes. Our lives now revolve around this place."

The intensity of the caring demonstrated by the staff's willingness to support students in their extracurricular endeavors was unquestionable, but as with individual help and friendly joking in the classroom, gender differences were again apparent in the caring demonstrated by attendance at students' activities. Although many teachers attended the boys' varsity football and basketball games, it was much more rare to see more than a handful of teachers at girls' athletic events or at the less-recognized boys sports. Elaborate schoolwide rallies were held on the afternoons of football games, but women athletes were recognized only at an end-of-the season multisport rally that generated little enthusiasm from the student body. While I frequently heard teachers laughing and talking with men athletes about their athletic endeavors, I did not observe a single instance of the women athletes in the classes I observed being recognized by a teacher. Although individual performances of men athletes were often highlighted on morning announcements on the day after a game, even when a team had lost a contest, the scores of women's games were frequently not even mentioned.

As with the other forms of caring that I have discussed, the extensive involvement of teachers in extracurricular activities is primarily a gesture of recognition and support for male students.

THE COSTS OF INDIVIDUALISTIC CARING

Students at St. Tarsisius High School are learning that they are cared for while also learning themselves how to care for others. Many female and minority students of St. T.'s are learning their roles as observers and supporters of caring directed at others, while white male students are learning of their entitlement to the care of their teachers and peers. Care is directed toward nurturing academic success and, in the case of obvious personal crises such as automobile accidents or pregnancies, toward broader aspects of the students' personal lives. But from the organizational norms of the school and from the examples of their teachers, students learn that the more quiet, collective crises grounded in the social, economic, political, and gendered dimensions of their lives lie beyond the boundaries of the school's definitions of caring, because at St. T.'s (and most likely, at other schools organized around a distinctive "ethos"), organizational norms define caring as relational work negotiated between individual teachers and individual students. As with my former student and her houseplants, there may be costs for extending unexamined forms of caring.

The teachers at St. Tarsisius, for example, may want to question why they and their students do not wonder whether they need to learn more about the "realities of the others" so that they would be able to care more completely for students who are from backgrounds different from their own. Beyond the easy personal familiarity that teachers demonstrate with white male students, there is also much to be learned about what it is like to negotiate society as members of groups on the margins. I observed, for example, discussions of racism in religion and social studies classes, but these discussions were usually centered around abstract situations in different times and places. I heard no public discussion of racial issues within the school or the community in any class or at any other school function that I attended. Students insisted that there was little sexism in the school, while white students and many African-American students that I interviewed were adamant that there was little racism. Students admitted that white students sometimes told racist jokes, but that African-American students "just laughed along." White students explained that African-American and white kids got along well together, even though individuals from the two groups very rarely socialized outside of school. White students did not perceive the subtle differences in interaction between African-American students and the almost exclusively white teaching staff, and they did not comment upon the overrepresentation of African-American students in the lower level courses. African-American students explained that they and their friends did less well academically in the school because they just did not work hard enough.

Thus, the unseen and unintended consequences of caring defined individualistically were that, for many students at St. T.'s, interpretations of their lived experiences within and outside of the school remained unfocused and questions about school practices remained unarticulated. For example, although most African-American students said that they did believe that they were treated fairly, they also sometimes wondered aloud if they were being overly sensitive when they did perceive what might be signs of subtle racism. One such instance occurred after cheerleading tryouts in the spring of the year when one African-American female student discussed in an interview what I had overheard many other students discussing in the halls and cafeteria: "You know, I've yet to see our cheerleading team with more than one black person on it. And it just seems like—like one graduated, she graduates this year, and they had tryouts, and another black cheerleader made the squad. And you know, you just sit there, and look at that, and it looks really odd. You really can't say that—and like I said, I didn't even try out for cheerleading, but I don't know."

It is certainly not unusual for minority students to experience such confusion in predominantly white schools, but in a school in which "caring" is an explicitly held value, questions might be raised about why this young woman, one of the most articulate and talented individuals in the school could not "Just say that this looks really odd" to the teachers and peers that she believes care for her.

As a consequence of the individualistially defined caring at St. T.'s, African-American students may readily request assistance with a homework assignment, but they are much more hesitant to request help in interpreting behaviors that appear to be racist. Young men learn to claim for themselves the care and nurturing of others, but they are learning little about how they might care for their classmates. In the pleasantness of days at St. T.'s, young women do not learn to recognize the subtle but pervasive denigration that they experience within the warmth, and they do not learn to raise questions about their role as audience to the caring extended to the males. These are not the messages that the staff would consciously chose to convey to their students.

IMPLICATIONS FOR INQUIRY AND FOR CHANGE

Although the study sheds light on the dynamics of one particular school, I would like to suggest that an exploration of the caring of well-intentioned teachers, as I have begun to do in this study, may suggest a small area of common ground upon which researchers who amply demonstrate the compelling need for school reform, and teachers, who have too often been charged with implementing the reforms envisioned by others, might meet.

More and more frequently, researchers, and especially critical scholars, acknowledge the necessity of working in collaboration with teachers if schools are to be transformed into more just places. Yet the discourse of critical scholars over school reform is generally limited to curricular, structural, and attendant political issues. Many of these scholars have yet to note, as Janet Miller (1990) has noted, that the facilitation of "empowerment" and "emancipation" are generally not the conceptualizations that teachers use to describe the purposes of their work. Instead, as Miller, observes, and as the teachers of St. Tarsisius demonstrate in an exemplary way, teachers speak of caring for kids and of wanting to help them to grow and learn.

I believe that taking more seriously the "caring" that teachers bring to their work offers a potentially rich avenue of inquiry into the workings of schools. As teachers and researchers work together to create more democratic forms of schooling, both can work to broaden their understanding of the nature of the obstacles that stand in the way of students' "growing and learning." The political, curricular and structural changes that must be made if schools are to serve all children well might come to be understood by teachers and researchers as necessary and logical extension of teachers' relational work with students. Framing politically grounded reforms within the understanding that reform will inevitably be implemented in the contexts of relationships that teachers build with their students suggests many questions for teachers and scholars to consider together.

There are many such issues for the staff of St. Tarsisius to consider. More so than in many other high schools, teachers at St. T.'s demonstrate a personal interest in their students' academic progress, their performance on the playing fields and stages of the school, and their everyday lives outside of the school. Yet genuinely caring teachers might also want to raise questions about the passive learning required by the academic tasks they so willingly help their students with, about the tracking policies that separate high and low achieving students from any extended contact with one another, and about an offering of extracurricular activities that designates female students as supportive observers rather than as full participants.

At St. Tarsisius, students *are* cared for as they proceed through the tasks and structures of the school day. The days at St. T.'s are pleasant, but the staff at St. Tarsisius—and other teachers striving to create communities within their schools and classrooms—may want to ask themselves whether they can be willing to settle for a warmth and pleasantness when such "caring" renders invisible the inequitable treatment of female and minority students and excludes from discussion the unpleasantness that permeates the realities of many students' lives. These are fundamental questions for teachers and researchers to consider together.

REFERENCES

Anyon, J. (1980). "Social Class and the Hidden Curriculum of Work." *Journal of Education* 162: 67–92.

Au, K. (1980). "Participant Structures in a Reading Lesson with Hawaiian Children." *Anthropology and Education Quarterly* 11: 91–115.

Becker, H., and Geer, B. (1970). "Participant Observation and Interviewing: A Comparison." In W. Filstead, ed., *Qualitative Methodology*. Chicago: Markham Publishing.

Bennett, K. (1991). "Doing School in an Urban Appalachian First Grade." In C. Sleeter, ed., *Empowerment Through Multicultural Education*. Albany: SUNY Press.

Blumer, H. (1969). *Symbolic Interactionism: Perspective and Method*. Englewood Cliffs, NJ: Prentice-Hall.

Bryk, A., and Driscoll, M. E. (1988). *The High School as Community: Contextual Influences, and Consequences for Students and Teachers*. Madison, WI: National Center on Effective Secondary Schools.

Bryk, A., Lee, V., and Smith, J. (1990). "High School Organization and Its Effects on Teachers and Students: An Interpretive Summary of the Research." In W. H. Clune and J. F. Witte, eds., *Choice and Control in*

American Education: The Theory of Choice and Control in American Education, Vol. 1. London: Falmer Press.

Chubb, J. (1988). "Why the Current Wave of School Reform Will Fail." *Public Interest* 90: 28–49.

———— and Moe, T. (1989). "Effective Schools and Equal Opportunity." In N. Devins, ed., *Public Values, Private Schools*. London: Falmer Press.

———— and Moe, T. (1990). *Politics, Markets, and American Schools*. Washington, DC: Brookings Institute.

Coleman, J. (1985). "Schools, Families, and Children. The 1985 Ryerson Lecture." University of Chicago.

————. (1990). "Choice, Community, and Future Schools." In W. H. Clune and J. F. Witte, eds., *Choice and Control in American Education: The Theory of Choice and Control in Education*, Vol. 1. London: Falmer Press.

———— and Hoffer, T. (1987). *Public and Private High Schools: The Impact of Communities*. New York: Basic Books.

Connell, R.W., Ashenden, D.J., Kessler, S., and Dowsett, G.W. (1982). *Making the Difference: Schools, Families, and Social Division*. Sydney: George Allen and Unwin.

Delpit, L. (1988). "The Silenced Dialogue: Power and Pedagogy in Educating Other People's Children." *Harvard Educational Review* 58: 290–298.

Everhart, R. B. (1988). *Practical Ideology and Symbolic Community*. New York: Falmer Press.

Fordham, S. (1988). "Racelessness as a Factor in Black Students' School Success: Pragmatic Strategy or Phyrric Victory." *Harvard Educational Review* 58: 54–84.

Fyans, L. J., and Maehr, M. L. (1990). *"School Culture," Student Ethnicity, and Motivation*. Urbana, IL: National Center for School Leadership.

Glaser, B. S., and Strauss, A. L. (1967). *The Discovery of Grounded Theory: Strategies for Qualitative Research*. New York: Aldine Publishing.

Goetz J. P., and Le Compte, M. D. (1984). *Ethnography and Qualitative Design in Educational Research*. Orlando, FL: Academic Press.

Grant, G. (1988). *The World We Created at Hamilton High*. Cambridge, MA: Harvard University Press.

Heath, S. B. (1982). "Questioning at Home and School: A Comparative Study. In G. Spindler, ed., *Doing the Ethnography of Schooling*. Prospect Heights, IL: Waveland Press.

Higgens, A. (1989). "The Just Community Educational Program: The Development of Moral Role-Taking as the Expression of Justice and

Care. In M. Brabeck, ed., *Who Cares: Theory, Research, and Educational Implications of the Ethic of Care*. New York: Praeger Publishing.

Hill, P. T., Foster, G., and Gendler, T. (1990). *High Schools with Character*. Santa Monica, CA: Rand Corporation.

Houston, B. (1989). "Prolegomena to Future Caring. In M. Brabeck, ed., *Who Cares: Theory, Research, and Educational Implications of the Ethic of Care*. New York: Praeger Publishing.

Lareau, A. (1987). "Social Class Differences in Family-School Relationships: The Importance of Cultural Capital." *Sociology of Education* 60: 73–85.

————. (1989). *Home Advantage: Social Class and Parent Intervention in Elementary* Education. London: Falmer Press.

Lee, V. E., Dedrick, R. B., and Smith, J. B. (1991). "The Effect of the Social Organization of Schools on Teachers' Efficacy and Satisfaction." *Sociology of Education* 64: 190–208.

Lesko, N. (1988). *Symbolizing Society: Stories, Rites and Structure in a Catholic High School*. London: Falmer Press.

Lightfoot, S. L. (1983). *The Good High School: Portraits of Character and Culture*. New York: Basic Books.

Marrett, C. (1990). "School Organizations and the Quest for Community." In W. H. Clune and J. F. Witte, eds., *Choice and Control in American Education: The Theory of Choice and Control in Education*, Vol. 1. London: Falmer Press.

Martin, J. R. (1989). "Transforming Moral Education." In M. Brabeck, ed., *Who Cares: Theory, Research, and Educational Implications of the Ethic of Care*. New York: Praeger Publishing.

Metz, M. H. (1986). *Different by Design: The Context and Character of Three Magnet Schools*. New York: Routledge and Kegan Paul.

Miller, J. (1990). *Creating Spaces and Finding Voices: Teachers Collaborating for Empowerment*. Albany: State University of New York Press.

Moll, L. C. (1992). "Bilingual Classroom Studies and Community Analysis: Some Recent Trends." *Educational Researcher* 21, no. 2: 20–24.

Newmann, F. (1990). "The Prospects for Communal School Organization." In W. H. Clune and J. F. Witte, eds., *Choice and Control in American Education: The Theory of Choice and Control in Education*, Vol. 1. London: Falmer Press.

Newmann, F., Rutter, R., and Smith, M. (1989). "Organizational Factors That Affect School Sense of Efficacy, Community, and Expectations." *Sociology of Education* 62: 221–238.

Noddings, N. (1984). *Caring: A Feminine Approach to Ethics and Moral Education*. Berkley: University of California Press.

Peshkin, A. (1986). *God's Choice: The Total World of the Christian Fundamentalist School*. Chicago: University of Chicago Press.

Puka, B. (1989). "The Liberation of Caring: A Different Voice for Gilligan's 'Different Voice'." In M. Brabeck, ed., *Who Cares: Theory, Research, and Educational Implications of the Ethic of Care*. New York: Praeger Publishing.

Rist, R. (1971). "Student Social Class and Teacher Expectations: The Self-Fulfilling Prophecy in Ghetto Education." *Challenging the Myths: The Schools, the Blacks, and the Poor*. Reprint series #5. Cambridge, MA: Harvard University Press.

Rutter, M., Maughan, B., Mortimore, P., and Ouster, J. (1979). *Fifteen Thousand Hours: Secondary Schools and Their Effects on Children*. Cambridge, MA: Harvard University Press.

Sadker, M., Sadker, D., and Long, L. (1989). "Gender and Educational Equality." In J. Banks and C. Banks, eds., *Multicultural Education: Issues and Perspectives*. Boston: Allyn and Bacon.

Salganik, L. H., and Karweit, N. (1982). "Voluntarism and Governance in Education." *Sociology of Education* 55: 152–161.

Shakeshaft, C. (1986). "A Gender at Risk." *Phi Delta Kappan* (March): 499–503.

Talbert, J. (1988). "Conditions of Public and Private School Organization and Notions of Effective Schools." In T. James and H. M. Levin, eds., *Comparing Public and Private Schools*, Vol. 1. *Institutions and Organizations*. London: Falmer Press.

Taylor, D., and Dorsey-Gaines, C. (1988). *Growing up Literate: Learning from Inner City Families*. Portsmouth, NH: Heinemann.

Wehlage, G. G., Rutter, R., Smith, G., Lesko, N., and Fernandez, R. (1989). *Reducing the Risk: Schools as Communities of Support*. London: Falmer Press.

CHAPTER 9

CARING IN ONE URBAN HIGH SCHOOL

Thoughts on the Interplay Among Race, Class, and Gender

LYNN G. BECK AND REBECCA L. NEWMAN

THE CHALLENGE OF RESEARCH ON CARING

Since the early 1980s, caring in educational settings has become a phenomenon that is attracting the interest of a small, but growing, number of researchers (see, e.g., Beck, 1992, 1994a; Brabeck, 1989; Dempsey and Noblit, 1993; Gilligan, 1982; Mercado, 1993; Noblit, 1993; Noddings, 1984, 1988, 1992; Van Galen, 1993; Walker, 1993). Virtually to a person, these authors introduce their work with a comment about the challenge of defining *caring* or labeling an act or an attitude as such. This challenge grows, in part, from the fact that caring is usually understood to be multi-faceted, involving motivation and action (Beck, 1994a; Kirkpatrick, 1986; Macmurray, 1961; Shogan, 1988), giving and receiving (Noddings, 1992), and the pursuit of both short-term happiness and long-range well-being of oneself and others (Noddings, 1984). It also derives from a growing awareness (see, e.g., Higgins, 1989; Puka, 1989; Purpel, 1988; Van Galen, 1993) that care—as an affective, nurturing phenomenon—cannot exist in the absence of an unrelenting spirit of critique that challenges established ways of thinking, traditional policies and practices, and existing structures (even that which claim to be "caring"). As Starratt (1991) aptly notes, persons seeking to care must also respond to insights gained from such a critique. Such responses are likely to involve what Matthew Fox (1990) calls "justice-making" (p. 11), something that involves the affirmation of "the sacred, inalienable rights of every individual, group, and people . . . [and] a continuous battle against hate, prejudice, or defamation of any person or group" (H. A. Cohen, 1965, p. 71, quoted in Fox, 1990, p. 12; see also Purpel, 1988, for an articulate discussion of the manifestations of care when it is coupled with a strong commitment to social justice).

Other aspects of caring—as an ethical perspective, an attitude, and an action or set of actions—make defining, recognizing, and conducting research on it quite challenging. For instance, when one takes a broad look at caring, attempting to understand it within social, cultural, political, and historical contexts, one must acknowledge that, under certain conditions, a commitment to care imposes potentially contradictory demands on persons. For example, one who cares would be concerned with responding to the expressed, felt needs of others, but also with pursuing generally recognized "good" outcomes such as physical and emotional health, the ability to find meaningful work, to engage in mutual, satisfying interpersonal relationships, and to act as a contributing member of society (Beck, 1994a; Gilligan, 1982; Noddings, 1984). Responsible "carers," over time, are almost certain to find themselves challenged by situations in which an individual's perceptions of her or his needs and the caregiver's understanding of conditions necessary for long-term health and happiness are at odds. They must seek to reconcile efforts to promote the latter, to—at the least—acknowledge the former, and to interact with the recipient of care so that she or he feels respect and support even in the face of disappointment or frustration. Researchers seeking to understand this phenomenon must, therefore, be sensitive to the nuances of care. They must consider external circumstances and the intent, cognition, emotions, and perceptions of all involved parties. Although not compromising the integrity of caring by assuming that words or labels that allude to this concept are actually linked to genuine care, they must, nevertheless, be open to the possibility that caring takes many forms and has many faces.

THIS INVESTIGATION

Site and Sample

In the investigation reported here, we sought to uncover and discover some of the forms and faces of caring in a large, urban high school in Los Angeles. We chose this site for our investigation quite deliberately. Previous research (Beck, 1994b) exposed us to Wilson High School,* an institution located in the heart of the Watts neighborhood within south central Los Angeles. At Wilson we found a school serving a neighborhood and student body whose racial composition is changing rapidly and dramatically. Once predominantly African-American, both the Watts community and its high school are now inhabited by a large population of Latinos. We also found a school serving students from four housing projects notorious for gang activity, drug use and sales, and related violence. The poverty of Wilson's students can be seen in the fact that the majority of its students qualify for Chapter 1 funding. (Wilson, in fact, has the largest percentage of such students among Los Angeles high schools.) At Wilson we also found a school where students, teachers, and administrators indicated that they felt safe and happy. We found a place where students—as they came to "check in" with the attendance office after being absent or regarding truancy problems—hugged the assistant principal and other staff members who were responsible for seeing that they were in class. We found students, staff, and parents wrestling with the meaning of racism and racial pride and struggling to discover and develop ways to come together in the spirit of genuine community. And we found people working together to discover ways to respect community norms regarding the roles of men and women, the behavior of gangs, and the like, while simultaneously pushing for responsible and just social and personal behavior.

Research Aims

We, therefore, chose Wilson as the site of this study because we expected to find there manifestations of caring (or, at least, manifestations of efforts to care) under challenging conditions. We were specifically interested in the interplay between care and three aspects of life at this school. First, because of the rapidly changing demographics of the Watts neighborhood and the concomitant changes in Wilson's student body, we suspected that cultural norms were likely to be quite varied in this setting. We wanted to see how—or if—persons cared across the represented ethnic cultures. Second, because the socioeconomic circumstances of Wilson's students and parents differed, in large measure, from those of the educators working there, we anticipated that we would find persons at-

---

* We have used pseudonyms for the name of the school and all persons we describe.

tempting to care also making efforts to understand perspectives not their own. We hoped to discover how they went about understanding the views of others and communicating care and respect. Finally, because one half of Wilson's students were women—African-American and Latino women from low socioeconomic circumstances—we were particularly interested in seeing how care, given and received, affected them. We assumed that "genuine" care would support the growth, development, and self-esteem of these women and that it would increase the number and quality of their educational, social, political, and vocational opportunities (Fox, 1990; Noddings, 1984, 1992; Starratt, 1991). We also knew, though, that several scholars have noted that a commitment to caring can serve as a rationale for encouraging women to embrace stereotypically female roles (Eugene, 1989; Puka, 1989; Van Galen, 1993). Therefore, we hoped to understand caring interactions involving Wilson's African-American and Latino female students. In each of these instances, we hoped to gain insight, not only into the acts and motives of those who seemed, at any point in time, to be caregivers, but also into the perceptions and responses of persons who were the intended recipients.

Data Collection and Analysis Strategies

To probe the forms of caring at Wilson High School, we visited this campus frequently over a nine month period (March through December 1993). During these visits, we spent over thirty hours shadowing the principal,* an activity that took us all over campus and enabled us to observe administrators, counselors, teachers, and students in a variety of settings. Additionally, we visited classes, the campus health clinic, the child care center, the community care center,** and the attendance office. During these visits, we conducted formal interviews with the principal, two assistant principals, the directors of the child care and the community care centers, a counselor, and a student. We also spoke at length with current and former district officials

---

* The principal we shadowed, Mary Story, left Wilson in August 1993 to take a regional superintendency. We shadowed her in our early phases of data collection. Beginning in September, most of our time was spent in the attendance office, community service center, and child care center.

** The community care center provides integrated services to selected at-risk ninth grade students and their families and to some of Wilson's teen parents.

who had direct supervisory responsibility for Wilson and with a Los Angeles based educator who recently completed an internship at this site. We had, in addition, the opportunity to engage in numerous informal conversations with teachers, students, classified staff, and parents.

Data were recorded in field notes and analyzed inductively (Merriam, 1988). In an earlier investigation (Beck, 1994b), one of us concentrated upon identifying characteristics of Wilson High School that indicated that this, indeed seemed to be functioning as a caring community. We, therefore, in this study, concentrated upon uncovering and understanding manifestations of caring at this school. As noted in an earlier section, we were especially interested in caring among and between persons from different ethnic cultures and different socioeconomic classes and caring as it affected the African-American and Latino women who constituted approximately half of the student body. We wanted to see both the forms and apparent outcomes of caring at Wilson to understand if, and how, caring occurs in such a setting.

In the sections that follow, we present the results of this analysis. To facilitate this discussion, we have divided our report into three sections. We begin with a discussion of forms of caring among persons of different races at Wilson. Our attention then turns to caring among individuals representing different socioeconomic classes. Finally, we consider caring given to and by female students. We do this with the recognition that many of the instances we describe actually involve interracial, transclass caring for and by women. Our decision to discuss a particular incident in any given section relates less to the "purity" of the example and more to a particular dimension of caring that, in our view, it exemplifies. In each of these sections we describe observed phenomena and then analyze characteristics of interactions, programs, or policies that seemed to contribute to care giving and receiving in this urban school.

FORMS OF CARING AT WILSON HIGH SCHOOL

Caring Among and Between Persons from Different Races

During the time of our study at Wilson, racial tension was high in Los Angeles. The civil unrest following the first verdict in the trial of the Los Angeles police officers charged with beating Rodney King had settled uneasily. Occasionally, persons and groups in the city seemed to be seeking solutions to the circumstances that had contributed to the disturbances. More often, though, individuals seemed to focus on finding ways to protect themselves, their families, and friends, in case additional trouble erupted. Frequently these protective tactics involved retreating into racial enclaves in which members sought to further their own interests and opportunities and undermine those of others.

Wilson and the Watts community are both places where evidence of past and present racial tension exists. The population of both school and community has changed in recent years. Once predominantly African-American, the neighborhood is now home to a large number of Latinos, many of them first generation immigrants from Central America. Differences in language and culture, coupled with an economic recession that has forced many of the citizens of Los Angeles to compete with one another for jobs and resources, have contributed, at times, to a sense of distrust and resentment among the citizens of this community.

Students, parents, faculty, and staff at Wilson noted that distrust, resentment, and occasional overt hostility had sometimes borne witness to the fact that the transition from being a school serving a large population of black students to one whose student body was now 65 percent Latino had not been easy. They also underscored, through both their words and actions, that part of Wilson's ethos is a commitment to confront racism and provide opportunities for building constructive, productive interactions and caring friendships among and between persons from different races.

On our first visit to Wilson, we entered the administrative offices to find the principal, Mary Story, herself a Jamaican immigrant of African descent, conversing in Spanish with a parent. This parent was concerned about getting records documenting an injury her daughter had received during physical education the previous year, so that the district's insurance could cover the young woman's visits to a physical therapist. Evidently her daughter was no longer a student at Wilson, and the fact that she was therefore not listed on the school district's roster had somehow caused a snag in processing paperwork. The parent, we later discovered, had been in this country for only a short time and felt quite unnerved at having to deal with the bureaucracy of the Los Angeles school district. Several times during the conversation she looked quite confused, as tears welled up in her eyes. Story spoke with her for forty minutes, often patiently reassuring the woman that her daughter was, indeed, covered and mapping out the steps the woman needed to take to gather the necessary documents. At the end of the conversation, the principal walked with the mother into a room next door and introduced her to another Latino mother, Mrs. Guttierez, who serves as a parent-school-community liaison. Mrs. Story explained the troubled mother's situation to Mrs. Guttierez, who immediately offered to help her be sure that she had all of the needed forms.

We were impressed by the manner in which Mrs. Story worked with this mother. She never became impatient and never displayed any frustration at attempting to communicate with someone who neither spoke her language nor had any familiarity with insurance and school policy. She showed the greatest respect for this mother who was so anxious to see that her daughter received the medical care she needed and deserved. Judging by the smiles and animated conversation occurring between this mother and Mrs. Guttierez, we sensed that this woman felt welcome and that she was satisfied that her concerns had been heard. We wondered, however, if this was an isolated incident—or perhaps an interaction that reflected the commitment of one person to care across racial differences.

Subsequent visits, conversations, and observations uncovered numerous examples of caring that transcended race. For example, we were impressed with the obvious effort to acknowledge the presence of non-English speakers by persons who spoke no Spanish. Signs were always printed in both languages, and at least one administrator and several secretaries and clerks were learning and using conversational Spanish, even though doing so was not an official job requirement. In turn, we observed parents with only limited English proficiency making great efforts to communicate in English. We were also impressed with what seemed to be great evenhandedness and affection demonstrated by African-American, Latino, and Anglo teachers and administrators as they interacted with young people from both represented races.

As we observed students in the yard during nutrition and lunch breaks, we noted that they seemed, in general, to be sitting and talking with others of their race. However, in classes and meetings, in a production staged by the leadership club for incoming students, and in the pick-up basketball games during the lunch hour, we found no such segregation. And we discovered that some students, administrators, and faculty were actively working to build a sense of a multiracial community. During one of our visits, we were standing on the grounds with Principal Mary Story when a young man came up and spoke, with great animation, to her. We could not overhear his words but we did hear her exclaim "Congratulations! That's just wonderful," as she patted his shoulder. After the student left, she reported the content of their conversation to us.

We were told that, three years ago, a group of African-American and Latino students had gotten into a fight on Wilson's large, open patio.

Because it was lunchtime, many students became involved in cheering on one group or another. Several outbreaks of pushing, shoving, and name calling occurred. The faculty and administration reacted quickly to break up and calm the crowd and, under Story's direction, escorted the Latino students into the gym and the African-American students into the auditorium. She, an African-American woman, took charge of the former group, and Mr. Gomez, a Hispanic assistant principal, joined the latter group. Both administrators invited the students to talk—about their feelings, their anger, their reactions, their fears, and the like. After impassioned conversations in both rooms, the adults then sought the students' ideas on ways they, as a school community, might deal with tension and misunderstanding. The students eventually determined that both groups needed representatives who could sit together, with adults if necessary, and address these issues in a consistent and productive manner. Such representatives were elected and began meeting regularly to examine ways to resolve problems and to encourage understanding and mutual respect.

Interestingly, one of the areas of tension related to the type of music played at athletic events and dances. Both racial groups had distinct preferences and resented it when music they did not care for was played. The student representatives, discussing this issue, hatched the idea of developing a musical group composed of both African-American and Latino students, which could represent the styles of both cultures. The name, Colors United, was chosen for this group, and some of the leading musicians within the school joined. As time transpired, this musical ensemble came to represent, not only Wilson's effort to accommodate the musical tastes of its students but also a commitment to racial harmony. The young man who had spoken with Principal Story had told her about a recent performance of Colors United at another high school in an ethnically diverse, but affluent section of town. Evidently the group was well received, and the student body of the other high school had decided that they, too, wanted to sponsor a similar musical group. The student was reporting this development—with great pride—to Story.

Characteristics of Interracial Caring at Wilson

As already noted, we conducted this study during a time of great racial tension. Our first visit to Wilson actually coincided with the announcement of the verdicts of the second, civil trial of the officers involved in the Rodney

King beating. The trial of the African-American men accused of beating Anglo truck driver Reginald Denny and at least one Hispanic service station attendant also occurred during the time of our investigation. We therefore expected to find a school bristling with efforts to quell potential disturbances. Instead we found a place of great openness—a place where faculty, staff, students, and parents seemed to be engaged in a great deal of talking and listening and in developing ways they might live and grow together. As we reflected upon our impressions and analyzed and reanalyzed our data, we concluded that two practices helped to contribute to the constructive forms of caring we observed. First, at Wilson, the reality that racial and cultural differences did exist was acknowledged, and persons with a concern or an insight, cognitive or affective, about these differences were given an opportunity to be heard by others. Second, in the case of problems, those most affected by them, Wilson's students, were involved in crafting strategies for addressing disagreements and differences. We will discuss these two practices at greater length in the remainder of this section.

Acknowledging Racial Differences and Confronting Actual and Potential Tensions. Our visits to Wilson forced us to confront something that, initially, surprised us. In earlier conceptual work (Beck, 1992; 1994a), we had virtually ignored the possibility that caring and conflict could occur together and that, in fact, one who cared might encourage the surfacing of disagreements and anger. Similarly, in our field work within elementary schools functioning as caring communities, we had not encountered much in the way of overt conflict. At Wilson, we found ourselves among persons who seemed quite comfortable in confronting one another and who would encourage discussion of difficult topics, such as the impact of race on the interactions within the school. The handling of the student disturbance described in the preceding section offers a vivid example of this, but we witnessed several other examples of persons confronting problems—and, if needed, one another—if they felt they had experienced actual or potential racism or injustice.

We sat in on one meeting among Mrs. Story and three counselors in which they addressed a disagreement about the best allocation of counselors' time. Two of the African-American counselors began to refer to a colleague who had a Spanish surname. Mrs. Story graciously, but firmly, cut the conversation short by noting that she did not feel comfortable talking about Mrs. Vasquez if she were not present. The others quickly agreed and decided to be sure that Mrs. Vasquez could attend the next meeting. Race was never mentioned in this meeting, but we questioned Story afterward, and she noted that perhaps there was a tendency on the part of two of the counselors to team up against their coworker. She added, "That's unacceptable. It's perfectly okay for them to feel frustrated, but they cannot act in unfair ways."

In a similar vein, Assistant Principal Joan Gregg told one of us that she loves her job and that "students are the best part—and adults are the worst." When pressed as to what she meant, she said that, unfortunately, "racism is alive and well at Wilson," in that some teachers have low expectations for students; low expectations that were, in Gregg's view, rooted in beliefs about poverty and race. When Gregg becomes aware that this is occurring, she told us, she works with teachers to see that "Wilson's students are treated like I would want my own daughter treated." Using direct discussions, various in-service opportunities, and the like, she said, she works with these teachers to encourage change, both in their pedagogy and in their underlying assumptions of deficiencies within the school community.

Involving Persons in Developing Solutions and Strategies. The incident in which students created a musical group, Colors United, to reflect their commitment to racial reconciliation offers a nice example of the attitude of many administrators, teachers, and students who believe that Wilson is a community and that, therefore, its members must be involved in solving problems that affect them. As Colors United began performing at other schools, group members noticed that many area high schools had extensive sound equipment for use in performances, while Wilson had virtually none. A young man spoke to Story about this, asking if anything could be done. Choosing to involve him and the others in solving this problem, Story suggested he seek funding for new sound equipment from Paramount, one of the school's Business Partners. The students did so, and Paramount agreed to donate the needed equipment. The handling of a different potentially inflammatory situation offers another example of this approach.

Following two shootings within local high schools, the school board instituted a policy of making random metal detector searches of students in all of the district's high schools. Faculty and administration at Wilson did not care for this policy. They felt that it would be ineffective in actually deterring students from bringing weapons to school; they suspected that it would be enforced with greater zeal in inner city schools than in those on the Westside or in the Valley (two of the more affluent areas within the district); and they feared that it would make students feel dehumanized and might promote hostile reactions against police or others representing the traditional authority structure. As they contemplated how to handle this situation, the administrators decided to meet personally with every class in the school. During these meetings, they explained the mandated procedures and invited students' views about ways they as a community might react. Students were sympathetic to the district's and board's need to seem to be doing *something* to deter students from bringing weapons to school, but indicated that they did not think these searches would do much (if any) good. With assurances from the adults that care would be taken to see that students were treated with respect during these random checks, they agreed to go along without complaint when the checkers showed up.

Students, however, wanted to continue the discussion, to determine if there were constructive ways they could help make Wilson a safer place. Eventually, they decided to place several "suggestion" boxes throughout the school. Students were encouraged to use these anonymously to report any suspicions of weapons in school and also to express concerns about other matters. These boxes are emptied and read at least twice a day. Every report of a possible weapon was acted upon, and Wilson's administrators have been able to maintain what seems to be a safe campus—without involving the police. All other concerns receive a direct response. If a student signs her or his name, the person in charge of the area of concern schedules a meeting to talk with this student. Unsigned suggestions are listed in a regular newsletter, with information about how the concern is being addressed and the name of the person the student should contact if she or he wants to pursue the topic in greater detail.

Caring Among and Between Persons from Different Socioeconomic Classes

Wilson High School has the reputation in the Los Angeles Unified School District of serving the poorest students from the city's poorest neighborhood. Many of the parents of these young people are unemployed, and according to Mary Story, many have had little in the way of formal education. Virtually all of Wilson's teachers and administrators live outside of the Watts neighborhood,* with a number hailing from the more affluent west side of the city; obviously, all are employed and well-educated. To obtain a

---

* We did no systematic checks on the residences of faculty. However, Mrs. Story indicated that most lived outside of the Watts community. Several teachers and other staff members were introduced to us as Wilson graduates, however, leading us to assume that they had, at one time, probably lived in the area.

California teaching credential, all of the faculty members had to pursue at least one year of university training after completing four years of college. According to Story, a large number of the staff hold master's degrees. We met two persons, an assistant principal and a counselor, who earned doctorates, and one individual, Assistant Principal Joan Gregg, who is "two-thirds of the way through a doctoral program at the University of Southern California." The differences between the socioeconomic status and educational levels of faculty and administrators and those of the students and parents within this community intrigued us. We wanted to understand how, and if, caring was manifested between and among these various individuals. We were aware of scholarship that suggests that a fair number of educators working with the children of poverty "have tended to attribute educational failures to deficiencies in the children" (Persell, 1993, p. 80; see also Hill, 1971; Stein, 1971). This assumption by educators has led to patronizing attitudes and actions, discriminatory tracking policies, a lowering of standards and expectations, and a tendency to do whatever was necessary to move these children through and out of the educational system expeditiously (Oakes, 1985; Persell, 1993; Powell, Farrar, and Cohen, 1985; Sedlak et al., 1986). We wondered if such beliefs and practices were prevalent at Wilson and how they shaped the quality of caring there.

Three persons with whom we spoke—Principal Story, Assistant Principal Gregg, and Mrs. Gunn, director of the campus child care center—reported that some persons at Wilson do, in fact, "feel that the students are unteachable and cannot achieve" and that, at times, these individuals "treat students poorly." Each of the respondents voicing this perspective implied that such attitudes and actions were linked to beliefs about poverty and the inhabitants of south central Los Angeles and not to race. (The women who expressed these views were, themselves, African-American.) All three, however, reported ways that they and others were working to encourage changes in these attitudes. During our visits we learned of few instances of patronizing, negative, or "elitist" behaviors. In contrast, we observed numerous interactions that demonstrated high expectations for Wilson's students and a high level of trust, respect, and acceptance for these young people and their families.

One negative situation to which we were privy involved a visit to a classroom with Mary Story. This visit occurred during the second visit one of us paid to Wilson. Story indicated that she was going to sit in on a class taught by a teacher she knew was doing a poor job and invited us to join her. She was in the process of collecting weekly data on this individual—

something required by contract—so that she could ask that he leave her school. On the way to this class, she said that this teacher "just didn't try" and that "he seemed to have given up." When we arrived, she asked the teacher if we might sit in, and he agreed. We sat for about forty-five minutes observing fifteen children halfheartedly working on worksheets in a rather disheveled room. On the walls were a number of posters—many of them torn, and some marked up. One, which was prominent in the front of the room, showed a large mansion overlooking the ocean. Below was a garage containing a fleet of Rolls-Royces and Jaguars; an inscription read "The Best Reason for an Education." The incongruity between the picture on the poster, the neighborhood around Wilson, and the message, which might be interpreted as being smug or sarcastic, struck us. We did not have the opportunity to talk, privately, with this teacher; however, we wondered if he assumed that these students could not possibly achieve and that, therefore, effort on his part would be wasted.

Mrs. Story expressed concern that we realize that "most of the teachers here are wonderful." To allow for a "test" of this statement, she invited us to visit several other classrooms, which contrasted markedly with the one just described. Several events suggested that many of the teachers viewed the students, not as deficient or "at risk," but, rather, as remarkably resilient. These teachers seemed consciously to look for ways to convey this view to students, encouraging them to believe in themselves, their strengths and abilities, their right to be heard, and their right to receive every opportunity promised to any citizen in a democracy.

In one class, we observed a reporter from the *Los Angeles Times* talking with students about the second verdict in the Rodney King beating trial. As the class ended, several students crowded around the teacher, voicing their ideas about the needs and concerns of their community. He listened and, gesturing toward the reporter, said, "Tell her." We watched him walk with the hesitant students toward the front of the room. When we left, one young man, a resident of a nearby housing project, was talking with great animation. The reporter, in turn, was listening intently, taking careful notes. Later we commented to Mrs. Story and the teacher that we thought we had seen a moment when that young man's voice had been heard. Both smiled, and one remarked, "These kids aren't heard very much, and they have so much to say. We just have to give them a chance."

On another occasion, we had a chance to visit with Wilson's art teacher. This woman took us outside to see a large and colorful mural that students had painted across one wall. We asked about the words "Seize the

Knowledge and Use Your Imagination" that figured prominently in the mural, and she smiled and explained:

> The kids thought of that. Some of the teachers weren't wild about it. I'm not sure why. I think they just thought it didn't make much sense. It did to me though, and regardless, the students understood what they were trying to say. It was important to them. So I insisted that the wall be done *their* way. They loved doing it. I just had to keep pushing them to get them to do all of the finishing work. You know how kids are. They wanted to paint it and to move on to something else, but I believed that this had to look good. It was their statement to themselves and to others. It had to look good.

We commented, again, on the fact that it seemed to be important that the students had control over this project, and this teacher replied "That doesn't happen to these kids a lot. For some reason, people feel like they can't handle things. It's important that we change that. They'll never believe in themselves if we don't."

During our time observing in Wilson's attendance office, we saw other examples of persons caring for students in ways that suggested that adults trusted and respected students and viewed them as capable of making good and productive decisions about their education and lives. We were, for example, impressed with the relaxed and friendly interchanges in this setting. Field notes taken by one of us read: "There is a fair amount of activity. Students and adults walk back and forth into and out of the area behind the counter and various offices. I am again struck by the relaxed atmosphere—the students waiting at the counter are quiet; the interchanges between young people and adults seem cheerful and friendly. Periodically, students come behind the counter and open drawers, look for things, take things out, and go on about their business without any challenge from adults."

The degree to which the students were trusted was impressive. Our experience in other settings has revealed that some attendance offices are not so open. Often there are strict policies governing access to things "behind the counter," and in a school where one of us did an administrative internship, a glass wall separated students from counselors, clerks, assistant principals, and others.

We found that this trust was manifested in other ways, also, and that students perceived that they were respected. Sam, a student, spoke with us at length about his impressions of the adults at Wilson. A former gang member, Sam explained that Wilson was the third high school he had attended. After a somewhat rocky past, he told us, he had moved in with his aunt. He commented "I'm not hanging out with those guys [the Bloods, a well-known gang] and I'm not having any problems living in Crips' [a rival gang] territory."

When asked how he felt about the way he was treated at Wilson, Sam stated, "I am treated respectfully. There's no 'where's your pass [giving students permission to be out of class] ?'" He went on to contrast his current situation with past experiences. He said that his old schools never called home if he was absent and that he could hang around the attendance office all day with no one paying attention to him. "Here," he noted, "You know what your responsibilities are and the school knows what its responsibilities are. So if you mess up, it's your own fault. Here they trust me, so I trust them." The degree to which Sam did, in fact, trust the adults at Wilson was evident when he spoke of one particular type of experience: "When they call my house if I'm not here, they're real friendly. My auntie has an answering machine, and sometimes I'll hear a voice start to leave a message like 'Hi Sam. If you're there, we're wondering why you're not in school today . . .' If I hear that, I pick up the phone and explain why I'm not there. *And they believe me.*"

For Sam, being trusted was a powerful experience, one to which he was apparently responding. He noted that he had been behind when he came to Wilson, but that he was catching up with other juniors. When asked about how his courses were going, he said "Okay," and pointed to his backpack on the floor. With very deliberate inflection, he said "I've got *books* in there. I never used to carry *them* around."

Characteristics of Caring Between Persons from Different Classes at Wilson

In many ways, our preceding discussion has alluded to factors that seemed to shape the powerful forms of caring that occurred between educators and students who, under many circumstances, might have been viewed as unmotivated, untrustworthy, and incapable of achieving. Here, however, we note two aspects of interactions at Wilson that struck us as especially important. We first discuss the fact that the adults we saw genuinely caring for students seemed to hold agency, not deficiency, models of these youngsters. Second, we explore the ways educators interacted with students in a highly personal manner, recognizing that young people had feelings, hopes, thoughts, and dreams just as they, themselves, did, and that these needed to be acknowledged and respected.

Assuming Agency, Ability, and Motivation. With both words and actions, many teachers and administrators at Wilson revealed that they viewed their students as quite capable of succeeding and that they believed that parents and students are able to make choices about education and should be given the opportunity to do so. Sam's story, offered in the preceding section, provides one example of this attitude. Faculty and staff want him to attend school, but they trust his judgment and that of his aunt (with whom he lives) about necessary absences.

Another incident also exemplified the belief that persons, regardless of their income or educational level, could and should be allowed to make informed decisions about their lives. While we were visiting with Assistant Principal Joan Gregg, one of the clerks beckoned to her and asked her to offer assistance to an adult and a young woman. The young woman was a Wilson student and the adult, her aunt, had come with her niece to enroll the young woman in independent study. Evidently there had been some problems with attendance, and the woman indicated that she did not *intend* to start sending her niece to school. Mrs. Gregg was very patient, warm, and friendly, and she stated that the family could have what they wanted, but that she would like for them to make an informed decision. She then said that some things about independent study made it a poor option for many students and that she was sure that the family and student wanted what was best. Noting that she was not an expert on this, she asked them to "give us five minutes of your time to hear our side of it" and arranged for them to speak with Dr. Oniko, a pupil services and dropout-prevention counselor. She also added that if, after getting this information, the family still wanted independent study, the school would make the placement. If, however, the family decided that this was not the best option, she and others would work "together" with the student and her aunt to find the best solution to their problem. We found two things about this interchange especially interesting. First, Mrs. Gregg went out of her way to try to find the best solution for a person who was probably not the easiest student to work with. Second, and more to the point, she arranged to provide the young woman and her aunt with good information and then to honor whatever decision they made.

Recognizing the Personhood of Students. We suggest that the fact that educators at Wilson seemed to believe that students and their families were capable and motivated is linked to the reality that many of the adults we met appeared very cognizant that their school was inhabited by *persons*. Persons who, like themselves, had a right to be treated with dignity and care. When discussing policies affecting students, teachers and administrators frequently made remarks that alluded to their belief that students "deserved" to be treated with the same respect as adults. On one occasion, Mrs. Story was talking about a district policy prohibiting students from bringing portable tape players with headphones to school. She commented, "I just think it's ridiculous. They know that they shouldn't use them in class, but why shouldn't they be able to listen as they walk to school or during lunch? After all, we adults want our Walkmans when we jog, but we don't think we can trust kids with them."

Mrs. Gregg noted another set of policies that seemed to emanate from the recognition, on the part of Wilson's administrators, that students needed and deserved to be treated with respect and to be shielded from humiliation. She pointed out that, under all circumstances, they tried to handle fights and other disturbances within the campus community, without involving police unless it was absolutely necessary. She noted that having students arrested "in front of other students" and led out in handcuffs (standard police procedure when they are called in) did no good and that students responded much better when their dignity was preserved even if they were being reprimanded.

We also noted a tendency—on the part of many of the adults at Wilson—to accept as important those issues about which students cared, even if they themselves did not share the same perspectives or concerns. We saw careful attention being paid to the types of music played at school dances, to encouraging a student who had forgotten dance steps in a program for ninth graders, and to seeing that every young woman who wished to attend the school formal had an opportunity to choose and borrow a party dress if she did not own one. These small and not-so-small behaviors bore witness to the respect for whole persons that seemed to drive many of the actions and policies at Wilson High School.

Caring For, About, and With Women

In chapters in Mary Brabeck's edited volume, *Who Cares? Theory, Research, and Educational Implications of the Ethic of Care* (1989), Toinette Eugene and Bill Puka offer a caution to those who might uncritically view "caring" as a kind of panacea for personal and educational problems. They suggest that, under certain conditions, caring may not be a response to perceived needs of others, but rather a "coping strategy" (Puka, 1989, p. 21) developed by women, minorities, and others who have been "orphaned, abandoned, alienated, and marginalized" (Eugene, 1989, p. 60) "to handle crises of hurt, domination, and rejection" (Puka, 1989, p. 21). In offering this perspective, these authors do not suggest that genuine caring is an undesirable phenomenon. They do, however, suggest that some behaviors that seem to be nurturing and supportive may, in fact, be encouraging women and minorities to accept rather than resist unjust, inhumane conditions.

Because one half of the students at Wilson were female and all were either Latino or African-American, we were especially interested in caring as it affected these individuals, fearing that they, in a sense, ran the risk of being doubly marginalized—by virtue of both race *and* gender. We wanted to see if efforts to care for these young women reinforced this situation or if, in contrast, caring was aimed at enabling female students to develop intellectually, emotionally, socially, and physically.

As we observed the day-to-day activities at Wilson, we saw no interactions that made us think that teachers and administrators treated women differently. During our visits during the lunch hour, for instance, we observed pick-up basketball games in which male coaches and students of both sexes participated. Every time, male and female students played together. We could detect no shift in the intensity of the games because women were playing, and we heard no gender-related comments. We saw many displays of affection between adults and students, but these never seemed to have sexual overtones. Frequent hugs, usually initiated by students, seemed linked to celebrations (as when one female Latino student hugged Mrs. Story when she found out she had received a special award and scholarship) or to gratitude on the part of the student for special attention from an adult. One young woman, for example, had been cutting school because she was convinced she was going to jail for violating parole on an auto theft charge. We saw her hug Dr. Oniko to thank him for getting her to return to school and working patiently with her through the first difficult day. And at least some women, apparently, were comfortable in leadership roles. We observed a student-run assembly that featured the officers of the "leadership club," three women (two Latino and one African-American) and two men (one Latino and one African-American). These students shared the platform and seemed quite comfortable in their working relationships.

These incidents impressed us, but none gave us a strong sense that we *understood* much about caring that specifically and directly affected women. As we visited the health services center, the child care center, and the community care center, we felt that we began to learn much more about the degree and quality of support for female students.

The community care center provides integrated services for at-risk ninth grade students and for teen parents. It is a part of California's Healthy Start program, a state effort to facilitate the development of multiagency, integrated services programs. The center is funded by Healthy Start and the participating agencies, which include the student health services center, the Watts Health Foundation, a local Hispanic service center, the school district, the county probation department, local and regional PTA organizations, and the county health department.

According to Mrs. Powers, community care center director, the school health services clinic—one of only three in the Los Angeles Unified School District and in operation for six years—provides general health care services for students whose parents enroll them in the clinic program and for the children of these enrolled students. Sexuality education and contraceptive services for men and women, and pre- and postnatal care for teen mothers are also available, although parents may choose whether or not such services are to be made available to their children. (Health care for students not enrolled in the health services clinic program is provided by the school nurse and does not include family planning services.) We were impressed by the "matter of factness" and nonjudgmental attitudes of persons working in both the health and community care centers. They seemed aware that many of Wilson's students were sexually active and were concerned with assisting students in making wise and safe decisions in this area. (During our visits, three persons told us that they estimated that at least 40 percent of Wilson's students were parents. They all indicated that they "wished" this figure were lower, but that they were concerned mainly with supporting young women and their families.) We were struck—especially—by the focus on the importance of *men* recognizing their responsibilities for their actions. We did not see women's issues being neglected, but neither did we feel that, here, acting in a sexually responsible manner was viewed as a predominantly female responsibility.

This point was exemplified when, on our first visit, we were introduced to a young man who serves as a peer counselor. We asked him what this involved, and he replied, "Well, I talk to students about things like pregnancy and sexually transmitted diseases. We go to classes and stuff, but we also just talk to individuals. They kind of listen better when it comes from us, sometimes." We later learned from Mrs. Powers that these counselors go through a fairly intensive training program to ensure that they possess both content knowledge and interpersonal skills. We also learned that a number of male students are involved in the program and that they are making conscious efforts to recruit more. Concerning this, she stated: "It's sometimes easy to concentrate upon the girls—because they get pregnant. And sometimes it's easier for them to come here for some reason or other. We want to be sure that we help the young men to *really* be responsible. Once they get involved, they're open and willing, but sometimes we have to encourage them—just a little—to give this a try. We have some wonderful men working with us in this program [offering the training], and that helps. They're great role models, and the students, in turn, become good role models for their peers."

At the child care center, we learned more about supportive services that particularly affect young women. This center is separate from the health center (although the staffs of both do much in the way of coordinated efforts). Founded in 1983, the child care center represents the results of efforts on the part of school and community leaders and of the members of Parents of Watts, an organization concerned about the quality of life for the children in this area. These groups united, applied for, and received a grant from the state to supply and staff a center. The school's only task was finding space. In the early days of the center's operation, many of the young mothers it served eventually dropped out of school, in spite of the extra support the center offered. In recent years, however, more and more mothers are staying and graduating, which means that there is relatively little turnover in the population the center serves—and that the waiting list to get in is longer. The center can accommodate only about twenty babies and preschoolers, so it is far from being able to meet the needs of Wilson's entire population of student mothers who might benefit from its services. Indeed, the attendance office reports that child care problems are a major cause of absenteeism at Wilson.

The child care center offers a rather comprehensive set of services for the children and their mothers. Children attend at no cost to the parent; however, every mother is asked to give one period a day to assist at the center for the length of time her child is in the program. Mrs. Gunn noted that they try to arrange this so that the mother can spend some time enjoying her baby, so that she can learn something about children and child care, and so that she feels that she is contributing to her child's growth and development. Ruefully, she admitted that they cannot always meet all of these goals, but, she added, "We keep trying." Mothers who have children in this program also attend two afterschool sessions a month, and they must complete a one year course called Infant Study, which is taught jointly by Mrs. Gunn and Wilson's home economics teacher. This class covers pregnancy, child growth and development, parenting skills, and self-esteem for parents and children. Instructors also spend some time helping students learn "how to access the 'system.'" Mrs. Joyce, the home economics teacher, stated that often young women "don't know where to go for help and how to ask for what they need," but indicated that the staff believed that this was slowly changing. Mrs. Gunn noted that this class is also open to nonparents as an elective. With some pride, she recalled several fathers and nonparenting male students who had enrolled.

Characteristics of Caring For, With, and About Women

As we analyzed our notes, seeking to code passages that especially related to care for women, several words kept recurring. These included *modeling, responsibility, accepting,* and *involving men as well as women.* At Wilson, we found a large number of women in leadership positions. These women, according to Principal Story and Assistant Principal Gregg, were aware of their potential to serve as role models and made conscious efforts to demonstrate that being a strong woman, a competent professional, and a nurturing wife and mother were not mutually exclusive options. We were also struck by the fact that the adults with whom we spoke seemed to accept that adolescents were, in fact, responsible for themselves and were concerned about equipping them to make good, developmentally sound decisions. This was done for both men and women. We saw no evidence of programs that focused on getting *women* students to "curb" or be careful with their sexual activity. Indeed, we did not observe this emphasis for either men or women. We did see programs concerned with getting information directly to students of both genders. In the sections that follow, we briefly discuss some of the characteristics of modeling and supporting responsibility as forms of caring at Wilson.

Modeling as a Form of Caring. At Wilson, when we were there, one half of the administrators were women. The principal and two of the assistant principals were African-American women. Two assistant principals were Latino men, and one was an Anglo man. The leadership council, an organization developed as a part of Wilson's commitment to site-based management, was composed of the principal, one assistant principal (who rotated on and off of the council), two parents (a Latino woman and African-American man), and two teachers, (a Latino woman and an Anglo man). Men and women, most of them Latino or African-American, worked in all arenas involving student counseling. The interaction among these adults was consistently professional and respectful; their interactions with students were straightforward, personal, and supportive. If our days at Wilson were at all typical, we came to believe that students had many opportunities to observe and participate in interactions that exploded gender stereotypes.

Two such interactions—one involving Principal Mary Story and one, Assistant Principal Joan Gregg—exemplify the types of exchanges we observed. In one, an African-American male teacher had asked a student to report to Mrs. Story because he believed that the student had been copying answers on a state-mandated standardized test. After the testing period ended, Mrs. Story walked the student back to class, and, in a private conversation, suggested to the teacher a "better" way to handle the incident next time. Evidently the teacher had torn up the answer sheet, something that would require that the student retake the entire test (an all-day procedure). Mrs. Story recommended that such a student be moved, but allowed to continue, saying "we'll deal with the cheating later. As it is, we don't even have any kind of evidence now. And he'll have to miss class for a day to retake the whole thing." The teacher, himself a Wilson graduate, disagreed and stated that he "knew" what it took to "turn kids around" and that they needed "something to open their eyes." Mrs. Story was unfailingly respectful of his perspective and praised his commitment to doing what was best for children, but she also continued to reaffirm that, in the future, situations such as this needed to be handled differently. The entire interaction was amicable and professional. We did not have the opportunity to speak privately with the teacher, but we never sensed that either Mrs. Story's gender or position inhibited his expressing his views. When we spoke with her later, we asked if such interactions were difficult for her—especially if they involved men—and she replied, "Oh sometimes, not for me, really, but I think they're hard for them. But you just have to be professional and do what's best for kids."

When we met Assistant Principal Joan Gregg, we noticed several pictures of a young infant in her office. In response to our comments, she told us, "We just adopted her last spring. It was a wild time. I took a leave—just to get used to being a mom and to get her settled." She then added: "All of the kids have been so interested in her. I bring new pictures in so they can see how she's growing. It's kind of neat because many of them have children, and they can see that I understand—and that it's possible to be a good mom and to work and to even go back to school." (Gregg is working on her doctorate.)

Assuming Responsibility, Providing Information and Support, and Respecting Decisions. At several urban schools, we have heard adults says that students need "*to learn* responsibility." At Wilson, we did not hear these words. Rather, we heard and saw numerous affirmations of the belief that young people *were* responsible for their lives and their decisions and that the job of educators was to assist them in handling that responsibility wisely. These assumptions, in our view, contributed to what seemed to be a powerful and empowering kind of caring for women at Wilson.

Adults at Wilson who worked in the child care and community service centers, as well as in the school health clinic, whether teachers, administrators, or staff members, appeared to start with the belief that students' bodies, identities, and choices belong to the students themselves. They conveyed this belief in the documents they produced, in the programs they sponsored, and in their daily interactions with students. They provided information directly to young people and encouraged them to make their best decisions. They reminded them in numerous ways that no one else— not a parent, nor a sexual partner, nor a teacher, nor a counselor—could or should control them, and they accepted decisions once they had been made. We suspect that such attitudes and actions, although important for all students, are likely to have an especially powerful impact on women's views of themselves. Literature (e.g., Butler, 1993; J. Cohen, 1993; Morrison, 1970; Spelman, 1982) suggests that the formulation of a strong sense of self is an especially challenging task for adolescent women of color.

With some pride, several adults told us of the ways young people had responded to these attitudes and actions. Mary Story pointed out one female student, walking across campus with a toddler and an infant, and said, "A few years ago, she never would have graduated. She's planning on going to community college this fall to become a nurse's aide." Mrs. Powers noted that several fathers who are not students at Wilson "and who are older—at least in their twenties," have been coming to the community care center, inquiring about and enrolling in parenting classes. Dr. Oniko, in turn, told of calling a young woman at home, telling her that they at Wilson would try to support her if she would come back to school. To his surprise, she turned up the next day and has, with some difficulty, been attending regularly for over a year and a half.

More powerful evidence of the responses to caring was seen in the yard and in the classes of Wilson High School. We overheard an animated conversation among teachers and two young women about the kinds of books they preferred. We heard one student tell of her pleasure at reading about Fannie Lou Hamer, an early leader in the Civil Rights Movement. We observed young women speaking out to a reporter from the *Los Angeles Times* in the class we described earlier. We sat in on a meeting in which a counselor reported that forty Wilson students would be attending summer sessions at colleges throughout the United States and that she and Mrs. Story had collected enough "frequent flyer" miles from friends and acquaintances to purchase all of the tickets to get the young people to and from their destinations. And we watched Dr. Oniko meet on an hourly basis with a young woman who was feeling like she would probably be sent to jail and, therefore, did not need to be at school. We learned that, in addition to counseling her, he was going to court with her and was confident that, with his support, she would be able to remain at Wilson.

CLOSING THOUGHTS

We discovered Wilson High School when one of us was assigned to shadow Principal Mary Story. As we drove through the neighborhood surrounding the school, we were struck by the powerful evidence of the ways poverty and racial tension were affecting this community. Gang graffiti covered walls that often surrounded shells of buildings or burned lots, stark reminders of the 1992 Los Angeles riots. Customers and employees in the businesses still in operation were virtually hidden from sight by the thick metal almost cage-like bars that covered windows and open doors. Often outside, unemployed men congregated on sidewalks and in alleys talking quietly or simply sitting. It was for us, therefore, an unexpected delight to find, in the middle of this community, an urban high school where adults and children were caring for one another, respecting each other, and sharing information and power. We found persons confronting stereotypes and prejudices based upon gender, race, and class, attempting in both personal interactions and through programs and policies to overcome these stereotypes. And we saw many positive results of such efforts.

As we reflected upon the meaning of the caring we felt we saw at Wilson, we found ourselves considering the applicability of Michael Apple's call for educators to "look for the subtle connections between educational phenomena, such as curriculum, and the latent social and economic outcomes of the situation" (Apple, 1990, p. 34). Did the caring we were seeing merely serve to pacify students, to soften their edges, and defuse what might otherwise be justifiable anger against society?

We know little about what happens to Wilson's students when they leave—the school itself has only bits of anecdotal information of this nature, so we cannot *know* that Wilson's brand of caring empowers rather than merely pacifies its students, but we think that we see evidence for the former. Many of the stories we have told are of caring that is not afraid of confrontation, nor of sticking up for principle, nor of pushing young people to do what they ought to do. Sam, the young man we met in the attendance office, understood this truth about Wilson.

He told us that he liked Wilson because *they paid attention and were organized*. His former schools never called his home when he was absent; they never noticed students at all, unless they caused problems, he said. At Wilson, he reported, *the school knew its responsibilities and he knew his*. If a student is absent, he said, the school needs to find out why and to pursue students who should be in school—while respecting the student's right to be absent when necessary. This could be done, he felt, while still treating students respectfully, like responsible human beings. It is up to students, on the other hand, to do their part, too, he told us. His part, he understood, was to attend, to study, to get into geometry next year, to graduate.

Wilson is not a perfect school. It may never be featured on the nightly news for overwhelming academic performance. There is a high dropout rate; teens get pregnant and have children; graffiti sometimes appears on an external school wall; some teachers seem to have given up; and some parents do not appear to care very much. It is, however, a school that is doing something about all of these issues to help all of the students have the best possible opportunities in life. Counselors and administrators visit homes to encourage students to attend and to see if there are family issues that might need to be addressed. Young women are supported through pregnancy and motherhood in a myriad of ways. Men and women students are given information about sexuality decisions and are asked to remember that they—

and they alone—are responsible for their choices and their bodies. Adult educators of both genders and all races function, for the most part, as colleagues and as friends, and youngsters are given the opportunity to learn and practice communication skills so that they, also, may interact in this manner. Self-esteem is emphasized and people are heard.

It may be that one of the keys to the development of this kind of atmosphere lies in the foundational beliefs and assumptions of many who work at Wilson. They do not feel disadvantaged because they work in what is known as "the poorest high school in Los Angeles." They see themselves coming to a school—and to a community—rich with possibilities and deserving of opportunities to achieve these. They view students, parents, and persons working and living in the Watts neighborhood as partners—partners who work with them to create a genuine community in this urban setting—even as they, themselves, attempt to teach the young people they serve.

REFERENCES

Apple, M. W. (1990). *Ideology and Curriculum*, 2d ed. New York: Routledge.

Beck, L. G. (1992). "Meeting Future Challenges: The Place of a Caring Ethic in Educational Administration." *American Journal of Education* 100, no. 4: 454–496.

———. (1994a). *Reclaiming Educational Administration as a Caring Community*. New York: Teachers College Press.

———. (1994b). "Creating a Caring School Community: One Principal's Story." In J. Murphy and K. S. Louis, eds., *Reshaping the Principalship: Insights from Transformational Reform Efforts*. Newbury Park, CA: Corwin Sage.

Brabeck, M. M., ed. (1989). *Who Cares? Theory, Research, and Educational Implications of the Ethic of Care*. New York: Praeger Publishing.

Butler, J. E. (1993). "Transforming the Curriculum: Teaching About Women of Color." In J. A. Banks and C. A. M. Banks, eds., *Multicultural Education: Issues and Perspectives*, pp. 149–167. Boston: Allyn and Bacon.

Cohen, H. A. (1965). *A Basic Jewish Encyclopedia*. Hartford, CT: Hartmore House.

Cohen, J. (1993). "Constructing Race at an Urban High School: In Their Minds, Their Mouths, Their Hearts." In L. Weis and M. Fine, eds.,

Beyond Silenced Voices: Class, Race, and Gender in United States Schools, pp. 289–308. Albany: SUNY Press.

Dempsey, V., and Noblit, G. W. (1993). "The Demise of Caring in an African-American Community: One Consequence of School Desegregation." *Urban Review* 25, no. 1: 47–61.

Eugene, T. M. (1989). "Sometimes I Feel Like a Motherless Child: The Call and Response for a Liberational Ethic of Care by Black Feminists." In M. M. Brabeck, ed., *Who Cares? Theory, Research, and Educational Implications of an Ethic of Care,* pp. 45–62. New York: Praeger Publishing.

Fox, M. (1990). *A Spirituality Named Compassion.* San Francisco: Harper.

Gilligan, C. (1982). *In a Different Voice: Psychological Theory and Women's Development.* Cambridge, MA: Harvard University Press.

Higgins, A. (1989). "The Just Community Educational Program: The Development of Moral Role-Taking as the Expression of Justice and Care." In M. M. Brabeck, ed., *Who Cares? Theory, Research, and Educational Implications of an Ethic of Care,* pp. 197–215. New York: Praeger Publishing.

Hill, S. I. B. (1971). *Race, Class, and Ethnic Biases in Research on School Performance of Low Income Youth.* Doctoral dissertation, University of Oregon, Eugene.

Kirkpatrick, F. G. (1986). *Community: A Trinity of Models.* Washington, DC: Georgetown University Press.

Macmurray, J. (1961). *Persons in Relation.* New York: Harper and Brothers.

Mercado, C. I. (1993). "Caring as Empowerment: School Collaboration and Community Agency." *Urban Review* 25, no. 1: 79–104.

Merriam, S. B. (1988). *Case Study Research in Education: A Qualitative Approach.* San Francisco: Jossey-Bass.

Morrison, T. (1970). *The Bluest Eye: A Novel.* New York: Holt, Rinehart and Winston.

Noblit, G. W. (1993). "Power and Caring." *American Educational Research Journal* 30, no. 1: 23–38.

Noddings, N. (1984). *Caring A Feminine Approach to Ethics and Moral Education.* Berkeley: University of California Press.

———. (1988). "An Ethic of Caring and Its Implications for Instructional Arrangements." *American Journal of Education* 96, no. 2: 215–230.

———. (1992). *The Challenge to Care in Schools: An Alternative Approach to Education.* New York: Teachers College Press.

Oakes, J. (1985). *Keeping Track: How Schools Structure Inequality.* New Haven, CT: Yale University Press.

Persell, C. H. (1993). "Social Class and Educational Equality." In J. A. Banks and C. A. M. Banks, eds., *Multicultural Education: Issues and Perspectives,* pp. 71–89. Boston: Allyn and Bacon.

Powell, A., Farrar, E., and Cohen, D. K. (1985). *The Shopping Mall High School: Winners and Losers in the Educational Marketplace.* Boston: Houghton Mifflin.

Puka, B. (1989). "The Liberation of Caring: A Different Voice for Gilligan's *Different Voice.*" In M. M. Brabeck, ed., *Who Cares? Theory, Research, and Educational Implications of the Ethic of Care,* pp. 19–44. New York: Praeger Publishing.

Purpel, D. (1988). *The Moral and Spiritual Crisis in Education: A Curriculum for Justice and Compassion in Education.* Granby, MA: Bergin and Garvey.

Sedlak, M. W., Wheeler, C. W., Pullin, D. C., and Cusick, P. A. (1986). *Selling Students Short: Classroom Bargains and Academic Reform in the American High School.* New York: Teachers College Press.

Shogan, D. (1988). *Care and Moral Motivation.* Toronto: Ontario Institute for Studies in Education.

Spelman, E. V. (1982). "Theories of Gender and Race: The Erasure of Black Women." *Question: A Feminist Quarterly* 5, no. 4: 36–62.

Starratt, R. J. (1991). "Building an Ethical School: A Theory for Practice in Educational Leadership." *Educational Administration Quarterly* 27, no. 2: 185–202.

Stein, A. (1971). "Strategies for Failure." *Harvard Educational Review* 41, no. 2: 158–204.

Van Galen, J. (1993). "Caring in Community: The Limitations of Compassion in Facilitating Diversity." *Urban Review* 25, no. 1: 5–24.

Walker, E. V. S. (1993). "Interpersonal Caring in the 'Good' Segregated Schooling of African-American Children: Evidence from the Case of Caswell County Training School." *Urban Review* 25, no. 1: 63–77.

CHAPTER 10

CARING AS EMPOWERMENT

School Collaboration and Community Agency

CARMEN I. MERCADO AND MEMBERS OF THE BRONX
MIDDLE SCHOOL COLLABORATIVE

In the fall of 1989, Marceline Torres and I embarked upon a partnership that has transformed our personal and professional lives and given a new purpose to our activities as educators and as women. Our biographies converged in an institutional setting where academics from minority backgrounds are largely underrepresented. It was both pride in my accomplishments and concern about the academic progress of her middle school students, most of whom are Latinos, that led Marceline to invite me into her world as a teacher. Since my first visit in June 1989, Marceline's classroom has become my classroom, my refuge, and my training ground. Professionally, it is where I go on a regular basis to share my world as a college professor, my passion as an educational ethnographer, and my experiences being the first college-educated member of my immediate family. Mostly, I go there to learn, to create meaning my life, and to renew my commitment to this kind of work.

Because of our cultural background and because of our experiences growing up in economically and politically powerless communities—and not just because we are women—our concern has always been to help others we meet so that they do not have to struggle alone. We agree with Walsh

(1991) that, because we are culturally inscribed beings, it is our collective and individual pasts and presents that compel us to challenge conceptions and act on reality. This may also explain why our families have played a key role in our collaborative work. In addition to the parents and caretakers of students, who serve as authorities to be consulted for research, members of our respective families have also participated in our activities, including my father and Marceline's mother and son. Making our families a part of our professional lives introduces different ways of relating in settings and activities where other relational norms prevail.

However, our collaborative has also evolved into a multiethnic community that cuts across a number of important distinctions, including class, ethnicity, and language. Graduate students, some of whom come from privileged backgrounds, have also participated in our activities. We strive to be inclusive so that we may all benefit from the talents, interests, and abilities of others, no matter who they are or where they come from. For students in an inner city middle school, this means an opportunity to extend the boundaries of their insular existence, to relate to others whose lives may be very different from their own. Belonging and being included are significant themes for each of us in different ways.

As we have described in another article (Mercado, 1992), Marceline and I come together to engage her sixth graders in inquiry-based learning, and to examine how this affects youngsters at a critical juncture in their social, emotional, and academic development. Specifically, we employ collaborative-intervention research (Moll and Diaz, 1987) to explore what happens when adolescent students from underprivileged communities engage in the habits of mind of ethnographic researchers and use academic forms of literacy to learn about topics of personal significance. Variations on this approach to literacy are being used increasingly with culturally and linguistically diverse students who are learning English or who have a history of underachievement (Brice-Heath, 1985; Moll and Diaz, 1987; Trueba, 1987).

To date, the major focus for our analysis has been describing our pedagogical practices and the literacy-related outcomes measured by standardized tests. We have been placed in the position of having to demonstrate or justify the potential for academic excellence among these students, even though we do not feel that these practices fully explain the changes that have been documented. We believe that it is our way of relating to one another that is an important influence on students' academic accomplishments. Because students perceive that we care about them as individuals, they are willing "to put

more effort into their work," to accomplish what many consider to be beyond their capabilities. However, in the process of engaging in these experiences, their capacity to care is also nurtured and developed. We agree with
Noddings (1991, 1992) and Greene (1986) that the ethics of care is as fundamental as promoting literacy and academic learning.

Our purpose in this chapter is to examine our approach to collaborative pedagogy, learning, and research to describe how our activities lead to
affirmation and empowerment for students between the ages of eleven and
fifteen, who are primarily Latino (65 percent) and Afro-Caribbean/Ameri-
can (30 percent). In the second part of the chapter, we will examine some
of the moral and ethical issues that surfaced from our activities as well as
some of the tensions that are inherent in collaborative learning and research. According to Noddings (1991, 1992), caring is a way of being in a
relationship, not a specific set of behaviors. It involves "total engrossment"
in the needs of others, evident in intensive looking and listening to really
see, hear, and feel what the other person is trying to convey. However,
Noddings suggests that caring is not unconditional acceptance of another
because it also involves helping others to grow. Moreover, although caring
leads to nurturing the capacity to care, it does not always assure ethical results. This analytic framework is one of the several we have used to name
what we do and understand what we are accomplishing in one inner-city
middle school setting.

I (Carmen I. Mercado) patterned the texts of our individual voices to
construct a narrative that would not exist without collective effort. As such,
the identities of the many voices that may be heard throughout this document are acknowledged whenever it is possible to so in a respectful manner.
You will meet students such as Angel and Sonia, who like Marceline and
me, are of Puerto Rican ancestry as well as students like Njeri who is of
Afro-Caribbean decent. You will hear the voices of parents like Eric's
mother and of future teachers like Patricia, Pamela, and Ellie; you will also
hear many other anonymous voices who have influenced and have been influenced by our work.

WORKING TOGETHER, LEARNING TOGETHER

Within our community, everyone is to some extent responsible for teaching,
documenting, and sharing. We work in a way that blurs distinctions among
collaborative pedagogy, collaborative learning, and collaborative research and

in a way that blurs distinctions between novice and expert, student and teacher, parent and teacher, teacher and researcher. This is as significant for youngsters, who are sensitive about what they know and insecure about their capabilities, as it is for their adult collaborators who want to make a difference in a setting where isolation, control, and failure are the norm.

COLLABORATIVE PEDAGOGY

Virginia Woodward (1985) describes an approach to pedagogy that captures the essence of how Marceline and I have worked together during my regular Friday visits: "In collaborative pedagogy, both the researcher and the teacher are active participants in the classroom setting. Each participant is making curricular decisions based on beliefs. The researcher is not there to tell the teacher what her curricular decisions should be. Rather, the role calls for mutual sharing: sharing our instructional strategies, sharing our observations of the children's linguistic and cognitive processes as transactions occur in the language event, and sharing the planning and implementation of ongoing language events. By this definition the researcher role and the teacher role meld into the one role of teacher/researcher for both participants" (p. 770).

Four years ago, when Marceline invited me to participate in the life of her classroom, neither of us had a very clear idea of how this would play out with her middle school students. I was initially concerned about whether young adolescent students would be interested in learning about my academic life. My misgivings, which not based on direct experiences but on stories told by others, proved to be unfounded. I soon gained confidence and began to derive great pleasure from my encounters with young people who are surprised to learn that I am one of their own.

Our collaborative pedagogy has evolved over the past four years and reflects shared understandings that we have created together over time. At first, I was responsible for organizing our research activities, which enabled me to introduce two variations to the traditional interactional pattern that prevails in middle schools. Students' concerns were elicited as a way identifying their research focus and research groups of students having similar interests or affinities were formed. Giving students the power to direct our pedagogy created opportunities for us to observe and learn from and about students, essential to our roles as teacher-researcher or researcher-teacher.

During our sessions together students meet with their research groups to support one another, which includes sharing their work and planning activities. Sometimes I lead discussions with the whole class to address common concerns or upcoming events as I do when we are making preparations for a conference presentation. Most of the time, however, I am another adult in the classroom who is there to consult with students about their work or listen to those who simply want to chat. I also make copies of primary sources that may not be accessible to students, as I did when I brought in copies of research articles from newspapers and journals, and surveys used by agencies such as the Census Bureau. Although this is how research occurs during our Friday meetings, from the beginning Marceline created other opportunities to do research. She organized visits to local institutions; she assigned homework requiring students to interview family members; and she encouraged students to observe and take notes during local trips. Because Marceline has made research a way of learning, last year, she was officially designated the coordinator of the school's research program, a program that consists of the students in her official class. Marceline has been especially masterful in creating a climate for our activities. For example, relating to students that they will be doing "college work" with her college professor, a researcher, peaks their interest and builds students' excitement in anticipation of my first visit. Students are literally shocked to meet me as most expect me to be a balding man who wears glasses and a white coat. To satisfy their initial curiosities of who I am and why I want to visit them, they are given an opportunity to interview me in a manner that is not unlike a presidential press conference. Although no limitations are imposed on the types of questions that may be asked, students usually elicit my opinion on issues that concern them and inquire about aspects of my personal and professional life. These first exchanges are crucial as they are intended to allay fears about doing "college work," a term that both intimidates and excites students, and to make clear that I come to be with them because "I want to and not because I have to": "Dr. Mercado comes to us every Friday. . . . She don't get paid or any thing for working with us. She does it because she loves us and our working together" (Njeri, 2/91).

The following excerpt from an interview conducted in September 1991, captures the general tone of this significant encounter, which also gives glimpses of the way Marceline and I relate to one another and to our young collaborators.

MT: Welcome Dr. C.M. Are you prepared to answer all these inquiring reporters today

CM: Well, I'm certainly going to try

MT: Who'd like to ask Dr. C.M. the first question?

S_1: Where do you go when you are done working?

CM: I never stop working. This is my life. This is not like a job where people go to work at nine and go home at five. This is my life so I never stop thinking about what I am doing Your teacher knows well because she never stops thinking about what she is doing, right Mrs. Torres?

MT: That is correct.

CM: Weekends, all the time—with our parents, with other teachers, with friends—we are always talking about you, always thinking about you.

MT: Very good. Does that answer your question?

S_1: Yeah.

S_2: What does research mean to you?

CM: That's a very important question. You know, sometimes your questions are so important, so profound, that they are very difficult to answer with a few words. Research means a lot because as a human being I was born to be a researcher . . .

Being a researcher means being a learner. So research is something that we all do all the time only we don't call it research . . . Research to me is a very important way of helping to tell your story, what happens—here (in classrooms) so that other people know how wonderful you are . . . because in the newspapers what do we read? . . . we read about the crime and the problems. We need people to tell about the good things that are happening.

Research allows me to do that. Research is also important because for me research means making changes, helping to make things even better.

The way I do research now is by sharing it with people like you so that you can become researchers also . . .

Did I answer your question?

S_3: Would you like to retire?

CM: No! . . . I can't think of retiring because what I do is something that I love and, when I don't do this, when I don't go out to talk to students like you, I don't feel very important.

I don't feel like I'm doing something . . .
Did I answer your question? . . .
S_4: Why do you like (inaudible)
CM: Why do I like children?
S_4: . . . teaching?
CM: I always played at being a teacher, but I never wanted to study to be a teacher. I like teaching because I like to learn and share what I know. I also like it because it means working with people like you. I don't have children of my own so you're like my children. . . .
Did I answer your question?

Our collaborative approach to pedagogy did not introduce new ways of relating to students in Marceline's classes. She has always been known to be very sensitive and responsive to students, which is why Patricia chose to be mentored by Marceline during her formal student-teaching experience: "I have come to respect and admire the perseverance of MT (Marceline) . . . among what would be insurmountable obstacles for other teachers, MT continues to inspire her students by not only providing them with real teaching, but also truly caring about their lives and the lives of their families. She accepts every challenge. I don't think she knows the word *No*, especially when it comes to her students and her parents" (Patricia, 3/92).

Working together has served to validate and reinforce Marceline's ways of relating in a setting where her actions are considered by some to "go beyond the call of duty" and by others as "crazy." However, we have also created new opportunities to engage in relations of care through activities that are more academically challenging than the curriculum Marceline is expected to implement. In particular, our research activities have broadened students' opportunities to have a voice and be heard. In sharing with students how I take observational notes, which we refer to as "scribe" notes, they learn to capture interactions and activities the way "real researchers do." Scribe notes have developed into a significant mechanism for eliciting students' perceptions and giving them a forum to make their voices heard, especially for students who prefer to "write it" than "say it," as surprisingly many do. It is no coincidence that the term *scribe* or *scribing* is both a variant of the Spanish word *escribir* and a reference to the historical importance of scribes. The words we use are always imbued with personal meanings. The scribe notes presented here illustrate the potential value of this activity while giving another glimpse of the way we work together. It should be noted that students take scribe notes as we are engaged in our activities; we typically do not require them to rewrite these notes.

10:14   10/30/94

Dr. M. was impressed with our notes again. And she said that there is a difference and last year some students said that "research is hard but fun" I think so too. Mrs. Torres said that she like to take note from students and mix them together to make a story. Mrs. Torres said, "This is something that gets [me] excited. Your words are very valuable," and Dr. M. wrote it down on the blackboard. And when you quote some it show that you are listening. It show what others say that is important. You are authorities. Dr. M. said to Epi, "Did they quoted you or misquoted you," and Epi said, "they misquoted me," and Dr. M. said, "she takes them in our [notes] to collect and show them to her student." And they are impressed. 10:32 (A.M.)

Indicating the duration of activities and quoting the exact words people use suggest that students are learning about the rigors of research, but they are also learning that we respect them and value what they know.

Because our activities are organized around student-directed groups, Marceline and I have played an important role in helping students negotiate relationships with peers. Having come to understand the challenges of working collaboratively through firsthand experiences, it did not come as a surprise when we found similar concerns among students. Perhaps what surprised us most was the seriousness with which students brought these concerns to our attention. Although as adults we may prefer to work alone because some individuals are more difficult to relate to than others—which is also true for our young collaborators—students have also made us aware that it is preferable to work alone if a valued friendship is at stake. Caring about the relationships they have with others is often more important than working collaboratively, despite the social and cognitive advantages they agree are possible. Being engrossed in the needs of students enables us to be responsive to them, which also conveys that their needs are our top priority. This may explain why Marceline has been described as a teacher who is different because she "always has time to listen" and why students use the words *patient* and *understanding* to characterize the way I relate to them.

We have also played an important role in helping students to assess the progress they are making. What began as a way of assessing our conference presentations developed into a more systematic examination of students' progress that we initiated in the second year. The graduate students who joined us at this time played a key role in helping to organize student portfolios, which we used to make the middle school students aware of their progress. Through the individual conferences we organized to discuss these documents, students are given another opportunity to clarify or elaborate upon their intended meanings and to discuss what they were doing. Although our purpose has always been to create awareness of their accomplishments, we made important discoveries in the process. We found evidence for the unevenness that often characterizes students' work, which has led us to interrogate the data and to explore other explanations for the patterns we were finding.

Essentially, in this process of responding to student concerns and trying to understand their behaviors over time we deepened our understanding of the knowledge and abilities that underachieving students possess that often goes unnoticed in school settings. We also learned what it is like to walk in Marceline's shoes, and to see the classroom through her eyes. The common experiences we share gives us a compelling reason to talk, which we do all the time—in English, Spanish, and a combination of the two languages; with classroom participants with other professionals, and with our families. Dialogue serves many important purposes. It is the means through which we share information and develop understandings about what has occurred, but it is also is the means through which relations of care are established and sustained. "[D]ialogue is a common search for understanding, empathy, or appreciation . . . it is always a genuine quest for something undetermined. . . . Dialogue serves not only to inform the decision under consideration; it also contributes to a habit of mind—that of seeking adequate information on which to make decisions. Dialogue serves another purpose in moral education. It connects us to each other and helps to maintain caring relations" (Noddings, 1992, p. 23).

I recently discovered that this aspect of our work has the most meaning for Marceline. Conversations are an important means of connecting to others; they help lessen the isolation this teacher feels in a setting where "no one has time" to listen to students, parents, and teachers. Collaborative pedagogy serves as a vital source of support for individuals like Marceline, who are on a neverending quest to understand their students, a daunting pursuit when we consider that each student evidences distinctly different needs. Sharing our individual observations of and conversations with students, we made some surprising discoveries. Patricia called our attention to Tyrone's articulateness and quiet assertiveness, which she discovered through the letters he had written to her, and Ellie made us aware of Nadia's indignant reaction when she realized that we had not corrected her misspelling of the word *research*. Marceline has come to depend upon our different sets of eyes to help her understand more fully each student in her class, realizing how very difficult it is for any teacher to get to know all students equally well no matter how caring and sensitive that teacher may be.

Our collaborative research also gives Marceline a purpose for engaging in focused and systematic observations of students as they participate in their research activities. Even though Marceline has always been attentive and responsive to the needs of her students, her multiple responsibilities pull her in many directions at the same time. For a variety of reasons that are beyond this teacher's control, intensive looking, contemplation, and reflection are a rare luxury in this middle school.

I have learned as much about the middle school students in Marceline's class as I have about her concerns as a teacher. Disclosing my vulnerabilities and acknowledging Marceline's expertise, particularly in terms of how she relates to young adolescent students, has contributed significantly to equalizing perceived differences in status and knowledge. Entering the classroom as the college professor, I was consulted about any number of problems and expected to know most if not all of the answers. This has, however, changed through time. It is clear that we have learned from each other and that we are making discoveries together.

It has been interesting to observe how our collaborative activities have affected Marceline's practice. I have seen her make research an integral part of her pedagogy, and she has begun to use ethnographic procedures to document and examine her relationship with the parents and caretakers of her students. She has grown increasingly confident about and proud of her capabilities as a researcher; she has begun to walk in my shoes.

Similarly, Marceline has also been an influence on me. Through her efforts I am more knowledgeable about the organization of middle schools and working with young adolescent students. In particular, through her knowledge of the lives of students I have learned the most, especially about the many outside influences that affect students in the classroom and that explain momentary disinterest and preoccupation. It was also through Marceline's professional network that I met the editor of our first publication. Walking in each other's shoes is no minor accomplishment in teacher-researcher collaboratives, as Warren Little (1990) reminds us. Not only has our mutual sharing led to mutual learning, but we have also contributed to each other's personal and professional growth.

COLLABORATIVE LEARNING

"We are not working alone. We are working together. . . . They learn from us and we learn from them." Although this is how students and adults describe our collaborative approach to learning and research, our interdependence is important for socioemotional and sociocognitive reasons.

Students find it significant that they are trusted to work in *research groups* they organize and to seek out assistance from adults, when *they determine* it is needed. They insist that we treat them differently from other teachers because we "do not tell them what to do," "trust them to work on their own" (Sonia), and allow them to "discover things for themselves" (Maigen). This is an uncommon way of learning in a setting where interaction is suppressed and, for the sake of order and control, keeps students busy and, therefore, out of trouble with "boring board work." This is a major obstacle to creating challenging learning environments in inner-city middle schools, where there is a fear of violence and, because of poor performance on standardized tests of achievement, low expectations of what students are capable of accomplishing. Challenging perceptions and established ways always brings some repercussions from those who worry or are angered that students will not learn what they have to learn or that they are being given too much freedom. Learning to deal with these reactions is part of learning to work in the best interest of students and surviving in hostile environments.

In eliciting what students consider worthy of study, to have a focus for their research activities in the same manner that researchers are guided by their curiosities and concerns, students reveal what they know. As these questions reflect, students have serious concerns. They want to understand what they see happening in their neighborhoods and among family and friends:

Why are there so many homeless people?
Where so diseases come from?
Why do people take drugs if they know it is bad for them?
Why are so many girls having babies at a young age?
Why is there so much abuse and abandonment?

They also want to understand bigotry, violence, and injustices, as Amanda articulated with passion and conviction: "If I could learn about anything in the world, I would like to know why people kill each other. Why do they do that? And why are people so prejudiced. I would really like to know. When I saw the news on Monday, about a little six-year-old girl who got killed, I wanted to cry. That's why I would like to know why other people kill each other. And also I saw a woman who didn't like Black people and I didn't like that one bit" (10/90).

Although these topics do not form part of the traditional school curriculum, as Maigen said, they are important because it helps teenagers to deal with the "real world." For their adult guides, however, these topics are a painful reminder that our society has failed to care about all of its citizens in the same way, which is one of the reasons why this type of work is so emotionally draining. Through their research activities, students come to these understandings on their own as they begin to question why schools do not teach them what they need to know and how to overcome the problems of their community.

As activities get underway, students gradually reveal what they know about their topics, their observational and analysis skills, and their resourcefulness. Because they have not had the opportunity to be in control of their own learning in academic settings, we give special emphasis to research as a way of coming to know. Our role is to guide students to elicit information from a variety of sources to maintain careful accounts of their procedures, to interrogate and make sense of their data, and to seek out alternative explanations for what they are finding.

Because sharing is a nonthreatening and natural means of leaning when everyone is given the opportunity to share, students are encouraged to share their observational notes, to explain their surveys and interviews, and to share the charts and visuals they devise. Sometimes anonymous copies of these documents are shared with the permission of students and discussed during our sessions together. During our second year we began to use seventh graders who had been in Marceline's sixth grade class to orient sixth graders who were being initiated into research. We found that peers are an especially positive influence in our activities. Angel is among the students who, as a seventh grader, addressed sixth graders about "doing research with Mrs. Torres and Dr. Mercado." He has played an important role in our research activities throughout the three year period that he attended this middle school, a school he insisted on attending even after his family had moved out of the district. His participation illustrates the types of long-term relationships we cultivate with students. As the excerpt on page 211 illustrates, engaging in research has been an especially potent force in getting students to assume a more active role in their own learning, evident in students' words, actions, and posture.

It is instructive that what Angel choose to emphasize during his talk was the connection between research and social action and the need to care about others. This is a point that he has repeatedly emphasized, as he did in the survey he designed ("Test Your Caring") and the short story he wrote ("Who Cares?") about a boy named Angel who "is trying to stop the homeless problem in New York City." We were surprised when, on a number of occasions, we heard Angel admit that "research helped him find his true inside . . . the Angel that cares." Although the issue of "care" had not been explicitly discussed during our research activities, Angel's renewed interest in caring may illustrate Noddings's contention that students learn to care when they see others showing that they care. Relating to students in this way teaches them that they are important and that they have a responsibility to act on behalf of others who are less fortunate than they are. It is a significant theme in the writings of these youngsters. Here are excerpts from Angel's presentation of December 14, 1990:

Jerry: How do you feel about research?

Angel: I feel that if I didn't do research I would have kept on making fun of the homeless just like I did . . . throwing them bottles . . . telling them that they stink . . . calling them bums, that they should take a bath. . . . I'm lucky that I'm doing research on them . . . It showed me if a was a homeless I wouldn't like people saying that I stink . . . and—need new clothes

Keith: What got you interested in the homeless?

Angel: No one was doing it and I was curious

Jessica: Did it help you with your grades?

Angel: Yes, when I did research I just didn't do it from books

Epi: Did you find out why people are homeless? Why they are lying on the street?

Angel: Yes! Drugs, teen pregnancy, No one to help them with problems. They give up

Luis: You know, when you were talking about throwing rocks to the homeless, why did you stop?

Angel: Because I learned. I put myself as being a homeless. Then I went to some of the homeless that I knew . . .

Angela: When you interviewed a homeless lady, weren't you scared they were going to do something to you?

Angel: I knew her. My mother used to give her food. When I interviewed her I was half scared.

Anthony: Did you even tell the people, why didn't you get a job?

Angel: When I interviewed the homeless people they realized that somebody cared.

Luis: Why do you like this topic so much?

Angel: I don't know why I like this topic . . . I want to do it again this year.

Jeffery: Are you proud of what you are doing?

Angel: Yes I'm proud because if . . . if you need help. I'll be here every Friday

> I love doing research. Last year when I was in the sixth grade I did a little research on a very big thing called "teen agers having babies." The reason I like doing research in this subject is mainly because it helped me talk—a few girls out of it and so how to stop it from happening again (Njeri, 2/91).

Although, this emphasis may reflect norms of relating that are culturally determined, it may also reflect ways of relating found among the poor and the powerless who live in communities where each day represents a struggle for survival. However, as Angel suggests, just as we learn to care when others care for us, we also stop caring when we do not feel that others care. Realizing that someone cares, reawakens the capacity to care, as Angel seems to have discovered. Through their research activities, students have made us aware that insensitivity to the needs of others is a serious problem in their community as it is in society in general. This is especially problematic in a community with an increasing number of employment, housing, and health problems; in a community where the percentage of AIDS-related deaths is one of the highest in the nation.

However, providing assistance takes on many forms. Providing emotional support is essential, as Patricia suggests in this account of the experiences of one student who was thrust into doing research when her class was suddenly disbanded in February.

> When Ee. first entered the class she was a loner and very, very shy. . . . She would huddle over herself. . . . Just from looking at her you could tell she wanted to be anywhere else but here. . . .

Through talking with Ee. privately we found out that she has a lot of responsibilities at home. She takes care of her younger brother and sister when her mother goes out. . . . Also her younger sister doesn't listen to Ee. and this makes her angry. . . .

. . . Ee. tried to do her homework but she never was able to finish all of it and she never participated in class. When I would go over to speak to her she appeared to sound disinterested. Watching her in class, always by herself . . . bothered me. Maybe it was because I always identify with that student. . . .

Most of the teachers never give homework, I guess they don't want to correct papers. However, in this class students get homework every night in almost all of their subjects. The Monday after vacation . . . Ee. came in with a note from her mother saying that Ee. couldn't do most of the homework because it was too difficult for her. . . . Ee. [wrote] that she didn't feel ready for sixth grade, how could she handle college work?

. . . By April . . . no matter what she did or how hard she thought she was trying, she just couldn't keep up. Ee. was very worried and frustrated. She was afraid that she . . . wouldn't be promoted to the next grade. At that time, I wasn't aware of how bad Ee. felt, she was so quiet and so difficult to talk to. It was on this day that Ee's mother came . . . in to switch Ee. to another class. The conference was the turning point for Ee. It included MT, Ee., her mother, her uncle, and me. From hearing her mother talk the decision . . . had already been made. Her mother didn't like to see Ee. struggle so much. Ee. would be up until midnight trying to do her homework, often in tears. She felt that what MT was doing was beyond the reach of her daughter. She said that her daughter is a slow learner. After spending most of the period talking about how this class was more difficult and that most teachers don't give homework because they don't care, and all the opportunities available in the class, and showing her mother Ee.'s report card where her grades hadn't dropped as much as Ee. feared, it seemed over. It wasn't until they were about to leave that her uncle spoke up for the first time. He spoke directly to Ee.'s mother and said, "Well if you want my opinion I think you are making a big mistake. Every time Ee.'s life gets hard you come in and pluck her out and save her. She is learning that all she has to do to get out of difficult situations is to get you to take her out. I think you are doing her more harm than good because life is not easy. I think she should stay. She has a wonderful opportunity to be in this class and to be challenged. She has a good teacher who obviously cares . . . and I am willing to help her with her homework." And then the focus of the conversation changed to how her uncle could help Ee. . . .

This event was the catalyst that changed Ee. . . . On May 13 we went on a class trip to the Bronx Post Office . . . to meet past Olympic athletes and sign a giant post card. . . . It was there that the change in Ee. became real. On the train, at the post office, Ee. was taking lots of notes. When the ceremony was over she was the first person to run up to (the Bronx borough president) to speak to him. Ee. was everywhere, asking questions and interviewing everyone. When it came time to practice for (our) Princeton (presentation) she was speaking in a proud, loud voice. More importantly, though, she was smiling. We had never seen her smile.

Being understanding and providing emotional support are especially important for students who get easily discouraged when required to work in unfamiliar ways, especially if other preoccupations fill their minds.

We have also played an important role mediating learning by guiding students to become more reflective and thoughtful about what they are doing and learning. For example, we have used audio and video recordings to analyze our presentations and examine our effectiveness in communicating with our audiences. We help students to draw their own conclusions and not just accept someone else's opinion of their performance or to depend on their recollections of what occurred. Recollections are often distorted because students are overly self-critical. Our goal is to build confidence calling attention to our strengths while at the same time challenging students to become self-aware, self-critical, and self-directed learners, as this unrevised example illustrates. "The tape recording wasn't the same as the real thing it was much more interesting than the tape recording. We just heard the tape and not all of it was heard. If you want to know what happened you should have went. I don't have any recommendations for these kids, only for S. never past [pace] while making a speech" (1/8/90).

Through these activities, middle school students are using a broad range of literacy practices that are associated with doing "real" ethnographic research, especially since this was the teacher's initial concern. Students record interviews and conversations; they participate in organizing and preparing agendas, project chronologies, data summaries, project abstracts, conference proposals, and research reports. They also write speeches and stories and correspond with others for a number of authentic purposes. Writing is at the service of learning, and it is also used in response to real communicative and expressive needs that grow out of research. Reading and rereading drafts of their writings enable us to learn about their thoughts and feelings, especially about what is significant to them—their families, their community, and their desire for a more humane and just society, as these excerpts taken from first drafts illustrate.

I love my family they care about me and love me they give me things I want. They are friendly. I love my sisters because they are all I have. . . . My family treats people like they are part of the family. . . .

Some kids use drugs because they have many problems with other people, Some kids use drugs because they have problems in school or problems with their parents, sometimes it is because they want to get high. Drug dealers may try to convince people that drugs are good for them and if they use drugs they could become a leader of a group or stronger than the others. Parents should show love for their kids so that they would think they are the most important persons in the world and they won't need drugs to feel better.

If I won 500 dollars I would help the babies who are in the hospital because their mother or father used some kind of drugs and know they also suffer because there mother or father used drugs. I think that if a mother or father use drugs they should not have a baby. . . .

We prefer to show first drafts of students' writings to contrast the difference between students' sensitivities and thinking with the academic forms of language used by those who are second language learners of English, but also those who are not. Listening to the deeper meanings behind the words, and not their accuracy and correctness, is an important way to build confidence and self-esteem, although eventually students expect us to go beyond this, as we shall explain further on.

COLLABORATIVE RESEARCH

It is evident that in this collaborative, we are all the researchers and we are all the researched (Lather, 1986). However, because we are centered in this work, collaborative research also requires that we assure data trustworthiness, which we attempt to do by relying on multiple sources of data, multiple perspectives, and multiple interpretive frameworks (Lather, 1986). We strive to be rigorous in our work because we want to represent the various interpretive perspectives we each bring and have about what we are accomplishing and because we want students to understand what doing research requires. However, because we make no effort to mask our emotions, we feel pressured to demonstrate that our work is no less rigorous, a major tensions that is inherent in doing this type of research.

Documenting and Writing

As Epi and other students have observed, "there is no research without notes." We all kept notes of our work together in black and white marble composition notebooks, a practice we settled on during the second year as a way of solving the problem of lost documentation that occurred when students kept their research work in a loose-leaf binder and the adults used notepads or sheets of papers for this purpose. The use of composition books proved significant in that it transformed research into a participatory activity in which we all share responsibility for recording events, evolving interests and concerns, and for chronicling our progress.

While individual students write to document how and what they are learning about their research topics, adults write to document what students as a collective are doing and what they are learning through these activities. The impressive collection of "scribe" notes that the students have produced has made it possible to examine our activities from multiple perspectives, enabling us to acknowledge both similarities and differences in perspectives. Seeking counterevidence is an important part of data analysis, of interrogating our data. Not only does this illustrate that knowledge is socially constructed, it also illustrates that we need each other to render a complete account of our activities. Understanding that we value and depend upon their contributions boosts students' self-confidence and self-esteem, as does discovering that "data is everywhere;" that it is "in people"; and that their families are important authorities on the topics they are studying.

Reflecting and Contemplating

Just as "there is no research without notes" (Epi, 3/91), there is no research without reflection. Reflection requires common experiences but also a written (notes), visual (photographs, videotapes), or auditory (audiotapes) record of past events. Buchmann (1990) makes a distinction between reflection and contemplation that we have found useful: "Reflection is looking backward in hopes that light will be thrown by thought on experience. . . . One reflects in order to see something that is not available to simple looking but requires the mirror of mind. . . . [Contemplation is] a quiet, absorbed kind of looking at what there is, rather than looking forward or backward in planning and reflection" (pp. 490–491).

We have engaged in both reflection and contemplation in collective ways. This has been essential to interpret our observations and understand how collaborative inquiry and learning are influencing each of us, in different ways. We share our perceptions and interpretations of what we are doing with students in the classroom and with individual members of our community of learners when we sit in our homes, at the college, on the telephone, or wherever we happen to be, all the time. Collective reflection also occurs during presentations at professional gatherings when we discuss what we are doing with audiences from other settings. We have learned, however, that collective reflection cannot occur without first having shared experiences.

The large collection of photographs we have amassed initially served to preserve our special occasions—working in groups, making conference presentations, participating in monthly research celebrations, going on field trips—much the way families mark and preserve special occasions and events. Now, they serve as a powerful tool for reflection, particularly since many of these capture students as they engage with peers in student-directed groups, with others we meet, and during an occasional moment of solitude. It is incredible how memories are aroused by this form of representation that captures subtleties of our interactions in surprising ways.

Reviewing the many photographs we have collected, enables us to examine past events in light of new understandings. Each source of data that we use presents unique opportunities to deepen our understandings of what individual students are doing and learning and what we are accomplishing. However, this requires that judgments be suspended as we gather insights from a variety of sources over time. It is easy to misjudge students needs and capabilities or what we are accomplishing together on the basis of limited evidence. Yet, sometimes we accumulate so much evidence that we feel like we are drowning in data.

Sharing Through Conference Presentations

From the very beginning, collaborative conference presentations were intended as a means of showing respect for our young collaborators by allowing them to participate in professional forums where research is presented. We wanted the words of our young collaborators to echo in the sacred halls of academia, where they are often the object rather than the subject of inquiry and analysis. Because we believe this is what empowerment really means, we have struggled to subsidize the cost of travel sometimes at personal expense, to assure the participation of students.

Every time we make a formal presentation, we have the opportunity to take stock of our accomplishments and reexamine and synthesize what we are doing collectively and individually. In the process of explaining ourselves to ourselves and others, misconceptions are clarified and ideas and ideologies articulated, elaborated upon, and connected in more powerful and memorable ways. Cognitive psychologists describe this as deep processing, but students simply refer to it as "going deeper into things." Moreover, as Noddings suggests, understanding why we have done things in a particular manner is also a means of strengthening the bonds that exists between us.

Presentations also enable us to profit from reviewing what we have done with professionals from other settings, creating additional opportunities to reinterpret our work. Ellie, one of the graduate students, spoke for all of us when, after her first presentation, she confessed: "I didn't know that what we were doing was so important!" We need these experiences to redefine ourselves and to draw strength from the validation we receive so that we may continue with activities that are often emotionally draining.

I very much enjoyed the presentation. . . . It gave me a warm feeling to listen to the voices of young adults discuss their views, feelings, and concepts about learning, teaching, and their community. What really made the presentation special was the interaction between the young adults and their two teachers. These two women were of the same culture as the students and this made the rapport more special. There was a relationship of academics and cultivation. These educators could relate to these youngsters more so than most because they know firsthand about their backgrounds, meaning how they relate to the world around them . . . (student-teacher, 3/90)

Adults who have heard the voices of these young people and have observed their ways of relating, have heightened our awareness of their compassion, seriousness, and intelligence.

I was very impressed with the students from the Bronx. They really showed me how much they care about their community. The children showed me that kids do care about what's going around them and when given the chance will produce wonders to let all know about it. (preservice teacher, 3/90)

From this presentation . . . I really got wonderful ideas about how to teach children more efficiently. First of all, teachers should be concerned about students' interests. Usually teachers do not consider what students like to learn. . . . Second, teachers should not only teach children to master some concepts and skills but also develop their thinking abilities so that students can solve problems by themselves . . . (preservice teacher, 3/90)

It was a pleasure to have you visit our school. We were all quite taken with your presentation. . . . Due to your research project, I've been given ideas for my next year's class which I know will contribute to their education . . . (teacher, 5/90).

In the process, students have gained a great sense of self-worth and pride that comes from knowing that they have met a challenge and that others respect them: "When we first did a conference at Fordham University, it felt good for people to listen to us and want to see us again so they can get more information on our research and how it works" (Njeri, 1/90).

It is empowering for students to know that they have knowledge that can be of help to others, especially teachers. However, we would not have gained from the knowledge of these learners had we not treated them with respect, had we not let them show us what they knew, had we not carefully attended to their words.

Finally, our conference presentations have made it possible for us to connect with a broader community of educators and researchers; connecting to others is an important means of lessening the isolation that affects each of us in different ways. It was at a conference that we met a teacher with similar social concerns, leading several months later to a powerful exchange when her economically advantaged students from a private school in Manhattan visited the Bronx middle school. These visitors were especially taken by the articulateness of students, who did not require index cards to remind them of what they wanted to say and who captivated them with their seriousness, enthusiasm, and humor. We have all gained much from participating in these activities together.

Sharing Through Professional Publications

As the teacher educator, professional writing has always been one of my major responsibilities and a personal goal for reasons that began with but have now gone beyond the need to "publish or perish." I have come to view professional writing as a means of affirming myself as well as fulfilling an important social responsibility. Because of who we are and what we are accomplishing together, I am committed to collaborative writing. When people learn and work together, they must share the responsibility for writing together as well. There is no other way to capture the different views and interpretations that are part of collective activity, however difficult this may be to accomplish.

To achieve the representation of everyone involved, we have begun to experiment with different ways of creating narratives, using portions of individual pieces and quotations from our research journals and other documents that we create or collect. Because I am able to devote more time to this endeavor, I have assumed responsibility for selecting and arranging the quotations taken from individual journals into a text, as I have attempted to do in this chapter. However, as the person who crafts the text, I am also responsible for sharing what is created with members of the collective, to verify that the document represents what we are doing to everyone's satisfaction. This procedure is made complex by the fact that the drafting process usually extends over a period of time. Nevertheless, data that are presented have been shared in some form at one of the many public forums we address.

In this narrative, we have sought to describe how we have attempted to create relations of care through our collaborative approach to pedagogy, learning, and research. Our relations of care have been created and sustained over time through our words and our actions. It is these relations of care that have been an important influence on the academic accomplishments of students in one middle school setting and their adult collaborators.

FINDINGS: LEARNING FROM COLLABORATIVE PEDAGOGY AND RESEARCH

All participants in this collaborative are learning from one another, no matter the level of experience or the background of the individual—shedding new light on what it means to learn from "more capable others" (Vygotsky, 1978). In particular, we have learned that being together, being real, being open, and being fair were important influences on our accomplishments. Although we perceived them as ways of demonstrating care and concern for one another, our struggles to be together, to be real, to be open, and to be fair also contributed to the tensions that we have each experienced in our collective efforts, as we shall explain in the following section.

Being Together

In our work, doing research gives a purpose for our collaboration, for coming together—but caring is really at the heart of what we do. Because I care, I take the time to participate in the life of the classroom—to hang out, to listen, to talk, and to share common experiences—even when other responsibilities draw me away. Because she cares, Marceline is willing to give freely of her time to meet with me, to talk endlessly on the phone about our activities, and to attend two- and three-day conferences with her students, without compensation. Because they cared, the graduate students continued to visit the middle school students long after their course requirements were completed. Being together is significant because it is equated with caring and because it presents opportunities to learn to care in different ways, as we discovered from reading Eric's mother's writings. I translated this excerpt from the Spanish version that was submitted to us.

> When Mrs. Torres asked me if I would like to accompany the class on the trip, I was happy but at the same time I felt insecure because she told me that I had to speak in public. I felt timid. When I got to know the group better. I began to feel more secure and confident.
>
> The children offered me the security that I needed when it was my turn to speak. They did it so well that I told myself that I had to do it well because I did not want to let them down.
>
> I was proud to be able to share with everyone and learn from each one of them. All the love and respect that they offered me is something that I will never forget. More important is the self-assuredness that I have acquired and the patience that I am always going to try to have with everything and everyone. Well that patience and respect for everyone is evident in the way Dr. Mercado and Mrs. Torres relate to others. . . .
>
> I have learned something very important, that our society needs all of us to resolve the daily problems that we have in and out of our country.

As Eric's mother suggests, coming together allows each of us to give and to receive caring and to have our own caring nurtured. Mutuality characterizes all of our activities, which is why they are so emotionally powerful and empowering.

However, being there is not always easy. Although giving freely of my time is an important way of demonstrating that I care, sustaining weekly visits without relying on release time or any other form of time compensation becomes increasingly difficult. Unfortunately, we did not anticipate this development when we embarked upon this venture with a great deal of enthusiasm and devotion but little else. Although we have been strengthened by the struggles we have shared, they have also taught us a vital lesson. Commitment to collaborative partnerships requires us to officially protect time to "be there," but also to talk openly about what "not being there" requires, so that it is not equated with abandonment.

Being Real

Being real is as important for young adolescent students as it is in our relationships with others. It is essential for building relations of care and trust. *Being real* means being honest and truthful about your life, your beliefs, your feelings and emotions. *Being real* means sharing personal things about yourself—even your age, as Laila noticed I did. When she commented that "the college teacher is nice and truthful with us and tells us her personal things," I realized the significance of my revelation.

Further, *being real* also means being authentic and genuine in the sense that what you do has real meaning and purpose to you and others. No doubt our activities took on added significance when the adult collaborators engaged in the very same activities as the students and when our families became a part of our professional lives.

However, *being real* also means stripping away at the layers of lies students have been told about who they are and what they can accomplish and about the poor preparation they have received. On one occasion, when a student revealed that he came from a "bad family" because everyone was a high school dropout, I admitted that I, too, came from a family in which only one member graduated from high school, but I didn't think that I came from a bad family. I ended our brief exchange by asking the student to consider what our two families had in common and left him to ponder this. He eventually came around with another interpretation that demonstrated that he had given careful thought our brief interchange. It is a delicate matter to strip away at the layers of lies that rob students of their dignity and sense of self-worth and alienates them from their families.

It is also a delicate matter to challenge students who are easily discouraged to do harder work, while at the same time building their self-confidence and self-esteem. We try to encourage students by focusing on their positive accomplishments, especially as we embark upon what they consider "hard work," however, students want to be corrected. They want to be shown how to improve their speaking skills and their writing. This is what caring means to them, as this exchange illustrates.

Sitting at the table at the back of the classroom, [Ei. and I] discussed many different issues such as family, school, the one that was of greatest interest to me was a discussion we had about his writings in his portfolio. He had, of late, stopped writing as much as he had been writing in the beginning. When I expressed my disappointment, he looked uncomfortable, shrugged his shoulders, and said that he "had a lot of work in other classes." I said that I noticed he was slacking off in the research area as well and he told me that he had been thinking about this at home. . . . I told him that he was adept at higher level tasks, thinking critically, tying things together, summarizing. But I felt that he was weak in taking notes as someone was talking. He had very little scribing in his portfolio and I rarely saw him writing in his notebook as we spoke. He admitted that he was "afraid to miss something while he's writing." Marcy, who had joined us at this point, suggested Ei interview Angel about his scribing technique. . . . on April 26, Ei. wrote the following: "Pamela and I were talking about alot of things. She told me that I use to do more work then know I think its true. . . . We also talked about taking notes I need help to I decided to tell Angel to help me. I think this talk help me think." (Pamela, 4/20/91)

Being Open

Being open means being approachable and making it possible for others to communicate with you because you are perceived as being accepting of both others and other viewpoints, even when these are different from your own. "The capacity for moral agents to talk appreciatively with each other regardless of fundamental differences is crucial to friendships, marriage, politics, business and world peace. We see evidence every where that this capacity is sorely underdeveloped, and yet we have so far given the task little attention in educational circles" (Noddings, 1991, p. 157).

Through our activities, students have come in contact with others who offer unique learning opportunities, especially individuals whose lives are very different from their own. For example, Pamela, one of the graduate students, chose to discuss Native American storytelling rather than dealing with some of the social issues students had identified. Because of her knowledge of this topic, she awakened interests and curiosities she did not know the students had, making it a worthwhile experience for her and for the six students with whom she shared her passion.

However, being open is a formidable challenge. Sometimes, being too open and sensitive to the emotional reactions of others results in lost opportunities to challenge prevailing perceptions by presenting contrasting or opposing viewpoints, to push social and cognitive boundaries. We experienced this when we discussed issues such as teenage pregnancy and parenting with students who tend not to explore the long-term consequences for teen parents and their offspring. Among adults, this occurred when we discussed students' reading problems, school failure, and grade retention in terms other than "blaming the victim." This is an issue that became of increasing concern as we extended membership in our community across a number of boundaries, as I described in my journal: "I am still grappling with the tension of having to negotiate different interpretations that we each have of what we are doing, which affects the preparation of the oral and written reports, but also the openness with which we discuss topics and situations that may engender conflicting viewpoints or theories such as why "minority" children fail. Basically, what I fear most is not conflict over ideology but that our different perspectives may get in the way of our developing relationship" (6/91).

We are all learners when it comes to dealing with sensitive issues in a manner that is both respectful and empowering. Most of us are conditioned to view these types of disagreements as conflicts and destructive rather than as positive forces in learning, in cognitive development, and in social relationships. The problem is that engaging in difficult conversations requires trust, and building trust takes time.

Being Fair

Adolescent students are generally concerned about issues of fairness: what is right and what is wrong, what is just and what is unjust. As should be evident by now, among the students in the middle school, this concern with fairness is not limited to issues affecting them directly. They are concerned about treating others justly even when life has not been fair to them. We were all moved when evidence of this surfaced quite unexpectedly during our first conference presentation, when one student disclosed how she had learned about AIDS: "I interviewed a lady but I didn't tell anybody because it was a secret. The way it started was because her daughter is a friend of mine and I was talking to them about my research project. It's seems that she was very amazed and wanted to help me in any way she can. She started to tell me how her T-cell count went up and down and that was no good. I really can't explain myself on why she did tell me she had HIV and why did she trust me. Well I guess it was her daughter who told her that I could keep a secret." I was not prepared for the explanation that this student provided when I asked why she had not shared this interview with us previously. "I haven't written it down because I don't want to talk about her personal things. . . . I don't know why she trusted me" (1/90).

In some cases, however, students learned about the need to treat others fairly through their research work, even if adhering to the norm of privacy had other types of consequences for them. Angel's words provide other examples of this concern: "I used to throw rocks at the homeless . . . but I learned that there are many reasons why people are homeless. . . . (12/91). If we work collaboratively we can end homelessness" (01/91). Research helped me find my true inside . . . the one who cares" (12/91).

As their adult collaborators, we, too, faced similar issues as we began to consider how our well-intentioned actions have negative consequences for the lives of the students. Every time students travel to professional gatherings held at hotels where, as Angel said, "we were like rich people," this possibility exists. Laila hinted at one potential outcome of border crossings when she said, "They're looking at us as if we don't belong." I had had a similar experience when we traveled to Washington, D.C., to present at a national conference of bilingual educators. Our rooms were changed rather suddenly from the exclusive top floor of a luxury hotel used as the conference headquarters because one individual's efforts to ensure our comfort were undone by another who responded to other interests.

Collaborative work that is respectful of and openly acknowledges the contributions of all participants creates different kinds of problems. Every time students stand in front of an audience and talk openly about their research topics and about what they are learning, this possibility exists. This was brought home to me rather strongly when, during a recent presentation at Hunter College, some students candidly read and told stories of sexual abuse in their families and among close friends. Although it is important for students to decide what they want to share and how they want to share it because this affirms that we believe in their capabilities and judgments, with public disclosure comes public exposure. In doing away with notions of anonymity, we may unintentionally be making students publicly vulnerable. We did not consider this possibility at the outset because only by embarking upon a new course of action does one become aware of potential hazards along the way. However, as we discover what these hazards are, we must deal with them openly with the students and with ourselves. There is a moral obligation in efforts such as this; it is what being fair requires. It is ironic that outcomes of this kind are inherent in work that involves the researched in a democratic process of inquiry characterized by negotiation, reciprocity, and empowerment (Lather, 1986). As Noddings says, relations of care do not guarantee ethical results.

CONCLUSIONS

In our work, collaboration occurs on many levels, and it reflects the belief that collective activity is essential to accomplish complex tasks no matter what you know, who you are, and where you work. However, collective activity is also the means by which we build each other's confidence and self-esteem, help each other grow, and work to make a difference in the lives of others. In the process of engaging in the habits of mind of educational ethnographers, students from underprivileged communities learn to take control over their own learning and come to understand that collective action is essential to transform the character of teaching and learning in schools, as well as the quality of life in our communities and in our society. Ethnography is an empowering way of creating awareness, building self-esteem, and nurturing the capacity to care. Our work demonstrates that affective concerns are inseparable from academic concerns and that each has an influence on the other (Noddings, 1991).

Through collaborative pedagogy, learning, and research, we have all gained a deeper understanding of students who most hear about and read about through the distorted images frequently presented in the media. We have also learned about what it takes to survive in hostile environments and how, through collective action, we can affect the lives of children in positive ways. In particular, the teacher gains new understanding of individual students through the perspectives of others who share in the life of the classroom. Through the support one receives, one lessens one's isolation and renews one's commitment to continue with the hard work of teaching. Similarly, parents and caretakers are learning to relate to all children, not just their own, in different ways as they become respected members of the classroom community. Prospective teachers learn that "teachers need to care about the lives of children" (Patricia, 3/91), and as the teacher educator, I have renewed my commitment to support the work of teachers. It is a myth to believe that experienced teachers have no needs, particularly those working in inner city schools. For those of us who have learned to be ashamed of who we are and where we come from, it is empowering to acknowledge our families and affirm who we are within the setting of the school. This way of relating has been most affecting to young adolescent students, who take pride in being treated as a part of our families, observing that "when we do research, we are like a family." Challenging students academically as they increase their understanding of complex social and political forces that affect their lives is an emotional process. It is difficult not to be emotional when schools are among the institutions that limit our opportunities for economic integration by failing to prepare our youth for serious academic work, yet they succeed in robbing us of our dignity, alienating us from our families, and making us feel ashamed of who we are (Walsh, 1991). We agree that "the world we inhabit is palpably deficient: there are unwarranted inequities, shattered communities, unfulfilled lives . . . [but] when we reach out we experience a kind of blankness. . . . Where are the sources of questioning, of restlessness? How are we to move the young to break with the given, the taken for granted—to move toward what might be, what is not yet?" (Greene, 1986, p. 127)

This chapter describes one approach for inspiring the young and the not so young to rise above apathy and low expectations to build a better world.

REFERENCES

Brice-Heath, S. (1985). "Literacy or Literate Skills? Considerations for ESL? EFL Learners. In P. Larson, E. L. Judd, and L. S. Messerschmidt, eds., *On TESOL '84: Brave New World for TESOL*. Washington. DC: TESOL.

Buchmann, M. (1990). "Beyond the Lonely, Choosing Will: Professional Development in Teacher Thinking." *Teachers College Record* 91, no. 4: 481–508.

Greene, M. (1986). "In Search of a Critical Pedagogy." *Harvard Educational Review* 56, no. 4: 427–441.

Lather, P. (1986). "Research as Praxis." *Harvard Educational Review* 56, no. 3: 257–277.

Mercado, C. I. (1992). "Researching Research: A Student-Teacher-Researcher Collaborative Project." In A. Ambert and M. Alvarez, eds.,

Puerto Rican Children on the Mainland: Interdisciplinary Perspectives, pp. 167–192. New York: Garland.

Moll, L.C. and Diaz, S. (1987). "Change as the Goal of Educational Research." *Anthropology and Education Quarterly* 18: 300–311.

Noddings, N. (1991). "Stories in Dialogue: Caring and Interpersonal Reasoning." In I. C. Witherell and N. Nodddings, eds., *Stories Lives Tell,* pp. 157–170. New York: Teachers College Press.

———. (1992). *The Challenge to Care in Schools.* New York: Teachers College Press.

Trueba, H. T. (1987). "Organizing Classroom Instruction in Specific Sociocultural Contexts: Teaching Mexican Youth to Write." In S. R. Goldman and H. T. Trueba, eds., *Becoming Literate in English as a Second Language,* pp. 235–252. Norwood. NJ: Ablex.

Vygotsky, L. S. (1978). In M. Cole, V. John-Steiner, S. Scribner, and E. Souberman, eds., *Minds in Society: The Development of Higher Psychological Process.* Cambridge, MA: Harvard University Press.

Walsh, C. E. (1991). "Pedagogy and the Struggle for Voice: Issues of Language." *Power and Schooling for Puerto Ricans.* New York: Bergin and Garvey.

Warren Little, J. (1990). "The Persistence of Privacy: Autonomy and Initiative in Teachers' Professional Relations." *Teachers College Record* 91, no. 4: 509–536.

Witherell, C. and Noddings, N. (1991). "Prologue: An invitation to our readers." In C. Witherell and N. Noddings, eds., *Stories Lives Tell,* pp. 1–12. New York: Teachers College Press.

Woodward, V. (1985). "Collaborative Pedagogy: Researcher and Teacher Learning Together." *Language Arts* 62, no. 7: 770–776.

Conclusion

DEBORAH EAKER-RICH, JANE A. VAN GALEN, AND ELLEN L. TIMOTHY

We undertook this project in the hope that the volume would expand upon the developmental and philosophical notions of caring within the grounded contexts of schools. We hoped to invoke a more sociological and critical look at enactments of caring. We wanted to address the question: What are the *possibilities* and the *implications* of caring across cultural differences found in schools today and within the traditionally unequal power relations around which schools are structured?

As we collected and reviewed the research and analyses presented here, engaged in dialogue with the authors, and reflected upon the prior literature, we envisioned this book as a dual intervention: into theory with considerations of the complications of multiple perspectives, and into practice with the clear demonstration that merely sentimental, unreflective caring is likely to be neither effective nor emancipatory.

Several themes emerged from our readings. First, throughout the diverse settings described in this text, caring is consistently revealed as an important value and desire. In these chapters, caring is significant whether explicitly invoked in the school culture (see Dempsey and Noblit, Walker, Van Galen, Mercado) or as the taken-for-granted basis undergirding decisions and interactions (see Blount, Streitmatter, Beck and Newman). Teachers and other stakeholders in education *want* to care (see Webb-Dempsey et al., King, Kissen). Students voice an appreciation of receiving care (see Walker, Van Galen, Beck and Newman, Mercado). Even as we move into a critique of caring, implicit in this work is caring's fundamental importance in schooling.

A second major theme drawn from the evidence in these chapters is that caring does not always "work": interpretations of what is caring and what is received as caring are not generalizable across the different borders of culture and social position. The chapters document examples of attempts at caring that, despite the best of intentions, in some way fail. Some do not survive because they are not recognized and preserved (the administrative styles described in Blount's chapter, and the African-American schooling in the chapters by Walker and Dempsey and Noblit), or are misunderstood, resisted, and resented (as in the interethnic interactions in Webb-Dempsey et al.), or are disabled by social fears and the constraints of norms (i.e., the predicaments of gay and lesbian teachers raised by King and Kissen).

These elaborations of the difficulties of caring across various borders support Noddings's suggestion that caring requires continuity. Caring relations seem more possible in homologous groups where the caregivers are embedded in the community or culture: where teachers walk home with a student to confer with the parents, where teachers speak at church as in Dempsey and Noblit; where there is a cultural correspondence between teachers and students as described by Walker; and where administrators have emerged from and maintain connection to the community served as depicted by Blount. Although these examples are unexamined here in terms of their possible social-reproductionist outcomes, they nevertheless offer the lesson that caring is facilitated in community.

Chapters looking at current schooling establish the difficulty of reaching consensus regarding what it means to care in the absence of traditional ties of community. For some time now, many students have traveled considerable distances from their own neighborhoods to attend school; when they arrive at school, students from increasingly diverse backgrounds may bring disparate definitions of *caring* to the setting. Those engaged in the work of creating caring schools will have to consider how to redefine and possible recreate community. The ever-shifting populations of many contemporary schools makes the challenge to create schools with "continuity of purpose, people, and place" (Noddings, 1992) more compelling than ever. Several chapters suggest that understanding and articulating the *history of a community* and the *cultural meanings* of *caring* for different members of the community of a school are essential facets of building continuity among the fragmented social lives of many students.

How are these understandings and articulations of perspectives (possibly different from one's own) to come about? In heterogeneous settings, we must take seriously what Noddings calls "the difficulty of apprehending the reality of others" (1984, p. 14). Feelings of caring and actions based on feelings are clearly not enough. Nor can we be confident in the correctness of our own suppositions of what is needed, as is so clearly shown in the essay by Webb-Dempsey et al. In the introduction we referred to Gilligan's questioning equating care with self-sacrifice; the authors of this book question equating care with self-"rightness." Several chapters specifically articulate the importance to those receiving care of being *themselves* received—of being authentically recognized and affirmed (Streitmatter, Beck and Newman, Mercado). To be effective at caring in settings of diversity, we must move from a "caring about," which connotes a generalizability and an objectification of the one receiving care, to a practice of "caring for," which implies a recognition and relationality with the one receiving care.

Thus, a third and major theme emerging from this volume is a requirement, summoned by diversity, that *sentimental caring* necessarily be distinguished from the *practice* of caring. Gilligan's early work warns of against the inaccuracies of equating care with feelings as opposed to thought, and she named care as an orientation. Noddings construed caring as a process located in education. This work, along with other recent work, has begun to elaborate its complexities with critical reflections on actual practice. At the moment we take actual educational practice into account, caring as an educational practice or process becomes confused and conflated with generalized feelings of caring. Almost everyone in education "cares." Everyone can cite an experience of caring and carries an understanding of what *caring* means. But the caring to which we each refer is formulated out of individual, social, and cultural variables. Although caring may be in some way universally desired, it is not uniformly understood. In heterogeneous settings, the feeling of care can come to conceal misunderstanding. If we instead consider caring as a process or practice, we can see a dynamic, a movement between differences. The theorized practice offers a way of more deeply reading the situation and the possibility of understanding.

It is precisely when the caregiver and the cared-for are nonsynchronous that sentimental caring becomes problematic. Caring *is* affective, and the seductively good feelings engendered combined with the position of care*giver* can too easily shore up one's self and generate a position of benevolence. Its own sense of "rightness" can become its downfall. Compare Van Galen's insights on the limitations of caring when it is defined and enacted as compassion—a feeling—with the project reported by Mercado in which "caring as collaboration" locates caring as an interaction.

We are brought out of sentimentality in caring relations by authentic recognition of the other. The theory of caring as an engaged practice suggests some pathways, and the chapters by Beck and Newman and by Mercado offer examples of how they might work. The educators they describe utilize essential components of the practice of caring as delineated by Noddings: modeling caring, the practice (by which she means the experience) of caring, confirmation of the cared-for, and dialogue. We grant that modeling, experience, and confirmation are important in caring relations, but it is the last component, dialogue, that shifts caring out of potentially mere sentiment and into a dynamic process required for successful caring in heterogeneous settings.

Thus emerges a fourth theme, which is also a strategy: *dialogue* is crucial to enable the translation of caring across various cultures and social positions. In dialogue, we are provided with a format for engagement, a format that brings into caring an element of reciprocity, listening as well as speaking, and negotiation of meanings. *Giving* care includes *receiving* information. The organizational structure and the interactions in the one urban high school described by Beck and Newman illustrate several possibilities of dialogical caring: students "own" their choices and conflict is articulated and negotiated. Conflict is shifted from the emotional and reactive domain into consciousness and thereby establishes an explicit level in which negotiation can occur. This is a determining step: differences, inequalities, responsibilities, and caring values are all made explicit and acknowledged. Likewise, Mercado's project of student participation in collaborative research facilitates students authoritative voice and teaches negotiation of meaning in a context of respectfulness. These are but two possible examples of the cared-for being authentically recognized, participating in self-naming, articulating their own knowledge—in short, having a voice in the dialogue.

Drawing on an understanding of caring as an orientation, Noddings developed the theory of caring as a relational process. By foregrounding the dialogic component in the practice of caring, we have begun to think of caring as a strategy for engagement. The nature of a strategy is twofold. First, it is not merely reactive, but is based on a plan. Second, strategy carries an acknowledgment that the plan cannot be executed in a rote manner, but requires art and skill to be successfully carried out. We have already pointed out the disfunctionality of caring as emotionality, without intentionality or "plan." Nor does caring work as a rationality or formula unmediated by the particularities of context. One consequence of a formulaic approach is the reinforcement of "distance" between the caregiver and the cared-for, increasing the possibility that the caring may be less appropriate. This can be seen in Streitmatter's important chapter, which looks at the caring of a formulaic, "equality" orientation compared to a more strategic approach to issues of gender as issues of equity. Likewise the failure to survive of the caring-oriented school leadership styles (as depicted by Blount) and of the caring contexts of segregated schooling (as described in Dempsey and Noblit and by Walker) are outcomes of formulaic applications of "equality" with little attention to the particular and actual realities of the cared-for. At the very least, these chapters should lead us to look more deeply at policy decisions intended to "equalize" social and cultural inequities, even those consciously designed with an explicated ethic of care at the core.

With reforms grounded in theories of caring, like reforms grounded in technorational approaches, it is too easy to confuse the means with the ends of the efforts at change. In few of the schools represented in these chapters have the actors articulated a clear sense of the purposes of their caring. The teachers, administrators, parents, students, and even the authors speak often of caring as being important for the well-being of individual students and the adults who work with them. This is a laudable goal in itself. Yet, several of the analyses have brought forward the problem in educational practice of interpolating this feeling uncritically into action. If we do not raise broader questions, the comfort associated with caring can too easily become—as an unnamed audience member in a conference session once posited—"just a more gentle form of the manipulation in which schools engage."

We are concerned that the rhetoric of caring can too easily be coopted in the service of making ill-functioning schools merely more pleasant places to be. An ethic of care, divorced from political analysis of the institutions in which caring is manifested, may, in some instances, effectively silence those who might, under a different ethic, raise issues of racism, sexism, classism, and homophobia (Puka, 1993; and Van Galen, this volume). Many of us believe that caring will at least make the world a better place and that is enough. But in an unjust world, we must ask: A better place for whom? At whose expense? For what purposes? A caring ethic grounded in the cultural assumptions and interaction styles of the dominant culture may merely serve as another social reinforcement of prescribed roles differentiated by race, class, gender, and sexual orientation. Caring may indeed produce the feeling of comfort and connectedness, but the *practice* of caring must function in realities as well as relationships of conflict and contradiction; such a practice must be grounded theoretically and politically.

The fifth theme emerging from the juxtaposition of writings in this volume is a need for caring to be informed by critical consciousness that insists on taking into account the social positioning and power relations inherent in relationship. In education, as we seek to receive and understand the cared-for, we are also facilitating the elaboration of the cared-for's understanding of self. This is caring about what happens beyond the moment of interpersonal interaction; it is about the cared-for living materially in the world. This is why the engaged dialogue component is not enough: "being heard' is a prerequisite to the work of caring that is empowering, not merely instrumental.

If caring is merely another mechanism by which to accomplish the same instrumental goals of schooling supported by a technorational logic, then we must question its validity for promoting any true reform in the nature of schooling and society. If, on the other hand, there is more than an instrumentality involved within conceptualizations of caring, it is worth exploring in more depth. Van Galen suggests in this volume that caring may be the place where reformers, policy makers, and teachers are able to find common ground and share a vision for school reform as a logical extension of relational work.

As a final note, we must raise the issue of how we, as academics and policy makers, are to act in caring ways. Academics, policy makers, and others who hope to work in the best interests of children by remaining in an advocacy, rather than a collegial, role with those working within schools would do well to heed Noddings's cautions against attempting to care "at a distance": "Because we are not in relation, our acts can easily degenerate into acts of false generosity. . . . [W]hen we have the power and desire to act at a distance, it is tempting to initiate and control. We are too impatient or too confident or too puffed up with our own righteous sense of responsibility to listen and encourage initiative from the outsiders. We overlook the possibility that others may want most the power to create their own meanings and explore their own possibilities" (p. 116). As those of us in the academy endeavor to help create school as centers of care for children, our roles may be that of arbitrator among various participants in the dialogue, or translator of the necessarily *context-specific* nature of caring. Our roles in the process will be effective only if they are negotiated in relationship with those on whose behalf we claim to work.

Many factors produce the practice of caring; it is, after all a human desire and a human need and so engages us at an emotive level. A pedagogy of caring is undeniably an affective pedagogy. As we try to make caring do the most good, we become intentional and utilize our intellect. We have been guided by philosophical formulations on the nature and meaning of caring, we recognize it as a practice, and we have learned to affirm it as engagement. Caring, by definition, involves a relation to "others." This book seeks to include and enhance our consciousness of each as an other; it seeks to add an ethical-political consciousness of the implications of caring. This ethical-political consciousness is not antithetical to emotive caring, although we may be led to question and rethink our own individual emotive habits. Rather, it is a challenge and an invitation to open ourselves to a caring that reaches more broadly, is felt more deeply, is more thoughtful and, ultimately, more satisfying.

REFERENCES

Noddings, N. (1984). *Caring: A Feminine Approach to Ethics and Moral Education*. Berkley: University of California Press.

———. (1992). *The Challenge to Care in Schools: An Alternative Approach to Education*. New York: Teachers College Press.

Puka, B. (1993). "The Liberation of Caring: A Different Voice for Gilligan's *Different Voice*." In M. J. Larrabee, ed., *An Ethic of Care: Feminist and Interdisciplinary Perspectives*. New York: Routledge.

Contributors

Lynn G. Beck is an assistant professor of education at the University of California, Los Angeles. Her areas of interest include ethics of educational leadership, the principalship, and the preparation of educational administrators. Recent publications include *Site based Management as a Reform Strategy* (with Joseph Murphy), *Ethics and Educational Leadership Programs: An Expanding Focus* (with Joseph Murphy) and *Reclaiming Educational Administration as a Caring Profession.*

Jackie M. Blount, an Asheville, NC native, studied music and physics at The University of North Carolina at Chapel Hill before teaching high school physics for four years. She then returned to Chapel Hill to pursue doctoral studies in the Social Foundations of Education. While there, she received a Spencer Dissertation Fellowship for her historical research on women and the superintendency. She is currently an Assistant Professor in the Department of Curriculum and Instruction at Iowa State University.

Dickson Corbett received his Ph.D. from The University of North Carolina at Chapel Hill. He is currently Co-Director of the Applied Research Project at Research for Better Schools in Philadelphia.

Van Dempsey is an Assistant Professor in Educational Foundations at West Virginia University. His interests include Appalachian culture and education, the moral nature of schooling and the sociology of education.

Deborah Eaker-Rich is an Assistant Professor in Educational Leadership at North Carolina State University. Her interests include qualitative research methodology, the culture and politics of schooling and the sociology of education. She is co-editor of *The Tapestry of Caring: Education as Nurturance* published by Ablex (1994).

239

James R. King teaches undergraduate and graduate courses in literacy and qualitative research at the University of South Florida. His research interests include gender and early childhood education, critical and queer theory, and the politics of "at-risk." He has been a classroom teacher and spent a 1989–90 sabbatical as a first grade teacher.

Rita M. Kissen is a member of the teacher education faculty at the University of Southern Maine and past president of the Portland, Maine chapter of Parents, Families and Friends of Lesbians and Gays (P-FLAG). She is currently working on a book about lesbian and gay teachers, which will be published by Heinemann in 1996.

Carmen I. Mercado is on the faculty of The Department of Curriculum and Teaching at Hunter College of the City University of New York. She is heavily involved with the Bronx Middle School Collaborative of which this work is a part.

Rhonda Mordecai-Phillips is a researcher at Research for Better Schools in Philadelphia.

Rebecca L. Newman is a doctoral student and research associate at the University of California, Los Angeles. Her research focuses on the educational experiences of homeless children and their families. Recent publications include "Educating Homeless Children: One Experiment in Innovation" (with Lynn G. Beck).

George W. Noblit is a Full Professor in Social Foundations at The University of North Carolina at Chapel Hill. His current interests include the moral nature of schooling, qualitative research methodology especially as used in collaborative community work, and the sociology of education.

E. Vanessa Siddler Walker is an Assistant Professor at Emory University in the Division of Educational Studies. She is a former Spencer Post Doctoral Fellow and recipient of the Young Scholars Award from the Conference of Southern Graduate Schools. In addition to numerous talks and articles on the subject of the segregated schooling of African-American students, she is also co-author of the edited volume *Facing Racism in American Education* (1990), and *Their Highest Potential: A Case Study of African-American Schooling in the Segregated South* (1996).

Janice L. Streitmatter currently is Associate Professor of Teaching and Teacher Education, and Associate Dean of the College of Education at the

University of Arizona. Her research focus is gender equity in schools, with a current emphasis on girls-only education.

Ellen L. Timothy is a doctoral student in the Education Program at The University of Washington, Bothell.

Jane A. Van Galen received her Ph.D. in the Social Foundations of Education from The University of North Carolina at Chapel Hill. She is currently the Director of the Education Program at The University of Washington, Bothell. Her interests include the sociology of education and teacher education.

Jaci Webb-Dempsey is a Research Assistant Professor and Director of Assessment for the Benedum Project at West Virginia University. Her interests include educational policy, qualitative research methodology and the cultural context of learning. She was previously a Research Associate for Applied Research at Research for Better Schools in Philadelphia.

Bruce Wilson is Co-Director of the Applied Research Project at Research for Better Schools in Philadelphia.

Index

243